CONTENTS

* *Bach's Fugue in G Minor, Organ "The Little Fugue"*
appears on page xiv.

Elgar's Symphony No. 2 in E flat (Op. 63)
appears on page xiv.

Tschaikowsky Melodie, Op. 42, No. 3 from
Souvenir D'Un Lieu Cher, Vn. & Pft,
appears on page xiv.

ACKNOWLEDGEMENTS

The Publishers have to acknowledge the following copyright permissions:

Items A 29, E 49, F 124–7, F 214–15, G 185–201, H 723–91, K 90–118, M 396–400, P 66, P 78–84, P 100–7, R 123–4, R 155–6, R 162, S 1523–34, S 1534a–g, S 1535–40, S 1546–7, S 1599–1608, T 119–22c, T 301–2, T 315–20 by permission of Schott & Co. Ltd., London, for all countries with the exception of Germany (where these works are controlled by B. Schott's Sohne, Mainz) and the U.S.A. (where these works are controlled by The Associated Music Publishers Inc., New York).

Items B 1728–37, C 584–8, D 269–94, D 300–38, D 350–425, D 434–69, S 145–61, S 166–71, S 1609–15 by permission of N. Simrock–Richard Shauer, London.

Items B 434–6, P 163–4, R 285–92 permission of D. Rahter–Richard Shauer, London.

Permission is also acknowledged from Messrs. Alfred Lengnick & Co. Ltd. as publishers for the British Empire for the following:–Items C 584, D 292–4, D 357–73, D 466–9.

Items S 812–15 by permission of Elkin & Co. Ltd., London. Permission is also acknowledged from Elkin & Co. Ltd., as publishers for the British Empire for the following:– M 18–20, M 23–6, M 37–45.

Items S 1094–5, S 1365–75, S 1376–92, S 1419–24, S 1425–30, S 1468–74, S 1475–9 by permission of the copyright owners, Peters Edition, London, Frankfurt and New York.

A Dictionary of
MUSICAL THEMES
Revised Edition

HAROLD BARLOW
SAM MORGENSTERN

Introduction by
JOHN ERSKINE

ff

faber and faber

LONDON · BOSTON

First published in the United States of America in 1948
by Crown Publishers, Inc.

First published in Great Britain
by Williams and Norgate Limited in 1949

Published by Ernest Benn Limited in 1952

Published by Faber and Faber Limited
3 Queen Square, London WC1N 3AU in 1983
Reprinted in 1986

Printed by Butler & Tanner Ltd,
Frome and London

British Library Cataloguing in Publication Data

A Dictionary of musical themes.
1. Music—Thematic catalogue
I. Barlow, Harold   II. Morgenstern, Sam
780   ML134
ISBN 0-571-11998-0

A Dictionary of Musical Themes
Revised Edition

INTRODUCTION

BY JOHN ERSKINE

THIS dictionary of musical themes, by Harold Barlow and Sam Morgenstern, supplies an aid which students of music have long needed. When the authors showed me the plan of it a year ago, or somewhat earlier, I applauded at once, and agreed to write a word of preface. We should now have something in musical literature to parallel Barlett's *Familiar Quotations*. Whenever a musical theme haunted us, but refused to identify itself no matter how much we scraped our memory, all we should have to do would be to look up the tune in Barlow and Morgenstern, where those ingenious dictionary-makers would assemble some ten thousand musical themes, with a notation-index or theme-finder, to locate the name of the composition from which the haunting fragment came, and the name of the composer.

After a brief but exciting conversation, Mr. Barlow and Mr. Morgenstern went off with my promise of a preface, as it were, in their pocket, leaving me very thoughtful — and inclined to become more thoughtful with each passing hour. I knew there had already been attempts to index music, and I was fairly familiar with the difficulties which had in the past tripped up bold experimenters. A dictionary such as Barlett's can classify quotations according to the subject with which they deal, and can arrange them in the usual index method by the letter-order of the opening words. But no method has been hit on to index musical sounds, nor the variations in pitch by which a theme is articulated. No method, that is, which permits the musical material of a theme to remain strictly musical.

I understood what Mr. Barlow and Mr. Morgenstern would try to do; since letters can easily be indexed, and musical notes cannot be, they would try to translate the notes into letters. After much thought I feared this would prove a task far beyond even their enthusiasm, and the result might be less useful than they hoped. But they put an end to my doubts by bringing to my study one day a section of the theme index, and challenging me to give them a theme they couldn't speedily locate. My conversion was prompt. I am glad to record here my confidence in the theory of this book, and my admiration for the manner in which the theory has been worked out.

As the authors are more than ready to admit, the ten thousand themes, more or less, which can be identified quickly and easily with the help of this book, do not encompass the entire literature of music, but they do include practically all the themes which can be found in compositions that have been recorded. It is hardly likely that a music student will be haunted by a theme from a composition not yet considered worthy of recording.

The authors believe, and I agree with them, that their dictionary of musical themes will be useful to the trained musician, even to the professional performer, who is more likely than the beginner or the amateur to have a firm grasp of the musical material which has gone into well-known masterpieces.

The book is divided into two parts. The first part contains ten thousand or more musical themes arranged by composers. The second part is the notation-index or theme-finder. If we consult the dictionary in order to locate a theme, we shall begin with the second part of the book, and conclude with the passage in the first part which gives the answer we have been looking for. But there are many occasions when a musician needs to refresh his memory about the themes in a given composition. Though he knows the name of the composition and of the composer, he may need to remind himself of the theme in the first movement, or the second, or the third. Of course he can go to his music shelves and consult his copy of the complete work. That is, if his music shelves are large enough to contain the scores of ten thousand sonatas or symphonies. I suspect that the convenience of the Barlow–Morgenstern dictionary will soon be recognized by serious students of musical literature.

How enormous that body of literature is, and how rapidly it increases, we sometimes forget. It is well within the truth to say that no pianist, no violinist, and no singer, pretends to have in his repertoire all the important compositions for piano, violin, or voice. Each musician has probably read over hundreds of pieces he would gladly include in his repertoire if life were long enough. A pianist who keeps in his repertoire, and in condition for performance, a thousand pieces of respectable length and difficulty, is an unusual artist. If his repertoire were three times as large, he would still be something of a specialist; the piano repertory has long since grown beyond human capacity to master completely. It recital programs do not seem more repetitious than they sometimes are, it is because of the helpful capacity of audiences to forget music which they themselves do not play. Sometimes they wish to recall at least a theme or two of what they have forgotten. From now on they will probably consult the Barlow and Morgenstern dictionary of themes.

The present volume does not contain themes from vocal music. To cover vocal as well as instrumental compositions, another volume would be needed as large as this.*

I have been speaking of trained musicians as well as of the average music lover. Both can use this dictionary without difficulty. The theme index is ingenious and, as I now believe, simple. If a theme or a tune is running through your head, and if your musical ear is good enough, you will be able to play it in the key of C major or C minor. Then if you write down the letters by which the notes are named, and find the resulting letter sequence in the index, you will be directed at once to the name of the original work and the name of its composer.

It is this process of identifying the theme when it is played by ear that seemed to me at first complicated and likely to discourage those who consult the dictionary. But I am confident now that once we have tried the method for ourselves, we shall find it extraordinarily simple.

Like any other dictionary of quotations, this book will perhaps be most useful to the young. Music is now a well-established subject in American education. Though many children in our schools are fortunately taught to play and sing, all of them — and this is equally their good fortune — are put in the way of listening to recorded music, to great masterpieces performed by great artists of yesterday and today. Not so long ago school children used to go along the street humming a snatch of ragtime or jazz. Nowadays the youngsters are just as likely to hum a passage from Schubert or Tschaikovsky, or whoever was the composer who last spoke to them from the disc in the music class.

"What is that you are humming?"

Sometimes the children remember, but more often, like the elders,

* *A Dictionary of Opera and Song Themes.*

they forget. But when they have learned to consult this dictionary, they will place the passage at once.

I believe this book is destined to a wide and increasing usefulness, both to mature music lovers now and to the army of children whom our schools are training to be the music lovers of tomorrow.

PREFACE

WHEN we began the research for this book, we both felt like the Sorcerer's Apprentice, for each theme that we found seemed to loose a crowd of others waiting for us. It looked as if this one book might stretch into volumes. However, the limits we set ourselves made the completion of the work seem possible within a lifetime.

This work contains about 10,000 themes. They have been chosen primarily from recorded, instrumental pieces. No vocal works, excepting those which in instrumental arrangement have become better known than their originals, have been included. We feel that the book contains almost all the themes the average and even the more erudite listener might want to look up.

Certain works we omitted because the scores were unavailable in libraries, and publishers who were more than helpful could not supply them. A few other works we left out because we could not, after great effort, secure copyrights. Though the book does not exhaust the subject, by far, we feel that we have compiled a fairly complete index of themes, not only first themes, but every important theme, introduction, and salient rememberable phrase of the work included. In certain modern works where a number of varied phrases could be construed as thematic, we tried to present them all. Naturally, in the development of a work certain phrases occur which are as rememberable as the themes themselves. To include these would amount to reprinting the pieces in their entirety. A few ultramodern works we left out. We felt that anyone likely to remember their themes, or more aptly their combinations of notes, would in all probability know their source. Consequently, these works would hardly fit into the scope of this volume.

Careful search through so many hundreds of works by different composers living in different eras in divers countries leads the research student to rather interesting generalizations. Permeating the work of many of the great and prolific composers we find certain combinations of notes, a certain "melos". This "melos" or melodic line seems to be a strong ingredient of their style. Schubert, Beethoven, Mozart, each has his ever-recurring theme song, but so disguised that it makes for artistic variety rather than monotony.

Many themes in compositions of the same period seem to possess similar melodic lines. In our notation key we had to carry some themes to seven or eight letters before their lines began to diverge. It is not that the composers were necessarily imitative. Melodic thinking of the period simply took on certain characteristics, rhythm and harmonic background giving these almost identical lines their variety.

Since the folk tune plays such an integral part in serious composition, one finds special national characteristics in the melodic lines of composers of various lands. Certain interval as well as rhythmic combinations make for Spanish, Russian, German, and French themes, and those of other countries too, of course. Identical motives are used again and again by composers, both consciously and unconsciously. The famous Mannheim motive (G C E♭ G C E♭ D C B C) as found in Beethoven's First Piano Sonata, Mozart's G Minor Symphony, and Mendelssohn's E Minor String Quartet, is probably the most obvious example of this. We found a rather wry footnote to the first page of one of Clementi's B♭ Major Piano Sonatas, stating that when he played this piece for Kaiser Franz Joseph, Mozart was in the audience. The theme of the Sonata is identical with the overture of The Magic Flute, which appeared a few years later. Mozart was famous for his phenomenal memory.

Parody quotations of themes, such as the Tristan Prelude in Debussy's Golliwogg's Cake Walk, are both plentiful and amusing. The Lullaby in Strauss's Domestic Symphony is a steal from a Venetian Boat Song by Mendelssohn, and whether Prokofieff knows it or not, the last half of the second theme in the second movement of his Sixth Piano Sonata bears more than a sneaking resemblance to Mendelssohn's Spring Song.

And so the research student becomes a tone sleuth.

The book should prove useful not only to those who are bothered by a theme and can't remember its source, but also to those who know the source but can't remember the theme. We ourselves shall certainly use it in both capacities.

A book of these dimensions could never have appeared without the aid and encouragement of a great many interested people. We owe a debt of deep and sincere gratitude first to Miss Gladys Chamberlain, Director of the 58th St. Music Library of New York City, who turned over the entire resources of that splendid organization to us, and gave us unreservedly of her time and advice. We want to thank the members of her staff, Miss Mary Lee Daniels, Miss Eleanor Chasan, Miss Lilly Goldberg, Mrs. Hilda Stolov, Mrs. Leah Silton, Mrs. Elsa Hollister, who were more than helpful.

In the music division of the main library of New York City, we wish to thank Mr. Philip Miller, and two of his indefatigable pages, George Klinger and Noel Schwartz.

Our thanks for the special kindness of James Blish, Mrs. Rose Gandal, Alex. M. Kramer, Robert Lowndes, Ben Meiselman, Dr. Rudolf Nissim, Herbert Weinstock, and the many music publishers and copyright owners who gave us assistance. We are indebted to Robert Simon, of Crown Publishers, for his constant encouragement in the undertaking; and to Miss Elizabeth Galvin, his assistant, without whom this book would probably never have appeared.

S. M.

New York, N.Y.
April, 1948

Fugue in G Minor, Organ
"The Little Fugue" Bach — B99a

Symphony No.2, Op. 63
Elgar
By permission of
Novello & Co., Ltd.,
London

1st Movement
1st Theme,
A — E73a

1st Movement
1st Theme,
B — E73b

1st Movement
2nd Theme,
A — E73c

1st Movement
2nd Theme
B — E73d

2nd Movement
Intro. — E73e

2nd Movement
1st Theme — E73f

2nd Movement
2nd Theme — E73g

3rd Movement
1st Theme — E73h

3rd Movement
2nd Theme — E73i

4th Movement
1st Theme — E73j

4th Movement
2nd Theme — E73k

Mélodie, Op. 42, No. 3
from Souvenir D'Un Lieu
Cher. Vn. & Ptt.
Tschaikovsky

T153a

xiv

ADAM, Adolphe (1803-1856)

La Poupée de Nuremberg
(The Nuremberg Doll)
Overture

Si J'Étais Roi
Overture

ALBÉNIZ, Isaac M. F. (1860-1909)

Suite Española, Pft.
   Cadiz (Saeta)
By permission of Associated
Music Publishers, Inc.

Cuba

Seguidillas

Sevillanas

Iberia I, Pft.
   Evocación
By permission of Associated
Music Publishers, Inc.
   Fête Dieu à Seville

Iberia II, Pft.
   Triana
By permission of Associated
Music Publishers, Inc.

2nd Theme — A19

Iberia III, Pft.
El Albaicin (El Polo)
By permission of Associated
Music Publishers, Inc.

A20

Iberia IV, Pft.
Jerez
By permission of Associated
Music Publishers, Inc.

A21

Malaga

A22

Cordoba (Nocturne), Pft.
By permission of Associated
Music Publishers, Inc.

1st Theme — A23

2nd Theme — A24

Pavana-Capricho, Op. 12, Pft.
By permission of Associated
Music Publishers, Inc.

1st Theme — A25

2nd Theme — A26

Sous Le Palmier, in E Flat (Tango Flamenco), Pft.
By permission of Associated
Music Publishers, Inc.

1st Theme — A27

2nd Theme — A28

Tango in D, Pft.
By permission of Associated
Music Publishers, Inc.

A29

ALFVÉN, Hugo (1872-1960)

Midsommarvarka (Swedish Rhapsody), Op. 19, Orch.
By permission of Associated
Music Publishers, Inc.

1st Theme — A30

2nd Theme — A31

3rd Theme — A32

4th Theme — A33

ARENSKY, Anton (1861-1906)

Suite No. 1, Op. 15, 2 Pfts.
Copyright by the Oxford
University Press
Reproduced by permission.

I. Romance
1st Theme — A34

2nd Theme — A35

II. Valse
1st Theme — A36

2nd Theme A37

Trio in D Minor,
Op. 32, Vn., Pft., & Vcl.
By permission of
International Music Co.

1st Movement
1st Theme A38

1st Movement
2nd Theme A39

2nd Movement
1st Theme A40

2nd Movement
2nd Theme A41

3rd Movement
(Elégie)
1st Theme A42

3rd Movement
2nd Theme A43

4th Movement
1st Theme A44

4th Movement
2nd Theme A45

ATTERBERG, Kurt (1887-1974)

Symphony No. 6,
in C, Op.31
By permission of Associated
Music Publishers, Inc.

1st Movement
1st Theme A46

1st Movement
2nd Theme A47

1st Movement
3rd Theme A48

2nd Movement
1st Theme A49

2nd Movement
2nd Theme A50

3rd Movement
1st Theme A51

3rd Movement
2nd Theme A52

AUBER, Daniel François (1782-1871)

Le Cheval de Bronze
Overture

1st Theme A53

2nd Theme A54

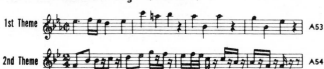

3rd Theme   A55

Le Domino Noir
Overture   1st Theme   A56

2nd Theme   A57

3rd Theme   A58

4th Theme   A59

Fra Diavolo
Overture   1st Theme   A60

2nd Theme   A61

3rd Theme   A62

La Muette De Portici
Overture   1st Theme   A63

2nd Theme   A64

AUBERT, Louis (1877-1968)

Habañera, Orch.   1st Theme   A65
Permission for reprint granted
by Durand & Cie, Paris.
Elkan-Vogel Co.,Inc.Philadelphia,
Copyright Owners   2nd Theme   A66

Suite Breve, Op. 6, Orch.
   I. Menuet   1st Theme   A67
Permission for reprint granted
by Durand & Cie, Paris.
Elkan-Vogel Co.,Inc.   2nd Theme   A68
Philadelphia,Copyright Owners,

   II. Berceuse   A69

   III. Air de Ballet   1st Theme   A70

2nd Theme   A71

3rd Theme   A72

AURIC, Georges (1899-)

Les Matelots (Ballet)
By permission of
the copyright owner.
Heugel & Cie, Paris.

1st Movement 1st Theme	A73
1st Movement 2nd Theme	A74
1st Movement 3rd Theme	A75
1st Movement 4th Theme	A76
2nd Movement	A77
3rd Movement 1st Theme	A78
3rd Movement 2nd Theme	A79
4th Movement 1st Theme	A80
4th Movement 2nd Theme	A81
5th Movement 1st Theme	A82
5th Movement 2nd Theme	A83
5th Movement 3rd Theme	A84

BACH, Johann Christian (1735-1782)

Concerto in C,
Op. 7 . No.1, Pft. & Str.

| 1st Movement | B1 |
| 2nd Movement Minuet | B2 |

Concerto in E Flat,
Op.7, No.5, Pft. & Str.

1st Movement 1st Theme	B3
1st Movement 2nd Theme	B4
2nd Movement	B5
3rd Movement	B6

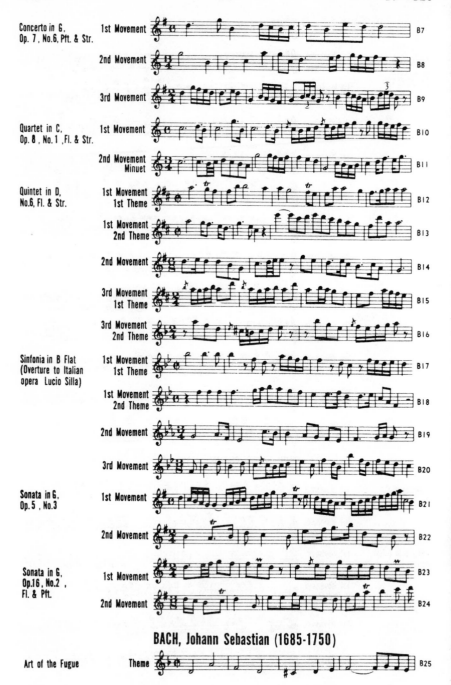

Christ Lag in Todesbunden
(Church Cantata, No. 4)
B26

Jesu, Joy of Man's
Desiring (from
Cantata 147)
1st Movement
1st Theme
B27

1st Movement
2nd Theme
B28

Eine Feste Burg Ist Unser Gott
B29

Komm Süsser Tod
(Schemelli No. 42)
B29a

Wachet Auf
Organ Chorale
B29b

Brandenburg
Concerto No. 1,
in F, 2 Hns.,
3 Oboes, Fg., Vn.,
Str. & Cembalo
1st Movement
B30

2nd Movement
B31

3rd Movement
B32

4th Movement
Minuetto,1st Theme
B33

4th Movement
2nd Theme
Trio
B34

5th Movement
B35

Brandenburg
Concerto No. 2,
in F, Tpt., Vn.,
Fl., Ob., Str.
& Cembalo
1st Movement
1st Theme
B36

1st Movement
2nd Theme
B37

2nd Movement
B38

3rd Movement
B39

Brandenburg
Concerto No. 3,
in G (2nd
Movement is
only a bridge)
1st Movement
B40

3rd Movement
B41

Brandenburg
Concerto No. 4,
in G, 2 Fl., Vn.,
Str. & Cembalo
1st Movement
B42

2nd Movement
B43

3rd Movement — B44

Brandenburg Concerto No. 5, in D, Fl., Vn., Str. & Cembalo

1st Movement — B45

2nd Movement — B46

3rd Movement — B47

Brandenburg Concerto No. 6, in B Flat, Viola Solos & Strings

1st Movement — B48

2nd Movement — B49

3rd Movement — B50

Concerto No. 8, in A Minor, Fl., Vn., Pft. & Orch.

1st Movement — B51

2nd Movement — B52

3rd Movement — B53

Concerto No. 1, in D Minor, Pft. & Orch.

1st Movement — B54

2nd Movement — B55

3rd Movement — B56

Concerto No. 2, in D, Pft. & Orch.

1st Movement — B57

2nd Movement — B58

3rd Movement — B59

Concerto No. 4, in A, Pft. & Orch.

1st Movement — B60

2nd Movement — B61

Concerto No. 5, in F Minor, Pft. & Orch.

1st Movement — B62

2nd Movement — B63

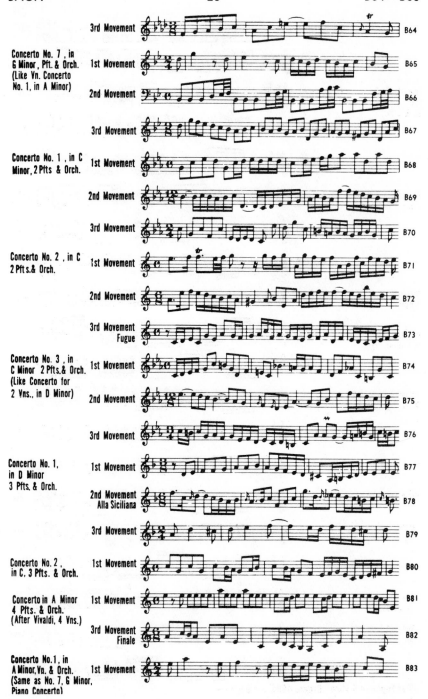

3rd Movement — B64

Concerto No. 7 , in
G Minor, Pft. & Orch.
(Like Vn. Concerto
No. 1, in A Minor)
1st Movement — B65

2nd Movement — B66

3rd Movement — B67

Concerto No. 1 , in C
Minor, 2 Pfts & Orch.
1st Movement — B68

2nd Movement — B69

3rd Movement — B70

Concerto No. 2 , in C
2 Pfts.& Orch.
1st Movement — B71

2nd Movement — B72

3rd Movement
Fugue — B73

Concerto No. 3 , in
C Minor 2 Pfts.& Orch.
(Like Concerto for
2 Vns., in D Minor)
1st Movement — B74

2nd Movement — B75

3rd Movement — B76

Concerto No. 1,
in D Minor
3 Pfts. & Orch.
1st Movement — B77

2nd Movement
Alla Siciliana — B78

3rd Movement — B79

Concerto No. 2 ,
in C. 3 Pfts. & Orch.
1st Movement — B80

Concerto in A Minor
4 Pfts. & Orch.
(After Vivaldi, 4 Vns.)
1st Movement — B81

3rd Movement
Finale — B82

Concerto No.1, in
A Minor, Vn. & Orch.
(Same as No. 7, G Minor,
Piano Concerto)
1st Movement — B83

*For Fugue in G Minor, Organ, B99a, see page xiv.

No. 3, in D — B104
No. 4, in D Minor — B105
No. 5, in E Flat — B106
No. 6, in E / 1st Subject — B107
Counter Subj. — B108
No. 7, in E Minor — B109
No. 8, in F — B110
No. 9, in F Minor — B111
No. 10, in G — B112
No. 11, in G Minor — B113
No. 12, in A — B114
No. 13, in A Minor — B115
No. 14, in B Flat — B116
No. 15, in B Minor — B117
Three-part Inventions (Also called Sinfonias) / No. 2, in C Minor — B118
No. 3, in D — B119
No. 4, in D Minor — B120
No. 7, in E Minor — B121
No. 9, in F Minor — B122
No. 11, in G Minor — B123

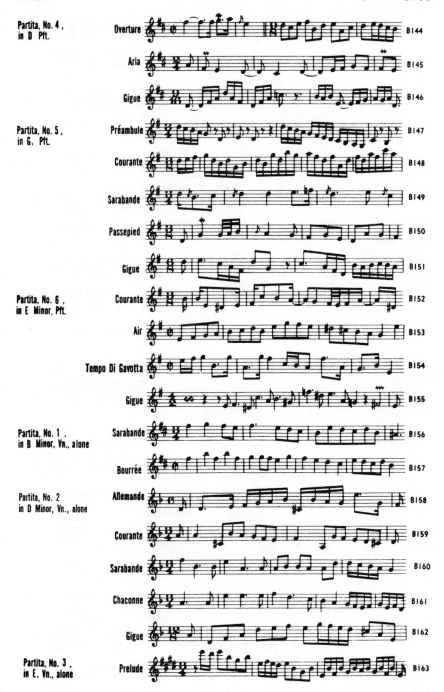

Partita, No. 4,
in D Pft. Overture B144

Aria B145

Gigue B146

Partita, No. 5,
in G, Pft. Préambule B147

Courante B148

Sarabande B149

Passepied B150

Gigue B151

Partita, No. 6,
in E Minor, Pft. Courante B152

Air B153

Tempo Di Gavotta B154

Gigue B155

Partita, No. 1,
in B Minor, Vn., alone Sarabande B156

Bourrée B157

Partita, No. 2
in D Minor, Vn., alone Allemande B158

Courante B159

Sarabande B160

Chaconne B161

Gigue B162

Partita, No. 3,
in E, Vn., alone Prelude B163

Loure	B164
Gavotte En Rondeau / 1st Theme	B165
2nd Theme	B166
Minuet	B167
Bourrée	B168
Gigue	B169
*Passacaglia, in C Minor, Organ	B170
Sonata No. 1 in B Minor, Fl. & Harpsi. / 1st Movement	B171
2nd Movement	B172
3rd Movement	B173
Sonata No. 2 in E Flat, Fl. & Harpsi. / Siciliana	B174
Sonata No. 1 in G Minor, Vn., alone / 1st Movement Adagio	B175
Fugue	B176
Siciliana	B177
Finale Presto	B178
Sonata No. 2, in A Minor, Vn., alone / Grave	B178a
Fugue	B179
Andante	B180
Allegro	B180a
Sonata No. 3 in C, Vn., alone / Adagio	B181

*Bach borrowed the theme from André Raison, a Paris organist in the reign of Louis XIV (1638—1715).

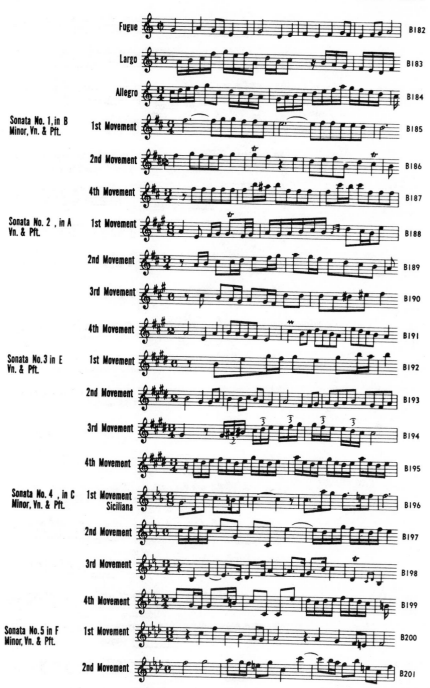

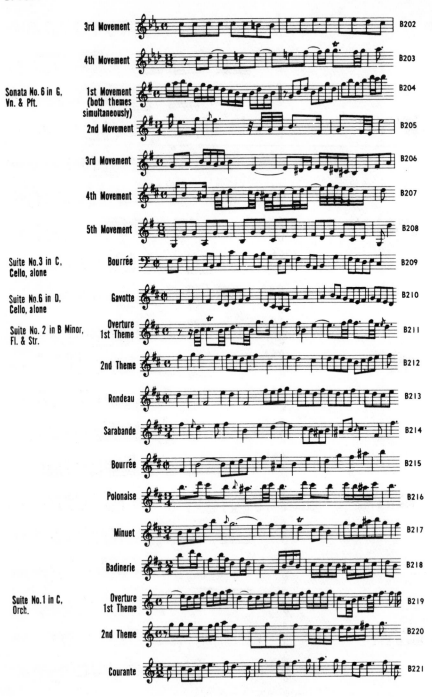

3rd Movement — B202

4th Movement — B203

Sonata No. 6 in G, Vn. & Pft.
1st Movement (both themes simultaneously) — B204

2nd Movement — B205

3rd Movement — B206

4th Movement — B207

5th Movement — B208

Suite No. 3 in C, Cello, alone
Bourrée — B209

Suite No. 6 in D, Cello, alone
Gavotte — B210

Suite No. 2 in B Minor, Fl. & Str.
Overture 1st Theme — B211

2nd Theme — B212

Rondeau — B213

Sarabande — B214

Bourrée — B215

Polonaise — B216

Minuet — B217

Badinerie — B218

Suite No. 1 in C, Orch.
Overture 1st Theme — B219

2nd Theme — B220

Courante — B221

Gavotte — B222
Forlane — B223
Minuet — B224
Bourrée — B225
Passepied — B226

Suite No.3 in D, Orch.
Overture 1st Theme — B227
2nd Theme — B228

"Air for the G String"
Air — B229
Gavotte 1st Theme — B230
2nd Theme — B231
Bourrée — B232
Gigue — B233

English Suite, No. 1, in A, Pft.
Sarabande — B234
Bourrée 1st Theme — B235
2nd Theme — B236
Gigue — B237

English Suite, No.2, in A Minor, Pft.
Prelude — B238
Allemande — B239
Courante — B240
Sarabande — B241

Bourrée I — B242

Bourrée II — B243

Gigue — B244

English Suite, No.3, in G Minor, Pft.

Prelude — B245

Allemande — B246

Sarabande — B247

Gavotte — B248

Musette — B249

Gigue — B250

English Suite, No. 4, in F, Pft.

Prelude — B251

Sarabande — B252

Minuet I — B253

Minuet II — B254

Gigue — B255

English Suite, No. 5, in E Minor, Pft.

Prelude — B256

Courante — B257

Sarabande — B258

Passepied I — B259

Passepied II — B260

Gigue — B261

BACH   35   B262—B281

Fugue No.11 B322

Prelude No. 12 B323

Fugue No.12 B324

Prelude No. 13 B325

Fugue No. 13 B326

Prelude No.14 B327

Fugue No. 14 B328

Prelude No. 15 B329

Fugue No. 15 B330

Prelude No.16 B331

Fugue No. 16 B332

Prelude No. 17 B333

Fugue No.17 B334

Prelude No.18 B335

Fugue No.18 B336

Prelude No. 19 B337

Fugue No. 19 B338

Prelude No. 20 B339

Fugue No. 20 B340

Prelude No. 21 B341

Fugue No. 21 — B342
Prelude No. 22 — B343
Fugue No. 22 — B344
Prelude No. 23 — B345
Fugue No. 23 — B346
Prelude No. 24 — B347
Fugue No. 24 — B348

Well Tempered Clavichord
Book II

Prelude No. 1 — B349
Fugue No. 1 — B350
Prelude No. 2 — B351
Fugue No. 2 — B352
Prelude No. 3 A — B353
B — B354
Fugue No. 3 — B355
Prelude No. 4 — B356
Fugue No. 4 — B357
Prelude No. 5 — B358
Fugue No. 5 — B359
Prelude No. 6 — B360
Fugue No. 6 — B361

Prelude No. 7   B362
Fugue No. 7   B363
Prelude No. 8   B364
Fugue No. 8   B365
Prelude No. 9   B366
Fugue No. 9   B367
Prelude No. 10   B368
Fugue No. 10   B369
Prelude No. 11   B370
Fugue No. 11   B371
Prelude No. 12   B372
Fugue No. 12   B373
Prelude No. 13   B374
Fugue No. 13   B375
Prelude No. 14   B376
Fugue No. 14   B377
Prelude No. 15   B378
Fugue No. 15   B379
Prelude No. 16   B380
Fugue No. 16   B381

Prelude No.17 — B382
Fugue No.17 — B383
Prelude No.18 — B384
Fugue No.18 — B385
Prelude No.19 — B386
Fugue No.19 — B387
Prelude No. 20 — B388
Fugue No.20 — B389
Prelude No. 21 — B390
Fugue No. 21 — B391
Prelude No. 22 — B392
Fugue No. 22 — B393
Prelude No. 23 — B394
Fugue No. 23 — B395
Prelude No. 24 — B396
Fugue No. 24 — B397

BACH, Karl Philipp Emanuel (1714-1788)

Abschied Von Meinem Silbermannischen Klaviere , Pft. — B398

Concerto No. 3 , in A Cello & Str. Orch. 1st Movement — B399

2nd Movement — B400

3rd Movement — B401

Solfeggio (Solfeggietto), Pft. — B402

Sonata No. 1 in
A Minor , Pft.   1st Movement — B403
(from Würtemberg Sonatas)

2nd Movement — B404

3rd Movement — B405

Sonata No. 4 in B Flat
Pft.   1st Movement — B406
(from Würtemberg Sonatas)

2nd Movement — B407

3rd Movement — B408

Sonata No. 1 in G,
Pft. (from Für Kenner   1st Movement — B409
and Liebhaber Collection
No. 2)

2nd Movement — B410

3rd Movement — B411

Sonata No. 3 in F Minor,
Pft. (from Für Kenner   1st Movement — B412
und Liebhaber Collection
No. 3)

2nd Movement — B413

3rd Movement — B414

Concerto in D, Orch.   1st Movement — B415

2nd Movement — B416

3rd Movement — B417

Symphony No.1   1st Movement — B418
in D,

2nd Movement — B419

3rd Movement — B420

Symphony No. 3, in C, Str. & Cembalo — 1st Movement — B421

2nd Movement — B422

3rd Movement — B423

BACH, Wilhelm Friedemann (1710-1784)

Concerto in D Minor, (also attributed to Vivaldi), Pft. — 1st Movement Intro. — B424

1st Movement Fugue — B425

2nd Movement — B426

3rd Movement — B427

Sonata in C, Harpsi. — 1st Movement — B428

2nd Movement — B429

3rd Movement — B430

Sonata in F (Concerto) 2 Pfts. — 1st Movement — B431

2nd Movement — B432

3rd Movement — B433

BALAKIREFF, Mily (1837-1910)

Islamey (Oriental Fantasy) Pft. — 1st Theme — B434
By permission of Associated Music Publishers, Inc.

2nd Theme, A — B435

2nd Theme, B — B436

Russia (symph. poem) — 1st Theme — B437

2nd Theme — B438

3rd Theme — B439

4th Theme — B440

Thamar (Tamara)
(symph. poem)
By permission of Associated
Music Publishers, Inc.

1st Theme — B441

2nd Theme — B442

3rd Theme — B443

4th Theme — B444

BALFE, Michael (1808-1870)

The Bohemian Girl
Overture

1st Theme — B445

2nd Theme — B446

3rd Theme — B447

4th Theme — B448

BANTOCK, Sir Granville (1868-1946)

The Pierrot of the Minute
Overture
By permission of Associated
Music Publishers, Inc.

1st Theme — B449

2nd Theme — B450

3rd Theme — B451

4th Theme — B452

BARBER, Samuel (1910-   )

Adagio for Strings, Op. 11
Copyright 1939 by
G. Schirmer, Inc.

B452a

Essay for Orchestra,
Op. 12
Copyright 1941 by
G. Schirmer, Inc.

1st Theme — B453

2nd Theme — B454

First Symphony
Op. 9
Copyright 1943
by G. Schirmer, Inc.

1st Theme — B454a

2nd Theme — B454b

3rd Theme — B454c

4th Theme — B454d

5th Theme — B454e

6th Theme — B454f

7th Theme — B454g

The School for Scandal
Overture
Copyright 1941 by
G. Schirmer, Inc.

1st Theme — B455

2nd Theme — B456

BARTÓK, Béla (1881-1945)

Allegro Barbaro, Pft.
By permission of the copyright
owner, Boosey and Hawkes, Inc.

1st Theme — B457

2nd Theme — B458

Bagatelle, Op.2, Pft. — B459

Burlesque (A Bit Drunk)
Op.8c, No.2 — B460

Concerto for
Vn. & Orch.
By permission of the copyright
owner, Boosey and Hawkes, Inc.

1st Movement
1st Theme — B461

1st Movement
2nd Theme — B462

2nd Movement — B463

3rd Movement
1st Theme — B464

3rd Movement
2nd Theme — B465

Contrasts, Vn., Cl.
& Pft.
By permission of the
copyright owner,
Boosey and Hawkes, Inc.

1st Movement
1st Theme
Recruiting Dance — B466

- 1st Movement / 2nd Theme — B467
- 2nd Movement / Relaxation — B468
- 3rd Movement / 1st Theme / Fast Dance — B469
- 3rd Movement / 2nd Theme — B470
- 3rd Movement / 3rd Theme — B471

Hungarian Folk Songs
Ungarische Volksweisen
(Arranged by Szigeti),
Vn. & Pft.
By permission of the copyright owner, Boosey and Hawkes, Inc.

- 1st Movement / 1st Theme — B472
- 1st Movement / 2nd Theme — B473
- 1st Movement / 3rd Theme — B474
- 2nd Movement / 1st Theme — B475
- 2nd Movement / 2nd Theme — B476
- 3rd Movement / 1st Theme — B477
- 3rd Movement / 2nd Theme — B478

Hungarian Sketches, No. 1
(Est a Szeklyeknel)

- 1st Movement / An Evening in the Village / 1st Theme — B479
- 2nd Theme — B480
- 2nd Movement / Bear Dance — B481

Quartet No. 1,
Op. 7, Str.
By permission of the copyright owner, Boosey and Hawkes, Inc.

- 1st Movement — B482
- 2nd Movement / Intro. — B483
- 2nd Movement / 1st Theme — B484
- 2nd Movement / 2nd Theme — B485
- 3rd Movement / Intro. — B486

RumanianFolkDances Pft. By permission of the copyright owner, Boosey and Hawkes, Inc.

BAX, Sir Arnold Trevor (1883-1953)

Fantasy-Sonata, Viola & Harp
Copyright 1922 Murdock, Murdock & Co., London. Carl Fischer, Inc., N. Y., Sole Agents for the U.S.A.

1st Movement 1st Theme — B507

1st Movement 2nd Theme — B508

2nd Movement — B509

3rd Movement — B510

4th Movement — B511

Mediterranean, Orch.
Copyright 1923 Murdock, Murdock & Co., London. Carl Fischer. Inc. N. Y. Sole Agents for the U.S.A.

— B512

Overture to a Picaresque Comedy
Copyright 1934 Murdock, Murdock & Co., London. Carl Fischer, Inc., N. Y., Sole Agents for the U.S.A.

1st Theme — B513

2nd Theme — B514

3rd Theme — B515

Sonata, Viola & Pft.
Copyright 1923 Murdock. Murdock & Co., London. Carl Fischer, Inc., N. Y., Sole Agents for the U.S.A.

1st Movement 1st Theme — B516

1st Movement 2nd Theme — B517

2nd Movement 1st Theme — B518

2nd Movement 2nd Theme — B519

3rd Movement — B520

BEETHOVEN, Ludwig Van (1770-1827)

Andante Favori, F — B521

Concerto No. 1, in C Op.15, Pft.

1st Movement 1st Theme — B522

1st Movement 2nd Theme — B523

2nd Movement 1st Theme — B524

2nd Movement 2nd Theme — B525

3rd Movement 1st Theme — B526

3rd Movement 2nd Theme — B527

3rd Movement 3rd Theme — B528

Concerto No. 2, in B Flat Op. 19, Pft.

1st Movement 1st Theme — B529

1st Movement 2nd Theme — B530

2nd Movement — B531

3rd Movement — B532

Concerto No. 3, in C Minor, Op. 37, Pft.

1st Movement 1st Theme — B533

1st Movement 2nd Theme — B534

2nd Movement — B535

3rd Movement — B536

Concerto No. 4, in G, Op. 58, Pft.

1st Movement 1st Theme — B537

1st Movement 2nd Theme — B538

2nd Movement — B539

3rd Movement 1st Theme, A — B540

3rd Movement 1st Theme, B — B541

3rd Movement 2nd Theme — B542

Concerto No. 5, in E Flat, Op. 73, "Emperor"

1st Movement 1st Theme — B543

1st Movement 2nd Theme — B544

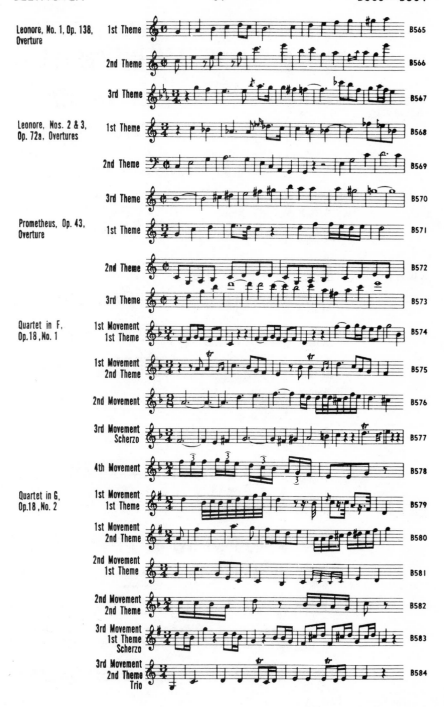

Leonore, No. 1, Op. 138, Overture — 1st Theme — B565
2nd Theme — B566
3rd Theme — B567

Leonore, Nos. 2 & 3, Op. 72a, Overtures — 1st Theme — B568
2nd Theme — B569
3rd Theme — B570

Prometheus, Op. 43, Overture — 1st Theme — B571
2nd Theme — B572
3rd Theme — B573

Quartet in F, Op.18, No. 1 — 1st Movement 1st Theme — B574
1st Movement 2nd Theme — B575
2nd Movement — B576
3rd Movement Scherzo — B577
4th Movement — B578

Quartet in G, Op.18, No. 2 — 1st Movement 1st Theme — B579
1st Movement 2nd Theme — B580
2nd Movement 1st Theme — B581
2nd Movement 2nd Theme — B582
3rd Movement 1st Theme Scherzo — B583
3rd Movement 2nd Theme Trio — B584

Quartet in B Flat, Op.18, No.6

1st Movement 1st Theme — B604

1st Movement 2nd Theme — B605

2nd Movement — B606

3rd Movement — B607

4th Movement La Malinconia Intro. — B608

4th Movement Theme — B609

Quartet in F Op.59, No.1 "Rasoumowsky"

1st Movement — B610

2nd Movement — B611

3rd Movement — B612

4th Movement — B613

Quartet in E Minor, Op.59, No.2 "Rasoumowsky"

1st Movement — B614

2nd Movement 1st Theme — B615

2nd Movement 2nd Theme — B616

3rd Movement 1st Theme — B617

3rd Movement 2nd Theme — B618

4th Movement — B619

Quartet in C, Op.59, No.3, "Rasoumowsky"

1st Movement — B620

2nd Movement — B621

3rd Movement — B622

4th Movement — B623

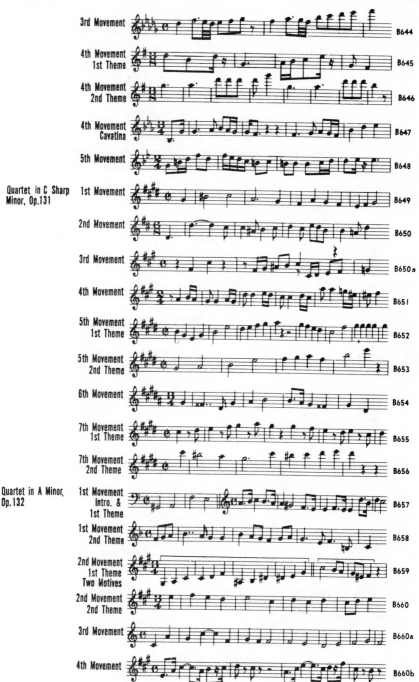

3rd Movement — B675
4th Movement — B676
5th Movement — B677
6th Movement — B678
7th Movement — B679

Serenade, Op. 8, Vn., Viola & Cello — 1st Movement — B679a
2nd Movement — B679b
3rd Movement Minuet — B679c
4th Movement 1st Theme — B679d
4th Movement 2nd Theme — B679e
5th Movement Alla Polacca — B679f
6th Movement — B679g

Sonata No. 2, in G Minor, Op. 5, No. 2, Cello & Pft. — 1st Movement Intro. — B679h
1st Movement — B680
2nd Movement — B680a

Sonata No. 3 in A, Op. 69, Cello & Pft. — 1st Movement — B681
2nd Movement 1st Theme — B682
2nd Movement 2nd Theme — B683
3rd Movement — B684

Sonata No. 4, in C, Op. 102, No. 1, Cello & Pft. — 1st Movement Intro. — B685

1st Movement — B686

2nd Movement — B686a

3rd Movement — B686b

Sonata in F
Op. 17, Horn & Pft. — 1st Movement — B687

2nd Movement — B688

3rd Movement — B688a

Sonata No. 1, in F Minor, — 1st Movement — 1st Theme — B689
Op. 2, No. 1, Pft.

1st Movement — 2nd Theme — B690

2nd Movement — B691

3rd Movement — 1st Theme — Minuet — B692

3rd Movement — 2nd Theme — B693

4th Movement — 1st Theme — B694

4th Movement — 2nd Theme — B695

Sonata No. 2, in A — 1st Movement — 1st Theme — B696
Op. 2, No. 2, Pft.

1st Movement — 2nd Theme — B697

2nd Movement — B698

3rd Movement — 1st Theme — B699

3rd Movement — 2nd Theme — B700

4th Movement — 1st Theme — B701

4th Movement — 2nd Theme — B702

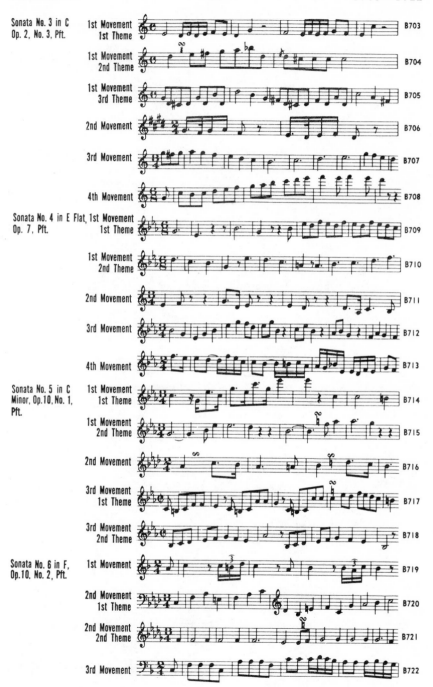

Sonata No. 3 in C
Op. 2, No. 3, Pft.

1st Movement
1st Theme — B703

1st Movement
2nd Theme — B704

1st Movement
3rd Theme — B705

2nd Movement — B706

3rd Movement — B707

4th Movement — B708

Sonata No. 4 in E Flat,
Op. 7, Pft.

1st Movement
1st Theme — B709

1st Movement
2nd Theme — B710

2nd Movement — B711

3rd Movement — B712

4th Movement — B713

Sonata No. 5 in C
Minor, Op. 10, No. 1,
Pft.

1st Movement
1st Theme — B714

1st Movement
2nd Theme — B715

2nd Movement — B716

3rd Movement
1st Theme — B717

3rd Movement
2nd Theme — B718

Sonata No. 6 in F,
Op. 10, No. 2, Pft.

1st Movement — B719

2nd Movement
1st Theme — B720

2nd Movement
2nd Theme — B721

3rd Movement — B722

Sonata No. 7 in D, Op. 10, No. 3, Pft.	1st Movement 1st Theme	B723
	1st Movement 2nd Theme	B724
	2nd Movement	B725
	3rd Movement Minuetto	B726
	4th Movement	B727
Sonata No. 8, in C Minor, Op. 13, Pft. "Pathetique"	1st Movement Intro	B728
	1st Movement 1st Theme	B729
	1st Movement 2nd Theme	B730
	2nd Movement 1st Theme	B731
	2nd Movement 2nd Theme	B732
	3rd Movement 1st Theme	B733
	3rd Movement 2nd Theme	B734
	3rd Movement 3rd Theme	B735
Sonata No. 9, in E Op. 14, No. 1, Pft.	1st Movement 1st Theme	B736
	1st Movement 2nd Theme	B737
	2nd Movement 1st Theme	B738
	2nd Movement 2nd Theme	B739
	3rd Movement	B740
Sonata No. 10, in G Op. 14, No. 2, Pft.	1st Movement	B741
	2nd Movement	B742

3rd Movement 1st Theme — B743
3rd Movement 2nd Theme — B744
Sonata No.11, in B Flat, Op.22, Pft. 1st Movement 1st Theme — B745
1st Movement 2nd Theme — B746
1st Movement 3rd Theme — B747
2nd Movement — B748
3rd Movement — B749
4th Movement — B750
Sonata No.12, in A Flat, Op.26, Pft. 1st Movement — B751
2nd Movement 1st Theme — B752
2nd Movement 2nd Theme — B753
3rd Movement — B754
4th Movement — B755
Sonata No.13 in E Flat, Op.27, No.1 (Sonata Quasi Una Fantasia) 1st Movement 1st Theme — B756
1st Movement 2nd Theme — B757
2nd Movement 1st Theme — B758
2nd Movement 2nd Theme — B759
3rd Movement — B760
4th Movement — B761
Sonata No.14 in C Sharp Minor, Op.27, No.2, Pft. (Sonata Quasi Una Fantasia) "Moonlight" 1st Movement Intro. — B762

1st Movement — B763

2nd Movement 1st Theme — B764

2nd Movement 2nd Theme — B765

3rd Movement 1st Theme — B766

3rd Movement 2nd Theme — B767

Sonata No.15 in D Op.28. Pft. "Pastoral"

1st Movement 1st Theme — B768

1st Movement 2nd Theme — B769

1st Movement 3rd Theme — B770

2nd Movement 1st Theme — B771

2nd Movement 2nd Theme — B772

3rd Movement 1st Theme — B773

3rd Movement 2nd Theme — B774

4th Movement — B775

Sonata No.16 in G Op.31, No.1, Pft.

1st Movement 1st Theme — B776

1st Movement 2nd Theme — B777

2nd Movement — B778

3rd Movement — B779

Sonata No.17 in D Minor, Op.31, No.2, Pft., "Tempest"

1st Movement 1st Theme — B780

1st Movement 2nd Theme — B781

2nd Movement 1st Theme — B782

2nd Movement
2nd Theme   B783

3rd Movement
1st Theme   B784

3rd Movement
2nd Theme   B785

Sonata No. 18 in E
Flat Op. 31,
No. 3, Pft.   1st Movement
1st Theme   B786

1st Movement
2nd Theme   B787

2nd Movement   B788

3rd Movement
1st Theme
Minuetto   B789

3rd Movement
2nd Theme   B790

4th Movement
1st Theme,
A   B791

4th Movement
1st Theme,
B   B792

Sonata No. 19 in G Minor
Op. 49, No. 1, Pft.   1st Movement
1st Theme   B793

1st Movement
2nd Theme   B794

2nd Movement
1st Theme   B795

2nd Movement
2nd Theme   B796

Sonata No. 20 in G
Op. 49, No. 2, Pft.   1st Movement
1st Theme   B797

1st Movement
2nd Theme   B798

2nd Movement   B799

Sonata No. 21 in C
Op. 53, Pft.
"Waldstein"   1st Movement
1st Theme   B800

1st Movement
2nd Theme   B801

2nd Movement
Intro.   B802

2nd Movement Rondo — B803

Sonata No. 22 in F Op. 54, Pft. — 1st Movement 1st Theme — B804

1st Movement 2nd Theme — B805

2nd Movement — B806

Sonata No. 23 in F Minor, Op. 57, Pft. "Appassionata" — 1st Movement 1st Theme — B807

1st Movement 2nd Theme — B808

1st Movement 3rd Theme — B809

2nd Movement — B810

3rd Movement 1st Theme — B811

3rd Movement 2nd Theme — B812

Sonata No. 24 in F Sharp, Op. 78, Pft. — 1st Movement 1st Theme — B813

1st Movement 2nd Theme — B814

2nd Movement — B815

Sonata No. 25, in G Op. 79, Pft. (Alla Tedesca) — 1st Movement — B816

2nd Movement 1st Theme — B817

2nd Movement 2nd Theme — B818

3rd Movement — B819

Sonata No. 26 in E Flat, Op. 81a, Pft. Les Adieux — 1st Movement Intro. — B820

1st Movement 1st Theme, A — B821

1st Movement 1st Theme, B — B822

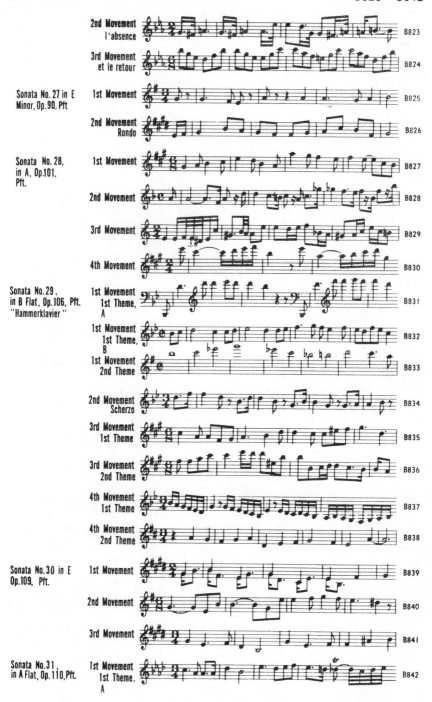

3rd Movement — B863

Sonata No. 5, Op. 24
Vn. & Pft.,"Spring"
1st Movement — B864

2nd Movement — B865

3rd Movement
Scherzo — B866

4th Movement — B867

Sonata No. 6 , in A
Op.30, No. 1,
Vn. & Pft.
1st Movement
1st Theme — B868

1st Movement
2nd Theme — B869

2nd Movement — B870

3rd Movement — B871

Sonata No. 7 in C
Minor, Op.30 , No.2
Vn. & Pft.
1st Movement
1st Theme — B872

1st Movement
2nd Theme — B873

2nd Movement — B874

3rd Movement
1st Theme — B875

3rd Movement
2nd Theme — B876

4th Movement — B877

Sonata No. 8 in G
Op.30, No.3
Vn. & Pft.
1st Movement — B878

2nd Movement — B879

3rd Movement — B880

Sonata No. 9 in A, Op. 47,
Vn.& Pft.
"Kreutzer"
1st Movement
Intro. — B881

1st Movement — B882

2nd Movement — B883

3rd Movement 1st Theme, A — B884

3rd Movement 1st Theme, B — B885

3rd Movement 2nd Theme — B886

Sonata No. 10 in G Op. 96, Vn. & Pft.

1st Movement 1st Theme — B887

1st Movement 2nd Theme — B888

2nd Movement — B889

3rd Movement Scherzo — B890

4th Movement — B891

Symphony No. 1, in C, Op. 21

1st Movement Intro. A — B892

1st Movement Intro. B — B893

1st Movement 1st Theme — B894

1st Movement 2nd Theme — B895

1st Movement 3rd Theme — B896

1st Movement 4th Theme — B897

2nd Movement 1st Theme — B898

2nd Movement 2nd Theme — B899

2nd Movement 3rd Theme — B900

3rd Movement 1st Theme — B901

3rd Movement 2nd Theme — B902

4th Movement 1st Theme — B903

4th Movement 2nd Theme — B904

Symphony No.2, in D Op.36

1st Movement Intro. — B905

1st Movement 1st Theme — B906

1st Movement 2nd Theme — B907

2nd Movement 1st Theme, A — B908

2nd Movement 1st Theme, B — B909

2nd Movement 2nd Theme — B910

2nd Movement 3rd Theme — B911

2nd Movement 4th Theme — B912

3rd Movement 1st Theme — B913

3rd Movement 2nd Theme — B914

4th Movement 1st Theme — B915

4th Movement 2nd Theme — B916

4th Movement 3rd Theme — B917

Symphony No.3, in E Flat, Op.55 "Eroica"

1st Movement 1st Theme — B918

1st Movement 2nd Theme — B919

1st Movement 3rd Theme — B920

1st Movement 4th Theme — B921

1st Movement 5th Theme — B922

1st Movement 6th Theme — B923

2nd Movement 1st Theme — B924

2nd Movement 2nd Theme — B925

2nd Movement 3rd Theme — B926

2nd Movement 4th Theme — B927

3rd Movement 1st Theme, A — B928

3rd Movement 1st Theme, B — B929

3rd Movement 2nd Theme — B930

4th Movement 1st Theme — B931

4th Movement 2nd Theme — B932

4th Movement 3rd Theme — B933

4th Movement 4th Theme — B934

Symphony No. 4, in B Flat, Op. 60

1st Movement Intro. — B935

1st Movement 1st Theme — B936

1st Movement 2nd Theme — B937

1st Movement 3rd Theme — B938

1st Movement 4th Theme — B939

2nd Movement 1st Theme — B940

2nd Movement 2nd Theme — B941

2nd Movement 3rd Theme — B942

Symphony No. 7 in A
Op. 92

Symphony No. 8
in F, Op. 93

1st Movement
2nd Theme — B1003

1st Movement
3rd Theme — B1004

1st Movement
4th Theme,
A — B1005

1st Movement
4th Theme,
B — B1006

2nd Movement
1st Theme — B1007

2nd Movement
2nd Theme — B1008

2nd Movement
3rd Theme — B1009

3rd Movement
1st Theme — B1010

3rd Movement
2nd Theme — B1011

4th Movement
1st Theme,
A — B1012

4th Movement
1st Theme,
B — B1013

4th Movement
2nd Theme — B1014

4th Movement
3rd Theme — B1015

Symphony No. 9,
in D Minor, Op. 125,
"Choral"

1st Movement
1st Theme — B1016

1st Movement
2nd Theme — B1017

1st Movement
3rd Theme — B1018

1st Movement
4th Theme — B1019

2nd Movement
1st Theme — B1020

2nd Movement
2nd Theme — B1021

2nd Movement
3rd Theme
A — B1022

2nd Movement / 3rd Theme, / B — B1023

3rd Movement / 1st Theme — B1024

3rd Movement / 2nd Theme — B1025

4th Movement / Intro. — B1026

4th Movement / 1st Theme — B1027

4th Movement / 2nd Theme — B1028

4th Movement / 3rd Theme — B1029

4th Movement / 4th Theme — B1030

Trio in B Flat, / Op.11, Cl., Cello & Pft. / Gassenhauer (Street Song) — 1st Movement — B1031

2nd Movement — B1032

3rd Movement — B1033

Trio in C Minor, / Op.1 , No.3, Str. — 1st Movement / 1st Theme, / A — B1034

1st Movement / 1st Theme, / B — B1035

1st Movement / 2nd Theme — B1036

2nd Movement — B1037

3rd Movement / 1st Theme — B1038

3rd Movement / 2nd Theme — B1039

4th Movement / 1st Theme — B1040

4th Movement / 2nd Theme — B1041

Trio in D, / Op.70, No. 1 / "Geister" / Vn, Cello, Pft. — 1st Movement / 1st Theme — B1042

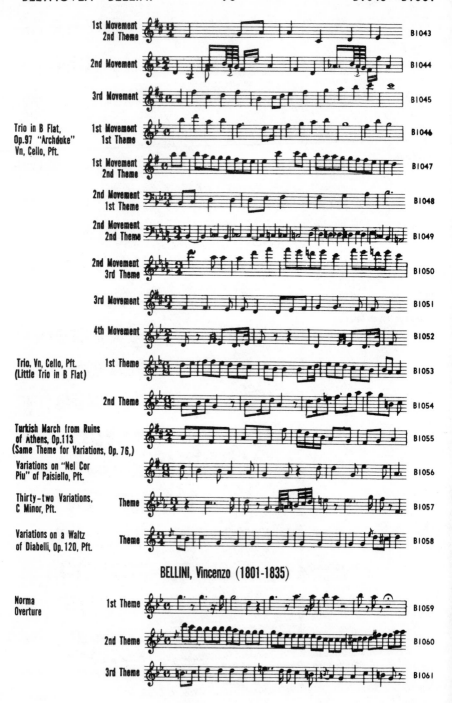

1st Movement 2nd Theme — B1043

2nd Movement — B1044

3rd Movement — B1045

Trio in B Flat, Op.97 "Archduke" Vn, Cello, Pft.
1st Movement 1st Theme — B1046

1st Movement 2nd Theme — B1047

2nd Movement 1st Theme — B1048

2nd Movement 2nd Theme — B1049

2nd Movement 3rd Theme — B1050

3rd Movement — B1051

4th Movement — B1052

Trio, Vn, Cello, Pft. (Little Trio in B Flat)
1st Theme — B1053

2nd Theme — B1054

Turkish March from Ruins of Athens, Op.113 (Same Theme for Variations, Op. 76,) — B1055

Variations on "Nel Cor Piu" of Paisiello, Pft. — B1056

Thirty-two Variations, C Minor, Pft.
Theme — B1057

Variations on a Waltz of Diabelli, Op.120, Pft.
Theme — B1058

BELLINI, Vincenzo (1801-1835)

Norma Overture
1st Theme — B1059

2nd Theme — B1060

3rd Theme — B1061

BERLIOZ, Hector (1803-1869)

Beatrice and Benedict Overture	Intro.	B1062
	1st Theme	B1063
	2nd Theme Variant of Intro.	B1064
	3rd Theme, A	B1065
	3rd Theme, B	B1066
Benvenuto Cellini Overture, Op. 23	1st Theme	B1067
	2nd Theme	B1068
	3rd Theme	B1069
	4th Theme	B1070
The Corsair Overture, Op. 21	1st Theme	B1071
	2nd Theme	B1072
	3rd Theme	B1073
Les Francs – Juges Overture, Op. 3	Intro. A	B1074
	Intro. B	B1075
	1st Theme	B1076
	2nd Theme	B1077
King Lear Overture, Op.4	1st Theme	B1078
	2nd Theme	B1079
	3rd Theme	B1080

4th Theme — B1081

5th Theme — B1082

Roman Carnival
Overture, Op.9   1st Theme — B1083

2nd Theme — B1084

3rd Theme — B1085

4th Theme — B1086

Romeo & Juliet,   1st Movement
Overture Op.17   Combat, Tumult — B1087

2nd Movement
Romeo Alone
1st Theme — B1088

2nd Movement
Fête at the Capulets
2nd Theme — B1089

4th Movement
Queen Mab Scherzo
1st Theme, A — B1090

4th Movement
1st Theme, B — B1091

4th Movement
2nd Theme — B1092

Fantastic Symphony,   1st Movement
Op.14   Reveries, Passions
Intro. A — B1093

1st Movement
Intro. B — B1094

1st Movement
1st Theme — B1095

1st Movement
2nd Theme — B1096

2nd Movement
A Ball
1st Theme — B1097

2nd Movement
2nd Theme — B1098

3rd Movement
Scenes in the Country
1st Theme — B1099

3rd Movement
2nd Theme — B1100

4th Movement
March to the Scaffold
1st Theme — B1101

4th Movement
2nd Theme — B1102

5th Movement
Witches' Sabbath
1st Theme — B1103

5th Movement
2nd Theme
Dies Irae — B1104

5th Movement
3rd Theme — B1105

Harold in Italy, On.16
Orch.
1st Movement
Harold in the Mountains
Intro. A1 — B1106

1st Movement
Intro. A 2 — B1107

1st Movement
Intro. B — B1108

1st Movement
1st Theme — B1109

1st Movement
2nd Theme — B1110

1st Movement
3rd Theme — B1111

2nd Movement
March of the Pilgrims — B1112

3rd Movement
Serenade
1st Theme — B1113

3rd Movement
2nd Theme — B1114

4th Movement
Orgy of the Brigands
1st Theme — B1115

4th Movement
2nd Theme — B1116

4th Movement
3rd Theme — B1117

BERNSTEIN, Leonard (1918 -)

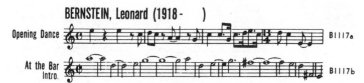

Fancy Free
Ballet
Copyright 1946 by
Harms, Inc.
Reprinted by
special permission.

Opening Dance — B1117a

At the Bar
Intro. — B1117b

Theme — B1117c

Pas de Deux — B1117d

Variation 1
1st Theme — B1117e

2nd Theme — B1117f

Variation 2 — B1117g

Variation 3
1st Theme — B1117h

2nd Theme — B1117i

Finale — B1117j

Jeremiah, Symphony
Copyright 1943 by
Harms, Inc.
Reprinted by
special permission.

1st Movement
Prophecy
1st Theme — B1117k

1st Movement
2nd Theme — B1117l

1st Movement
3rd Theme — B1117m

2nd Movement
1st Theme — B1117n

2nd Movement
2nd Theme — B1117o

3rd Movement
1st Theme — B1117p

3rd Movement
2nd Theme — B1117q

3rd Movement
3rd Theme — B1117r

BIZET, Georges (1838-1875)

L'Arlesienne
Suite No.1, Orch.

Overture
1st Theme — B1118

2nd Theme — B1119

Minuetto
1st Theme — B1120

2nd Theme — B1121

Countertheme to 2nd Theme — B1122

Adagietto — B1123

Carillon 1st Theme — B1124

2nd Theme — B1125

L'Arlesienne Suite No. 2, Orch.

Pastorale 1st Theme — B1126

2nd Theme — B1127

Intermezzo 1st Theme — B1128

2nd Theme — B1129

Minuetto — B1130

Farandole — B1131

Carmen, Opera

Prelude to Act 1 1st Theme — B1132

2nd Theme — B1133

3rd Theme (Toreador Song) — B1134

4th Theme (Fate Motive) — B1135

1st Intermezzo 1st Theme — B1136

2nd Theme — B1137

(Act II) Danse Bohème — B1138

2nd Intermezzo — B1139

3rd Intermezzo — B1140

Petite Suite, Op. 22
"Jeux D'Enfants"
Orch.

Marche — B1141

Berceuse (Doll) — B1142

Impromptu — B1143

Duo (Petit Mari, Petite Femme) — B1144

Galop (Le Bal) — B1145

Symphony No. 1.
in C

1st Movement 1st Theme, A — B1146

1st Movement 1st Theme, B — B1147

1st Movement 2nd Theme — B1148

2nd Movement 1st Theme — B1149

2nd Movement 2nd Theme — B1150

3rd Movement — B1151

4th Movement 1st Theme — B1152

4th Movement 2nd Theme — B1153

4th Movement 3rd Theme — B1154

BLOCH, Ernest (1880-1959)

Baal Shem, (Three Pictures of Chassidic Life) Vn. & Pft.

Vidui (Contrition)
Copyright 1924 by Carl Fischer, Inc., N. Y. — B1155

Nigun (Improvisation) 1st Theme
Copyright 1924 by Carl Fischer, Inc., N. Y. — B1156

2nd Theme — B1157

Simchas Torah
Copyright 1924 by Carl Fischer, Inc., N. Y. — B1158

Concerto grosso Str. Orch. & Pft. Obbligato
By permission of C. C. Birchard & Co., owners of the copyright.

1st Movement (Prelude) — B1159

Quintet, Pft. & Str.
Copyright 1924
by G. Schirmer, Inc.

Schelomo (Hebrew
Rhapsody), Cello & Orch.
Copyright renewal assigned
1945 to G. Schirmer, Inc.

Sonata, Vn. & Pft.
Copyright 1922
by G. Schirmer, Inc.

Suite, Viola & Orch.
Copyright 1921
by G. Schirmer, Inc.

4th Movement 2nd Theme — B1180
4th Movement 3rd Theme — B1181
1st Movement 1st Theme — B1182
1st Movement 2nd Theme — B1183
2nd Movement 1st Theme — B1184
2nd Movement 2nd Theme — B1185
3rd Movement — B1186
1st Theme — B1187
2nd Theme — B1188
3rd Theme — B1189
4th Theme — B1190
5th Theme — B1191
6th Theme — B1192
1st Movement — B1193
2nd Movement — B1194
3rd Movement — B1195
1st Movement 1st Theme — B1196
1st Movement 2nd Theme — B1197
1st Movement 3rd Theme — B1198
2nd Movement 1st Theme — B1199

2nd Movement
2nd Theme — B1200

3rd Movement — B1201

4th Movement — B1202

Israel, Symphony
Copyright 1925
by G. Schirmer, Inc.

1st Theme — B1203

2nd Theme — B1204

3rd Theme — B1205

4th Theme — B1206

5th Theme — B1207

Three Nocturnes,
Vn., Cello, & Pft.
Copyright by Carl Fischer, Inc., N.Y.
Reprinted by permisssion.

I — B1208

II — B1209

III — B1210

BOCCHERINI, Luigi (1743-1805)

Concerto in B Flat
Cello & Orch.

1st Movement
1st Theme — B1211

1st Movement
2nd Theme — B1212

2nd Movement — B1213

3rd Movement — B1214

Concerto No. 2 in D
Cello & Orch.

1st Movement — B1215

2nd Movement
1st Theme — B1216

2nd Movement
2nd Theme — B1217

3rd Movement
1st Theme,
A — B1218

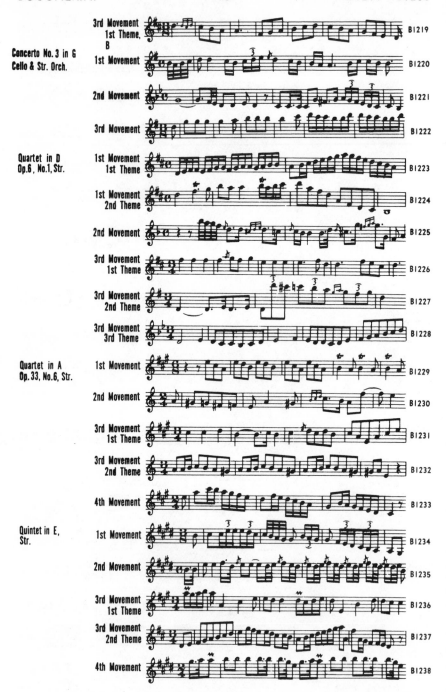

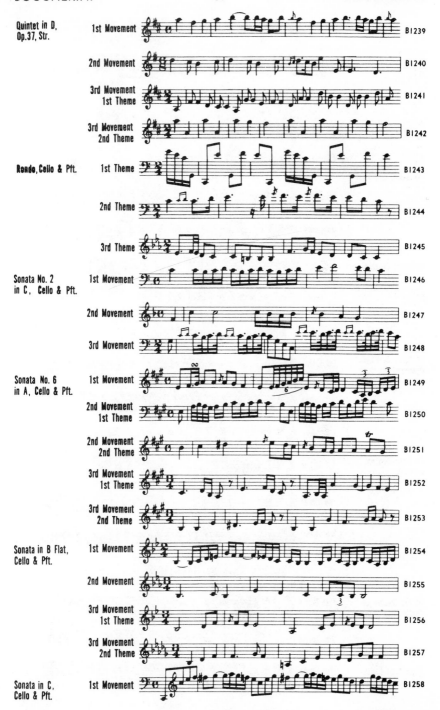

2nd Movement — B1259

3rd Movement — B1260

BOËLLMANN, Leon (1862-1897)

Suite Gothique,
Op. 25, Organ   1st Movement   Introduction-Choral — B1261

Permission for reprint
granted by Durand
& Cie, Paris.
Elkan-Vogel Co., Inc.   2nd Movement   Menuet Gothique — B1262
Philadelphia, Copyright
Owners

3rd Movement — B1263

4th Movement   Toccata — B1264

Variations Symphoniques,
Op. 63, Cello & Orch.   Intro. — B1265
Permission for reprint granted
by Durand & Cie, Paris.
Elkan-Vogel Co., Inc. Philadelphia,   Theme — B1266
Copyright Owners

BOÏELDIEU, François (1775-1834)

Le Calife De Bagdad
Overture   1st Theme — B1267

2nd Theme — B1268

3rd Theme — B1269

La Dame Blanche,
Overture,   1st Theme — B1270

2nd Theme — B1271

3rd Theme — B1272

BORODIN, Alexander (1833-1887)

On the Steppes of
Central Asia, Orch.   1st Theme — B1273

2nd Theme — B1274

Polovetsian Dances
from Prince Igor   1st Theme — B1275

2nd Theme

B1276

3rd Theme

B1277

3rd Theme

B1278

4th Theme

B1279

Quartet No.1, in A, Str.

1st Movement Intro.

B1280

1st Movement 1st Theme

B1281

1st Movement 2nd Theme

B1282

2nd Movement 1st Theme

B1283

2nd Movement 2nd Theme

B1284

2nd Movement 3rd Theme Fugato

B1285

3rd Movement 1st Theme

B1286

3rd Movement 2nd Theme

B1287

4th Movement 1st Theme

B1288

4th Movement 2nd Theme

B1289

Quartet No.2 in D, Str.

1st Movement 1st Theme

B1290

1st Movement 2nd Theme

B1291

1st Movement 3rd Theme

B1292

2nd Movement 1st Theme

B1293

2nd Movement 2nd Theme

B1294

3rd Movement 1st Theme Notturno

B1295

3rd Movement 2nd Theme — B1296

4th Movement 1st Theme — B1297

4th Movement 2nd Theme — B1298

Symphony No. 1 in E Flat

1st Movement 2nd Theme — B1299

1st Movement 2nd Theme — B1300

2nd Movement 1st Theme — B1301

2nd Movement 2nd Theme — B1302

2nd Movement 3rd Theme — B1303

3rd Movement 1st Theme, A — B1304

3rd Movement 1st Theme, B — B1305

4th Movement 1st Theme — B1306

4th Movement 2nd Theme — B1307

Symphony No. 2 in B Minor

1st Movement 1st Theme — B1308

1st Movement 2nd Theme — B1309

1st Movement 3rd Theme — B1310

2nd Movement 1st Theme, A — B1311

2nd Movement 1st Theme, B — B1312

2nd Movement 2nd Theme — B1313

2nd Movement 3rd Theme — B1314

3rd Movement 1st Theme — B1315

3rd Movement 2nd Theme — B1316

3rd Movement 3rd Theme — B1317

4th Movement 1st Theme — B1318

4th Movement 2nd Theme — B1319

Symphony No. 3 in A Minor (Unfinished) — 1st Movement 1st Theme — B1320

1st Movement 2nd Theme — B1321

1st Movement 3rd Theme — B1322

2nd Movement 1st Theme — B1323

2nd Movement 2nd Theme — B1324

2nd Movement 3rd Theme — B1325

2nd Movement 4th Theme — B1326

BOYCE, William (1711-1779)

The Power of Music, Overture — 1st Theme — B1327

2nd Theme — B1328

BRAHMS, Johannes (1833-1897)

Ballade, in D Minor, Op.10, No.1, Pft. — B1329

Ballade, in D Op. 10, No. 2, Pft. — 1st Theme — B1330

2nd Theme — B1331

Ballade, in G Minor, Op.118, No. 3, Pft. — 1st Theme — B1332

2nd Theme — B1333

Capriccio, in B Minor, Op. 76, No. 2, Pft. — B1334

Capriccio, in C Sharp Minor, Op. 76, No. 5, Pft. — B1335

Capriccio, in D Minor, Op. 116, No. 1, Pft. — B1336

Concerto No. 1 in D Minor, Op. 15, Pft. & Orch.
1st Movement 1st Theme — B1337
1st Movement 2nd Theme — B1338
1st Movement 3rd Theme — B1339
1st Movement 4th Theme — B1340
2nd Movement — B1341
3rd Movement 1st Theme — B1342
3rd Movement 2nd Theme — B1343
3rd Movement 3rd Theme — B1344

Concerto No. 2, in B Flat Op. 83, Pft. & Orch.
1st Movement 1st Theme — B1345
1st Movement 2nd Theme — B1346
1st Movement 3rd Theme — B1347
2nd Movement 1st Theme — B1348
2nd Movement 2nd Theme — B1349
2nd Movement 3rd Theme — B1350
3rd Movement — B1351
4th Movement 1st Theme — B1352
4th Movement 2nd Theme — B1353

2nd Theme — B1374

No. 5, in F Sharp Minor
1st Theme — B1375

2nd Theme — B1376

No. 6 , in D Flat — B1377

No. 7, in A — B1378

No.12, in D Minor — B1379

Intermezzo, in A Flat,
Op.76, No.3, Pft. — B1380

Intermezzo, in A Minor,
Op. 76, No.7, Pft. — B1381

Intermezzo, in A Minor,
Op.116, No.2, Pft. — B1382

Intermezzo, in C Sharp
Minor, Op.116, No.3, Pft. — B1383

Intermezzo, in E,
Op.116, No.4, Pft. — B1384

Intermezzo, in E Flat,
Op.117, No. 1, Pft. — B1385

Intermezzo, in B Flat
Minor, Op.117. No.2, Pft.   1st Theme — B1386

2nd Theme — B1387

Intermezzo, in A Minor,
Op.118, No.1, Pft. — B1388

Intermezzo, in A,
Op.118, No.2, Pft.   1st Movement — B1389

2nd Movement — B1390

Intermezzo, in E Flat   1st Movement
Minor, Op.118, No.6, Pft. — B1391

2nd Movement — B1392

Intermezzo, in B Minor,
Op.119, No.1, Pft. — B1393

Intermezzo, in E Minor, Op.119, No. 2, Pft. — 1st Theme — B1394

2nd Movement — B1395

Intermezzo, in C, Op.119, No.3, Pft. — B1396

Academic Festival, Overture, Op. 80 — 1st Theme — B1397

2nd Theme A — B1398

2nd Theme, B — B1399

3rd Theme — B1400

4th Theme — B1401

5th Theme Gaudeamus Igitur — B1402

Tragic Overture, Op. 81 — 1st Theme — B1403

2nd Theme — B1404

3rd Theme — B1405

Quartet in G Minor, Op.25, Pft. & Str. — 1st Movement 1st Theme — B1406

1st Movement 2nd Theme — B1407

1st Movement 3rd Theme — B1408

1st Movement 4th Theme — B1409

2nd Movement 1st Theme — B1410

2nd Movement 2nd Theme — B1411

2nd Movement 3rd Theme Trio — B1412

3rd Movement 1st Theme — B1413

Quartet in A,
Op. 26, Pft. & Str.

Quartet in C Minor
Op. 51, No. 1, Str.

Quartet in A Minor
Op. 51, No. 2, Str.

1st Movement 2nd Theme — B1434
2nd Movement — B1435
3rd Movement 1st Theme — B1436
3rd Movement 2nd Theme — B1437
4th Movement 1st Theme — B1438
4th Movement 2nd Theme — B1439

Quartet in C Minor
Op.60, Pft. & Str.

1st Movement 1st Theme — B1440
1st Movement 2nd Theme — B1441
2nd Movement 1st Theme — B1442
2nd Movement 2nd Theme — B1443
3rd Movement — B1444
4th Movement 1st Theme — B1445
4th Movement 2nd Theme — B1446

Quartet in B Flat
Op.67, Str.

1st Movement 1st Theme — B1447
1st Movement 2nd Theme — B1448
2nd Movement 1st Theme — B1449
2nd Movement 2nd Theme — B1450
3rd Movement 1st Theme — B1451
3rd Movement 2nd Theme — B1452
4th Movement — B1453

Quintet in F Minor, Op.34, Pft. & Str.
- 1st Movement 1st Theme — B1454
- 1st Movement 2nd Theme — B1455
- 1st Movement 3rd Theme — B1456
- 1st Movement 4th Theme — B1457
- 2nd Movement 1st Theme — B1458
- 2nd Movement 2nd Theme — B1459
- 3rd Movement 1st Theme — B1460
- 3rd Movement 2nd Theme — B1461
- 3rd Movement 3rd Theme — B1462
- 4th Movement 1st Theme — B1463
- 4th Movement 2nd Theme — B1464

Quintet in F, Op.88, Str.
- 1st Movement — B1465
- 2nd Movement — B1466
- 3rd Movement 1st Theme — B1467
- 3rd Movement 2nd Theme — B1468

Quintet in G, Op.111, Str.
- 1st Movement 1st Theme — B1469
- 1st Movement 2nd Theme — B1470
- 2nd Movement — B1471
- 3rd Movement — B1472
- 4th Movement 1st Theme — B1473

Quintet in B Minor, Op.115, Cl. & Str.

4th Movement 2nd Theme — B1474
1st Movement 1st Theme — B1475
1st Movement 2nd Theme — B1476
2nd Movement — B1477
3rd Movement — B1478
4th Movement — B1479

Rhapsody, in B Minor, Op. 79, No. 1, Pft.

1st Theme — B1480
2nd Theme — B1481

Rhapsody, in G Minor, Op. 79, No. 2, Pft.

1st Theme — B1482
2nd Theme — B1483

Rhapsody, in E Flat, Op.119, No. 4, Pft.

1st Theme — B1484
2nd Theme — B1485

Romance in F Op.118, No. 5, Pft.

1st Theme — B1486
2nd Theme — B1487

Serenade in D, Op.11, Orch.

1st Movement 1st Theme — B1488
1st Movement 2nd Theme — B1489
2nd Movement 1st Theme — B1490
2nd Movement 2nd Theme — B1491
3rd Movement 1st Theme — B1492
3rd Movement 2nd Theme — B1493

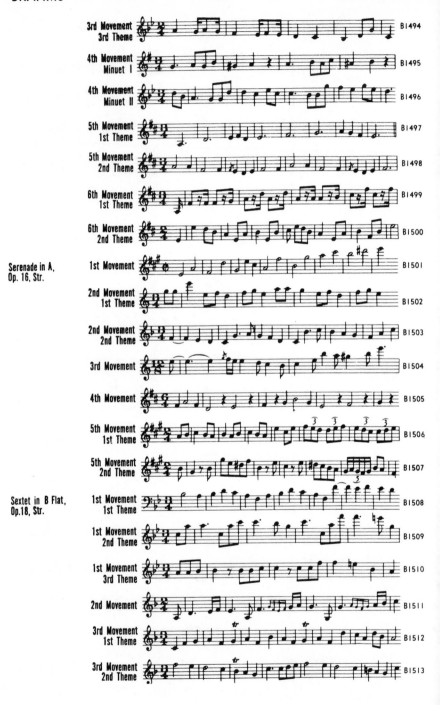

3rd Movement
3rd Theme — B1494

4th Movement
Minuet I — B1495

4th Movement
Minuet II — B1496

5th Movement
1st Theme — B1497

5th Movement
2nd Theme — B1498

6th Movement
1st Theme — B1499

6th Movement
2nd Theme — B1500

Serenade in A,
Op. 16, Str.

1st Movement — B1501

2nd Movement
1st Theme — B1502

2nd Movement
2nd Theme — B1503

3rd Movement — B1504

4th Movement — B1505

5th Movement
1st Theme — B1506

5th Movement
2nd Theme — B1507

Sextet in B Flat,
Op.18, Str.

1st Movement
1st Theme — B1508

1st Movement
2nd Theme — B1509

1st Movement
3rd Theme — B1510

2nd Movement — B1511

3rd Movement
1st Theme — B1512

3rd Movement
2nd Theme — B1513

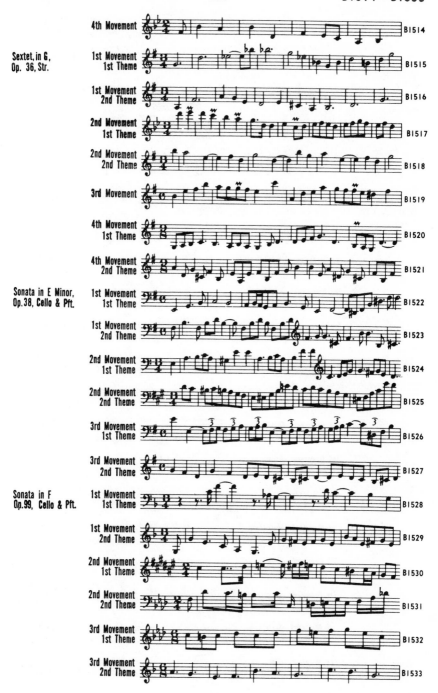

BRAHMS

4th Movement — B1514

Sextet, in G, Op. 36, Str.
1st Movement 1st Theme — B1515

1st Movement 2nd Theme — B1516

2nd Movement 1st Theme — B1517

2nd Movement 2nd Theme — B1518

3rd Movement — B1519

4th Movement 1st Theme — B1520

4th Movement 2nd Theme — B1521

Sonata in E Minor, Op. 38, Cello & Pft.
1st Movement 1st Theme — B1522

1st Movement 2nd Theme — B1523

2nd Movement 1st Theme — B1524

2nd Movement 2nd Theme — B1525

3rd Movement 1st Theme — B1526

3rd Movement 2nd Theme — B1527

Sonata in F Op. 99, Cello & Pft.
1st Movement 1st Theme — B1528

1st Movement 2nd Theme — B1529

2nd Movement 1st Theme — B1530

2nd Movement 2nd Theme — B1531

3rd Movement 1st Theme — B1532

3rd Movement 2nd Theme — B1533

4th Movement — B1534

Sonata in F Minor, Op. 120, No. 1, Cl. or Viola & Pft. By permission of Associated Music Publishers, Inc.

1st Movement — B1535

2nd Movement — B1536

3rd Movement — B1537

4th Movement — B1538

Sonata in E Flat Op. 120, No. 2, Cl. or Viola & Pft. By permission of Associated Music Publishers, Inc.

1st Movement 1st Theme — B1539

1st Movement 2nd Theme — B1540

2nd Movement 1st Theme — B1541

2nd Movement 2nd Theme — B1542

3rd Movement — B1543

Sonata in F Minor, Op. 5, Pft.

1st Movement 1st Theme — B1544

1st Movement 2nd Theme — B1545

2nd Movement 1st Theme — B1546

2nd Movement 2nd Theme — B1547

2nd Movement 3rd Theme — B1548

3rd Movement 1st Theme — B1549

3rd Movement 2nd Theme — B1550

4th Movement 1st Theme — B1551

4th Movement 2nd Theme — B1552

Sonata in G Op. 78, Vn. & Pft.

1st Movement 1st Theme — B1553

Sonata in A
Op.100, Vn. & Pft.

Sonata in D Minor,
Op.108, Vn. & Pft.

1st Movement 2nd Theme — B1554
2nd Movement 1st Theme — B1555
2nd Movement 2nd Theme — B1556
3rd Movement 1st Theme — B1557
3rd Movement 2nd Theme — B1558
1st Movement 1st Theme — B1559
1st Movement 2nd Theme — B1560
1st Movement 3rd Theme — B1561
1st Movement 4th Theme — B1562
2nd Movement 1st Theme — B1563
2nd Movement 2nd Theme — B1564
2nd Movement 3rd Theme — B1565
3rd Movement 1st Theme — B1566
3rd Movement 2nd Theme — B1567
1st Movement 1st Theme — B1568
1st Movement 2nd Theme — B1569
2nd Movement — B1570
3rd Movement — B1571
4th Movement 1st Theme — B1572
4th Movement 2nd Theme — B1573

Symphony No.1
in C Minor
Op.68

4th Movement — B1574

1st Movement
Intro. A 1
Both Themes
Simultaneous
Intro. A 2 — B1575 / B1576

1st Movement
Intro. B — B1577

1st Movement
1st Theme,
A — B1578

1st Movement
1st Theme,
B — B1579

1st Movement
1st Theme,
C — B1580

1st Movement
2nd Theme — B1581

1st Movement
3rd Theme — B1582

1st Movement
4th Theme — B1583

2nd Movement
1st Theme — B1584

2nd Movement
2nd Theme — B1585

2nd Movement
3rd Theme — B1586

2nd Movement
4th Theme — B1587

3rd Movement
1st Theme — B1588

3rd Movement
2nd Theme — B1589

3rd Movement
3rd Theme,
A — B1590

3rd Movement
3rd Theme,
B — B1591

3rd Movement
4th Theme — B1592

4th Movement
Intro. A — B1593

BRAHMS

4th Movement Intro. B — B1594

4th Movement Intro. C — B1595

4th Movement 1st Theme — B1596

4th Movement 2nd Theme — B1597

4th Movement 3rd Theme — B1598

4th Movement 4th Theme — B1599

Symphony No. 2 in D, Op.73

1st Movement 1st Theme — B1600

1st Movement 2nd Theme — B1601

1st Movement 3rd Theme — B1602

1st Movement 4th Theme — B1603

1st Movement 5th Theme — B1604

1st Movement 6th Theme — B1605

1st Movement Coda — B1606

2nd Movement 1st Theme — B1607

2nd Movement 2nd Theme — B1608

2nd Movement 3rd Theme — B1609

2nd Movement 4th Theme — B1610

3rd Movement 1st Theme — B1611

3rd Movement 2nd Theme — B1612

3rd Movement 3rd Theme — B1613

Symphony No.3
in F Op. 90

3rd Movement 4th Theme — B1614
4th Movement 1st Theme, A — B1615
4th Movement 1st Theme, B — B1616
4th Movement 2nd Theme — B1617
4th Movement 3rd Theme — B1618
1st Movement 1st Theme — B1619
1st Movement 2nd Theme — B1620
1st Movement 3rd Theme — B1621
1st Movement 4th Theme — B1622
2nd Movement 1st Theme — B1623
2nd Movement 2nd Theme — B1624
2nd Movement 3rd Theme — B1625
3rd Movement 1st Theme — B1626
3rd Movement 2nd Theme — B1627
3rd Movement 3rd Theme — B1628
4th Movement 1st Theme A — B1629
4th Movement 1st Theme B — B1630
4th Movement 2nd Theme — B1631
4th Movement 3rd Theme — B1632
4th Movement 4th Theme — B1633

Symphony No. 4
in E Minor, Op. 98

1st Movement
1st Theme
A — B1634

1st Movement
1st Theme
B — B1635

1st Movement
2nd Theme — B1636

1st Movement
3rd Theme — B1637

1st Movement
4th Theme — B1638

1st Movement
5th Theme — B1639

1st Movement
6th Theme — B1640

1st Movement
7th Theme — B1641

2nd Movement
1st Theme — B1642

2nd Movement
2nd Theme — B1643

2nd Movement
3rd Theme — B1644

3rd Movement
1st Theme
A — B1645

3rd Movement
1st Theme
B — B1646

3rd Movement
1st Theme
C — B1647

3rd Movement
2nd Theme — B1648

4th Movement
1st Theme — B1649

4th Movement
2nd Theme — B1650

4th Movement
3rd Theme — B1651

4th Movement
4th Theme — B1652

4th Movement
5th Theme — B1653

2nd Movement — B1674

3rd Movement 1st Theme — B1675

3rd Movement 2nd Theme — B1676

4th Movement 1st Theme — B1677

4th Movement 2nd Theme — B1678

4th Movement 3rd Theme — B1679

Trio in C Minor, Op.101, Vn., Cello & Pft.

1st Movement 1st Theme — B1680

1st Movement 2nd Theme — B1681

1st Movement 3rd Theme — B1682

2nd Movement — B1683

3rd Movement 1st Theme — B1684

3rd Movement 2nd Theme — B1685

4th Movement 1st Theme — B1686

4th Movement 2nd Theme — B1687

Trio in E Flat, Op. 40, Vn., Hn. & Pft.

1st Movement 1st Theme — B1688

1st Movement 2nd Theme — B1689

2nd Movement 1st Theme — B1690

2nd Movement 2nd Theme — B1691

2nd Movement 3rd Theme — B1692

3rd Movement 1st Theme — B1693

3rd Movement
2nd Theme — B1694

4th Movement
1st Theme — B1695

4th Movement
2nd Theme — B1696

Variations on a Theme
of Haydn, Op.56a, Orch.   Theme — B1697

Variations on a Theme
of Schumann, Op. 23, Pft. 4 Hands — B1698

Waltzes, Op. 39, Pft.

No. 1 — B1699

No. 2 — B1700

No. 3 — B1701

No. 4 — B1702

No. 7 — B1703

No. 8 — B1704

No. 9 — B1705

No. 10 — B1706

No. 11 — B1707

No. 12 — B1708

No. 14 — B1709

No. 15 — B1710

No. 16 — B1711

BRITTEN, Benjamin (1913-1976)

Peter Grimes,
Four Sea Interludes,
Op. 33a, Orch.

1st Interlude
Dawn — B1711a

By permission of the copyright owner,
Boosey and Hawkes, Inc.

2nd Interlude
Sunday Morning
1st Theme   B1711b

2nd Theme   B1711c

3rd Interlude
Moonlight   B1711d

4th Interlude
Storm
1st Theme   B1711e

4th Interlude
2nd Theme
A   B1711f

2nd Theme
B
(Simultaneous With A)   B1711g

3rd Theme   B1711h

4th Theme   B1711i

**Phantasy-Quartet,
Oboe, Vn., Viola & Vcl.**   1st Theme   B1711j
By permission of the copyright owner,
Boosey and Hawkes, Inc.

2nd Theme   B1711k

3rd Theme   B1711l

4th Theme   B1711m

Simple Symphony   1st Movement
Copyright by the (Boisterous Bourrée)
Oxford University Press   1st Theme   B1712

Reproduced
by permission.   2nd Theme   B1713

2nd Movement
(Playful Pizzicato)
1st Theme   B1714

2nd Theme   B1715

3rd Movement
(Sentimental Sarabande)
1st Theme   B1716

2nd Theme   B1717

4th Movement
(Frolicsome Finale)
1st Theme   B1718

2nd Theme   B1719

Variations on a Theme of Frank Bridge, Op. 10, Orch.
By permission of the copyright owner, Boosey and Hawkes, Inc.
Theme — B1719a

BRUCH, Max (1838-1920)

Concerto No. 1 in G Minor, Vn. & Orch.
Permission for reprint granted by Durand & Cie, Paris. Elkan-Vogel Co., Inc. Philadelphia, Copyright Owners.

1st Movement Intro. — B1720
1st Movement 1st Theme — B1721
1st Movement 2nd Theme — B1722
1st Movement 2nd Theme — B1723
2nd Movement 1st Theme, A — B1724
2nd Movement 1st Theme, B — B1725
3rd Movement 1st Theme — B1726
3rd Movement 2nd Theme — B1727

Concerto No. 2 in D Minor, Vn. & Orch.
By permission of Associated Music Publishers, Inc.

1st Movement 1st Theme — B1728
1st Movement 2nd Theme — B1729
2nd Movement 1st Theme — B1730
2nd Movement 2nd Theme — B1731
3rd Movement 1st Theme, A — B1732
3rd Movement 1st Theme, B — B1733
3rd Movement 2nd Theme — B1734

Kol Nidrei (Based on Traditional Hebrew Themes) Vn. & Pft.
By permission of Associated Music Publishers, Inc.

1st Theme — B1735
2nd Theme — B1736
3rd Theme — B1737

BRUCKNER, Anton (1824-1896)

Overture in G Minor
By permission of Associated
Music Publishers, Inc.

1st Theme — B1738

2nd Theme — B1739

3rd Theme — B1740

Quintet in F. Str.
By permission of
International Music Co.

1st Movement
1st Theme — B1741

1st Movement
2nd Theme — B1742

2nd Movement
1st Theme — B1743

2nd Movement
2nd Theme — B1744

3rd Movement — B1745

4th Movement — B1746

**Symphony No. 3
in D Minor**
Copyright by Lienau,
Licensed by
SESAC, Inc., N. Y.

1st Movement
1st Theme — B1747

1st Movement
2nd Theme — B1748

1st Movement
3rd Theme — B1749

1st Movement
4th Theme — B1750

2nd Movement
1st Theme — B1751

2nd Movement
2nd Theme — B1752

2nd Movement
3rd Theme — B1753

3rd Movement
1st Theme — B1754

3rd Movement
2nd Theme,
A — B1755

3rd Movement
2nd Theme
B — B1756

Symphony No.4. in
E Flat, "Romantic"
By permission of Associated
Music Publishers, Inc.

Symphony No.5, in
B Flat,
By permission of Associated
Music Publishers, Inc.

1st Movement 2nd Theme — B1797

1st Movement 3rd Theme — B1798

2nd Movement 1st Theme — B1799

2nd Movement 2nd Theme — B1800

3rd Movement 1st Theme — B1801

3rd Movement 2nd Theme — B1802

BULL, John (1563-1628)

A Gigge (Doctor Bull's My Selfe) Pft.-Harpsi. — B1803

The King's Hunt, Pft.-Harpsi. — B1804

BUXTEHUDE, Dietrich (1637-1707)

Chaconne, in E Minor, Organ — B1805

Passacaglia, Organ — B1806

Prelude & Fugue, No.6 in E Minor, Organ — 1st Theme Prelude — B1807

2nd Theme Fugue 1 — B1808

3rd Theme Fugue 2 — B1809

4th Theme Fugue 3 — B1810

Prelude & Fugue, No.8 in E, Organ — 1st Theme Prelude — B1811

2nd Theme Fugue — B1812

Prelude & Fugue, No.14, in G Minor, Organ — 1st Theme Prelude — B1813

2nd Theme Fugue I — B1814

BYRD, William (1543-1623)

Sellenger's Round, Harpsi.
Fitzwilliam Virginal Book No. 64 — B1834

La Volta, Harpsi.
Fitzwilliam Virginal Book No. 155 — B1835

Wolsey's Wilde, Harpsi.
Fitzwilliam Virginal Book No. 157 — B1836

CABANILLAS, Juan (1644-1712)

Passacalles in D Minor, Organ — C1

Tiento De Falsas, Del 4° Tomo, Organ — C2

CABEZÓN, Antonio de (1510-1566)

Tiento, Del 1° Tomo, Organ — C3

Tiento, Del 4° Tomo, Organ — C4

Variations on "El Canto Del Caballero" — C5

CADMAN, Charles Wakefield (1881-1946)

Thunderbird Suite, Orch.
(Music for a Production
of Norman Bel Geddes)
(Based on American
Indian Tunes)

Copyright by
White-Smith
Music Publishers
Co., Boston.

1st Movement From the Village — C6

2nd Movement Before the Sunrise — C7

3rd Movement Nuwana's Love Song (Blackfeet Indian Tune) — C8

4th Movement Night Song (Blackfeet Indian Tune) — C9

5th Movement Wolf Song (War Dance) — C10

CAIX d'HERVELOIS, Louis de (1670-1760)

Suite No. 1, in A,
Cello & Pft.

1st Movement La Milanese — C11

2nd Movement Sarabande — C12

3rd Movement Minuet — C13

4th Movement
L'Agréable — C14

5th Movement
Gavotte — C15

Suite No. 2 in D Minor
Vcl. & Pft.

1st Movement
Prelude — C16

2nd Movement
Allegro — C17

3rd Movement
Minuet — C18

4th Movement
Plainte — C19

5th Movement
La Neapolitaine — C20

CANNABICH, Christian (1731-1798)

Sinfonia in B Flat

1st Movement
1st Theme — C21

1st Movement
2nd Theme — C22

2nd Movement — C23

3rd Movement
1st Theme — C24

3rd Movement
2nd Theme — C25

CARPENTER, John Alden (1876-1951)

Adventures in a
Perambulator, Orch.
Copyright renewal assigned
1944 to G. Schirmer, Inc.

1st Movement
En Voiture
1st Theme — C26

1st Movement
2nd Theme — C27

2nd Movement
The Policeman
1st Theme — C28

2nd Movement
2nd Theme — C29

3rd Movement
The Hurdy Gurdy
1st Theme — C30

3rd Movement
2nd Theme — C31

3rd Movement 3rd Theme — C32

3rd Movement 4th Theme — C33

3rd Movement 5th Theme — C34

4th Movement The Lake — C35

5th Movement Dogs 1st Theme — C36

5th Movement 2nd Theme — C37

6th Movement Dreams — C38

Quartet in A Minor, Str.
Copyright 1928 by
G. Schirmer, Inc.

1st Movement Intro. — C39

1st Movement 1st Theme — C40

1st Movement 2nd Theme — C41

2nd Movement — C42

3rd Movement 1st Theme — C43

3rd Movement 2nd Theme — C44

CASELLA, Alfredo (1883-1947)

Il Convento Veneziano, Ballet
Copyright 1919 by
G. Ricordi & Co., Inc.

Ronde D'Enfants 1st Theme — C45

2nd Theme — C46

Pas Des Vieilles Dames — C47

La Giara, Ballet
By permission of Associated
Music Publishers, Inc.

Sicilian Dance "Chiovu" — C48

General Dance — C49

Finale — C50

Pupazzetti, Orch.
By permission of the copyright holders,
J. & W. Chester, Ltd., 11 Great Marlborough Street, London, W. 1.

1st Movement
1st Theme
Marcietta

C51

1st Movement
2nd Theme

C52

2nd Movement
Berceuse

C53

3rd Movement
Serenata

C54

4th Movement
Notturnino

C55

5th Movement
1st Theme
Polka

C56

5th Movement
2nd Theme

C57

Serenata
Cl., Fg., Tpt., Vn. & Cello
By permission of Associated Music Publishers, Inc.

1st Movement
Marcia

C58

2nd Movement
Minuet

C59

3rd Movement
1st Theme
Notturno

C60

3rd Movement
2nd Theme

C61

4th Movement
1st Theme
Gavotte

C62

4th Movement
2nd Theme
Musette

C63

5th Movement
Cavatina

C64

6th Movement
Finale-Tarantella

C65

Siciliana E Burlesca,
Vn., Cello, Pft.
Copyright 1919 by
G. Ricordi & Co., Inc.

1st Movement
Siciliana

C66

2nd Movement
Burlesca

C67

CHABRIER, Alexis Emmanuel (1841-1894)

Bourrée Fantasque,
Pft., Arr. for Orch., F. Mottl
By permission of
M M Enoch & Cie.,
Music Publishers,
27 Boulevard
des Italiens, Paris.

1st Theme

C68

2nd Theme,
A

C69

2nd Theme
B   C70

**España,
Rhapsody for Orch.**

By permission of
M M Enoch & Cie.,
Music Publishers,
27 Boulevard
des Italiens, Paris.

1st Theme   C71¹

2nd Theme   C72²

3rd Theme   C73

4th Theme   C74

5th Theme   C75³

Habañera, Pft. or Orch.

By permission of M M Enoch & Cie.,
Music Publishers,
27 Boulevard des Italiens, Paris.

    C76

Joyeuse Marche, Orch.

By permission of
M M Enoch & Cie.,
Music Publishers,
27 Boulevard
des Italiens. Paris

Intro.   C77

1st Theme   C78

2nd Theme   C79

3rd Theme   C80

**Gwendoline,
Overture**

By permission of
M M Enoch & Cie.,
Music Publishers,
27 Boulevard
des Italiens, Paris.

1st Theme   C81

2nd Theme   C82

3rd Theme   C83

Pièces Pittoresques, Pft.

No. 4
Sous Bois   C84

No. 6
Idylle   C85

No. 7
Danse Villageoise
1st Theme   C86

2nd Theme   C87

No. 8 , Improvisation   C88

No. 10 Scherzo-Valse
1st Theme   C89

1. Same as W98.   2. Same as W99.   3. Same as W100.

2nd Theme — C90

3rd Theme — C91

Le Roi Malgré Lui, Orch.
By permission of
M M Enoch & Cie.,
Music Publishers,
27 Boulevard
des Italiens, Paris

Prelude — C92

Danse Slave
1st Theme — C93

2nd Theme — C94

Fête Polonaise
1st Theme — C95

2nd Theme — C96

3rd Theme — C97

CHADWICK, George W. (1854-1931)

Symphonic Sketches
Copyright renewal assigned
1935 to G. Schirmer, Inc.

I. Jubilee
1st Theme — C98

2nd Theme — C99

3rd Theme, A — C100

3rd Theme, B — C101

4th Theme — C102

II. Nöel — C103

CHAMINADE, Cécile (1857-1944)

Air de Ballet, Pft. — C104

Callirhoë, in G
Air de Ballet, Pft. — C105

The Flatterer, Pft. — C106

Scarf Dance, Pft.
1st Theme   2nd Theme — C107

3rd Theme (Orch. Version) — C108

Serenade, Pft. — C109

Spanish Serenade, Vn. & Pft.
Arr. by Kreisler
© Foley — C110

CHAUSSON, Ernest (1855-1899)

Concerto in D
Pft., Vn. &
Str. Quartet
Op. 21
Copyright by Editions
Salabert Editions Salabert,
22 Rue Chaucat, Paris
Salabert, Inc.,
I East 57 St., N. Y.

1st Movement 1st Theme — C111

1st Movement 2nd Theme — C112

2nd Movement Sicilienne — C113

3rd Movement 1st Theme — C114

3rd Movement 2nd Theme — C115

4th Movement 1st Theme — C116

4th Movement 2nd Theme — C117

Poème, Op. 25, Vn. & Orch.
By permission of Associated
Music Publishers, Inc.

Intro. — C118

1st Theme — C119

2nd Theme — C120

3rd Theme — C121

Quartet, Op. 30
Str. & Pft.
By permission of
International Music Co.

1st Movement 1st Theme — C122

1st Movement 2nd Theme — C123

1st Movement 3rd Theme — C124

2nd Movement 1st Theme — C125

2nd Movement 2nd Theme — C126

3rd Movement 1st Theme — C127

3rd Movement 2nd Theme — C128

4th Movement 1st Theme — C129

4th Movement 2nd Theme — C130

Symphony in B Flat, Op. 20

1st Movement 1st Theme — C131

1st Movement 2nd Theme — C132

1st Movement 3rd Theme — C133

1st Movement 4th Theme — C134

2nd Movement 1st Theme, A — C135

2nd Movement 1st Theme, B — C136

2nd Movement 2nd Theme — C137

3rd Movement 1st Theme — C138

3rd Movement 2nd Theme — C139

CHAVEZ, Carlos (1899-   )

Concerto
Pft. & Orch.
Copyright 1942
by G. Schirmer, Inc.

1st Movement 1st Theme — C140

1st Movement 2nd Theme — C141

2nd Movement — C142

3rd Movement 1st Theme — C143

3rd Movement 2nd Theme — C144

Sinfonia India
By permission of the
copyright owners,
G. Schirmer, Inc.

1st Theme, A — C145

1st Theme, B — C146

2nd Theme — C147

3rd Theme — C148

4th Theme — C149

5th Theme — C150

CHERUBINI, Maria Luigi (1760-1842)

Les Abencerages
Overture — Intro. — C151

1st Theme — C152

2nd Theme — C153

3rd Theme — C154

Anacreon
Overture — Intro. — C155

1st Theme — C156

2nd Theme — C157

Medea
Overture — 1st Theme — C158

2nd Theme — C159

3rd Theme — C160

Der Wasserträger
(Les Deux Journées)
Overture — Intro. — C161

1st Theme — C162

2nd Theme — C163

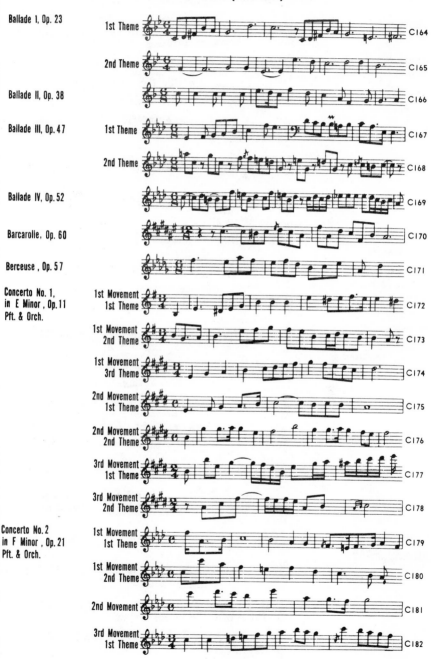

CHOPIN, Frédéric (1810-1849)

Ballade I, Op. 23 — 1st Theme — C164

2nd Theme — C165

Ballade II, Op. 38 — C166

Ballade III, Op. 47 — 1st Theme — C167

2nd Theme — C168

Ballade IV, Op. 52 — C169

Barcarolle, Op. 60 — C170

Berceuse, Op. 57 — C171

Concerto No. 1, in E Minor, Op. 11 Pft. & Orch. — 1st Movement 1st Theme — C172

1st Movement 2nd Theme — C173

1st Movement 3rd Theme — C174

2nd Movement 1st Theme — C175

2nd Movement 2nd Theme — C176

3rd Movement 1st Theme — C177

3rd Movement 2nd Theme — C178

Concerto No. 2 in F Minor, Op. 21 Pft. & Orch. — 1st Movement 1st Theme — C179

1st Movement 2nd Theme — C180

2nd Movement — C181

3rd Movement 1st Theme — C182

3rd Movement
2nd Theme — C183

Ecossaise, No. 1,
Op. 72, No. 3 — C184

Ecossaise, No. 2,
Op. 72, No. 4 — C185

Études, Op. 10
No. 1 in C — C186

No. 2 in A Minor — C187

No. 3 in E — C188

No. 4 in C Sharp Minor — C189

No. 5 in G Flat
"Black Key" — C190

No. 6 in E Flat Minor — C191

No. 7 in C — C192

No. 8 in F
Simultaneous { 1st Theme — C193
2nd Theme — C194

No. 9 in F Minor — C195

No. 10 in A Flat — C196

No. 11 in E Flat — C197

No. 12 in C Minor
"Revolutionary" — C198

Etudes, Op. 25
No. 1 in A Flat
"Harp" — C198a

No. 2 in F Minor — C199

No. 3 in F — C200

No. 4 in A Minor — C201

Impromptu, Op. 36 — C222

Fantaisie-Impromptu, Op. 66 — 1st Theme — C223

2nd Theme — C224

Mazurkas

No. 1 , Op. 6 , No. 1 — C225

5 , Op. 7 , No. 1 — C226

6 , Op. 7 , No. 2 — C227

7 , Op. 7 , No. 3 — C228

9 , Op. 7 , No. 5 — C229

13 , Op. 17, No. 4 — C230

14 , Op. 24, No. 1 — C231

15 , Op. 24, No. 2 — C232

17 , Op. 24, No. 4 — C233

19 , Op. 30, No. 2 — C234

21 , Op. 30, No. 4 — C235

23 , Op. 33, No. 2 — C236

24 , Op. 33, No. 3 — C237

25 , Op. 33, No. 4 — C238

26 , Op. 41, No. 1 — C239

27 , Op. 41, No. 2 — C240

Op.15 , No.1 in F — C260

Op.15 , No. 2 in F Sharp — C261

Op.15 , No. 3 in G Minor — C262

Op. 27 , No.1 in C Sharp Minor — C263

Op. 27 , No. 2 in D Flat — C264

Op. 32 , No. 1 in B — C265

Op. 32 , No. 2 in A Flat — C266

Op. 37 , No. 1 in G Minor — C267

Op. 37 , No. 2 in G — C268

Op. 48 , No.1 in C Minor — 1st Theme — C269

2nd Theme — C270

Op. 48 , No. 2 in F Sharp Minor — C271

Op. 55 , No. 1 in F Minor — C272

Op. 55 , No. 2 in E Flat — C273

Op. 62 , No. 1 in B — C274

Op. 62 , No. 2 in E — C275

Op. 72 , No. 1 in E Minor — C276

Andante Spianato & Polonaise, Op. 22 — 1st Theme Andante — C277

2nd Theme Polonaise — C278

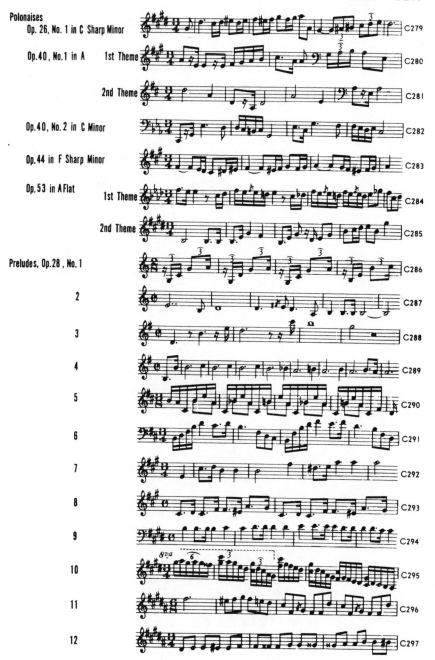

Polonaises
Op. 26, No. 1 in C Sharp Minor — C279

Op. 40, No. 1 in A — 1st Theme — C280

2nd Theme — C281

Op. 40, No. 2 in C Minor — C282

Op. 44 in F Sharp Minor — C283

Op. 53 in A Flat — 1st Theme — C284

2nd Theme — C285

Preludes, Op. 28, No. 1 — C286

2 — C287

3 — C288

4 — C289

5 — C290

6 — C291

7 — C292

8 — C293

9 — C294

10 — C295

11 — C296

12 — C297

13 C298

14 C299

15 "Raindrop" 1st Theme C300

2nd Theme C301

16 C302

17 C303

18 C304

19 C305

20 C306

21 C307

22 C308

23 C309

24 C310

Scherzo in B Minor, Op. 20 — 1st Theme C310a

2nd Theme C311

Scherzo in B Flat Minor, Op.31 — 1st Theme C312

2nd Theme C313

Scherzo in C Sharp Minor Op. 39 — 1st Theme C314

2nd Theme C315

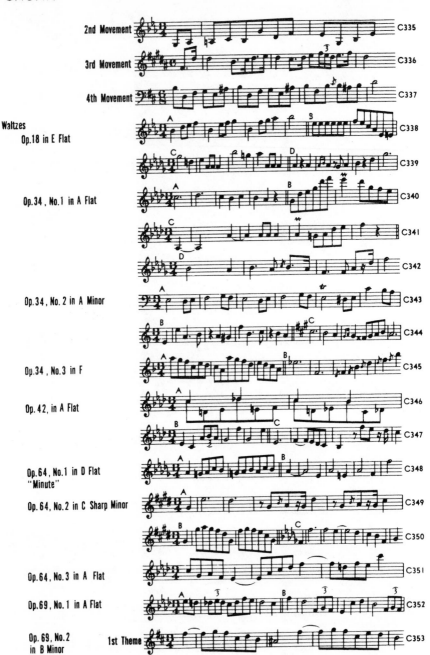

2nd Movement — C335
3rd Movement — C336
4th Movement — C337
Waltzes
Op.18 in E Flat — C338, C339
Op.34, No.1 in A Flat — C340, C341, C342
Op.34, No. 2 in A Minor — C343, C344
Op.34, No.3 in F — C345
Op.42, in A Flat — C346, C347
Op.64, No.1 in D Flat "Minute" — C348
Op.64, No.2 in C Sharp Minor — C349, C350
Op.64, No.3 in A Flat — C351
Op.69, No.1 in A Flat — C352
Op.69, No.2 in B Minor — 1st Theme — C353

2nd Theme — C354

Op.70 , No.1 in G Flat — 1st Theme — C355

2nd Theme — C356

Op. 70, No. 2 in F Minor — C357

Op.70, No. 3 in D Flat — C358

Waltz in E Minor, Posth. — 1st Theme — C359

2nd Theme — C360

Waltz in E, Posth. — C361

CIMAROSA, Domenico (1749-1801)

Il Matrimonio Segreto Overture — 1st Theme — C362

2nd Theme — C363

CLEMENTI, Muzio (1752-1832)

Sonata in B Flat , Pft. Op. 47, No. 2 — 1st Movement — C364

2nd Movement — C365

3rd Movement 1st Theme — C366

3rd Movement 2nd Theme — C367

Sonata in G Minor, Pft. Didone Abbandonata Op. 50 , No. 3 — 1st Movement Intro. — C368

1st Movement — C369

2nd Movement — C370

3rd Movement — C371

Sonata No. 1 in B Flat
2 Pianos, 4 Hands — 1st Movement 1st Theme — C372

1st Movement 2nd Theme — C373

2nd Movement — C374

3rd Movement — C375

Sonata No. 2 in B Flat
2 Pianos, 4 Hands — 1st Movement 1st Theme — C376

1st Movement 2nd Theme — C377

2nd Movement Tempo Di Minuetto — C378

COLERIDGE-TAYLOR, Samuel (1875-1912)

Othello Suite, Orch. — 1st Movement Dance 1st Theme — C387

1st Movement 2nd Theme — C388

2nd Movement Children's Intermezzo 1st Theme — C389

2nd Movement 2nd Theme — C390

3rd Movement Funeral March 1st Theme — C391

3rd Movement 2nd Theme — C392

4th Movement Willow Song — C393

5th Movement Military March 1st Theme — C394

5th Movement 2nd Theme — C395

Petite Suite de Concert Orch. — 1st Movement 1st Theme — C396

Le Caprice de Nanette

1st Movement
2nd Theme   C397

Demande et Réponse   2nd Movement
                     1st Theme   C398

                     2nd Movement
                     2nd Theme   C399

Un Sonnet D'Amour   3rd Movement
                     1st Theme   C400

La Tarantelle   3rd Movement
Frétillante   2nd Theme   C401

                     4th Movement   C402

COPLAND, Aaron (1900-   )

Appalachian Spring   1st Theme   C403
Ballet
By permission of the copyright
owner, Boosey and Hawkes, Inc. 2nd Theme   C404

                     3rd Theme   C405

                     4th Theme   C406
                     A

                     4th Theme,   C407
                     B

                     5th Theme   C408
Shaker Melody "The Gift
To Be Simple"

                     6th Theme   C409

Billy the Kid, Ballet Intro.
The Open Prairie   1st Theme   C410
By permission of the copyright
owner, Boosey and Hawkes, Inc. Intro.
                     2nd Theme   C411

Street in a Frontier Town Scene I
(Cowboy Tune)   1st Theme   C412

The Streets of Laredo   2nd Theme   C413

(Cowboy Tune)   3rd Theme   C414

(Cowboy Tune)   4th Theme   C415

The Card Game — Scene II, 1st Theme — C416

Macabre Dance — 3rd Theme — C417

Billy in Prison — 4th Theme — C418

Scene III — C419

Concerto for Orch. & Pft.
Copyright 1929,
Cos Cob Press, Inc.
1st Movement 1st Theme, A — C420

1st Movement 1st Theme, B — C421

1st Movement 2nd Theme — C422

2nd Movement 1st Theme — C423

2nd Movement 2nd Theme — C424

2nd Movement 3rd Theme — C425

2nd Movement 4th Theme — C426

Dance Symphony
Copyright 1931,
Cos Cob Press, Inc.
Intro. — C427

1st Movement 1st Theme — C428

1st Movement 2nd Theme — C429

1st Movement 3rd Theme — C430

2nd Movement 1st Theme — C431

2nd Movement 2nd Theme — C432

3rd Movement 1st Theme — C433

3rd Movement 2nd Theme — C434

3rd Movement 3rd Theme — C435

Music for the Theatre,
Small Orch.
Copyright 1932,
Cos Cob Press, Inc.

1st Movement
Prologue
1st Theme — C436

1st Movement
2nd Theme — C437

2nd Movement
Dance
1st Theme — C438

2nd Movement
2nd Theme — C439

3rd Movement
Interlude
1st Theme — C440

3rd Movement
2nd Theme — C441

4th Movement
Burlesque
1st Theme — C442

4th Movement
2nd Theme — C443

Nocturne, Vn. & Pft.
By permission of the copyright
owner, Boosey and Hawkes, Inc.

1st Theme — C444

2nd Theme — C445

Passacaglia, Pft.
By permission of the copyright
owner, Boosey and Hawkes, Inc. — C446

Piano Variations
Copyright 1932, Cos Cob Press, Inc.

Theme — C447

El Salon Mexico, Orch.
By permission of the copyright
owner, Boosey and Hawkes, Inc.

Intro. — C448

1st Theme — C449

2nd Theme
Trumpet Solo — C450

3rd Theme — C451

4th Theme — C452

5th Theme — C453

6th Theme — C454

7th Theme
Clarinet Solo — C455

Two Pieces, Str. Orch.
Copyright by Arrow
Music Press, Inc., N. Y.

1st Movement
Lento Molto
1st Theme — C456

1st Movement
2nd Theme — C457

2nd Movement
Rondino
1st Theme — C458

2nd Movement
2nd Theme — C459

Vitebsk, (Study on a Jewish
Theme) Vn., Cello & Pft.
Copyright 1934.
Cos Cob Press, Inc.

Theme — C460

CORELLI, Arcangelo (1653-1713)

Concerto Grosso in
G Minor, String &
Harpsi. Op. 6, No.8
Christmas Concerto

1st Movement
Intro. — C461

1st Movement
1st Theme — C462

1st Movement
2nd Theme — C463

2nd Movement — C464

3rd Movement — C465

4th Movement — C466

5th Movement
Pastorale — C467

Concerto Grosso in
B Flat, Op. 6, No.11
Str. Orch.

1st Movement
1st Theme
Preludio — C468

1st Movement
2nd Theme — C469

2nd Movement
Allemande,
A — C470

2nd Movement
Allemande,
B — C471

3rd Movement
Intro. — C472

3rd Movement — C473

4th Movement
Sarabande — C474

5th Movement Giga — C475

Sonata in G Minor, Op. 5 , No.5 Vn. & Harpsi.

1st Movement — C476

2nd Movement — C477

3rd Movement — C478

4th Movement — C479

5th Movement Gigue — C480

Sonata in E Minor, Op. 5 , No. 8 Vn. & Harpsi.

1st Movement Preludio — C481

2nd Movement Allemande — C482

3rd Movement Sarabande — C483

4th Movement Giga — C484

Sonata in D Minor, Op. 5, No. 12 "La Folia" — C485

Sonata Da Camera, B Flat, Op. 2, No.5 2 Vns., Viola Da Gamba, Harpsi.

1st Movement Preludio — C486

2nd Movement Allemande — C487

3rd Movement Sarabande — C488

4th Movement Tempo Di Gavotta — C489

Sonata Da Camera, G, Op. 2, No. 12 2 Vns., Viola Da Gamba, Harpsi. — C490

CORNELIUS, Peter (1824-1874)

Der Barbier Von Bagdad Overture

1st Theme — C491

2nd Theme — C492

3rd Theme — C493

COUPERIN, François (1668-1733)

Les Abeilles, Harpsi.   C494

La Bandoline, Harpsi.   C495

Les Baricades Misterieuses, Harpsi.   C496

Le Bavolet-Flotant, Harpsi.   C497

Les Bergeries, Harpsi.   Rondeau   C498

La Bersan, Harpsi.   C499

Les Calotins et Les Calotines, Harpsi.   C500

Le Carillon de Cythere, Harpsi.   C501

La Commére, Harpsi.   C502

Concert No. 8 in G, Dans Le Goût Théatral   1st Movement Overture 1st Theme   C503

2nd Theme   C504

2nd Movement Grande Retournele   C505

3rd Movement Air No. 1   C506

4th Movement Air Tendre No. 1   C507

5th Movement Air Léger No. 1   C508

6th Movement Loure   C509

7th Movement Air No. 2   C510

8th Movement Sarabande Brave Et Tendre   C511

9th Movement Air Léger No. 2   C512

Concert Royal, No.4 — 1st Movement / Prelude — C533
in E Minor, Chamber Orch.

2nd Movement / Allemande — C534

3rd Movement / Courante Françoise — C535

4th Movement / Courante à L'Italiéne — C536

5th Movement / Sarabande — C537

6th Movement / Rigaudon — C538

7th Movement / Forlane — C539

La Croûilli ou La Couperinéte, Harpsi. — C540

Le Dodo, Harpsi. — C541

Les Fastes de La Grande
Et Ancienne Ménestrandises, Harpsi. — C542
Act I (Les Notables et
Jurés-Ménestrandises)
Act II (Les Viéleux et — 1st Theme — C543
Les Gueux)

2nd Theme — C544

Act III (Les Jongleurs, Sauteurs, et Saltimbiques) — C545

Act IV (Les Invalides) — C546

Act V (Desordre et Deroute de Toute La Troupe) — C547

La Fleurie ou La Tendre Nanètte Harpsi. — C548

Les Folies Françaises Harpsi. — 1st Movement / La Virginité — C549

2nd Movement / La Pudeur — C550

3rd Movement / L'Ardeur — C551

4th Movement / L'Esperance — C552

5th Movement
La Fidelité — C553

6th Movement
Le Perseverance — C554

7th Movement
La Langueur — C555

8th Movement
Le Coqueterie — C556

9th Movement
Les Vieux Galans — C557

10th Movement
Les Coucous Bénévoles — C558

11th Movement
La Jalousie Taciturne — C559

12th Movement
La Frénésie — C560

Le Gazouillement, Harpsi. — C561

L'Himen-Amour, Harpsi. — C562

La Julliet,
Harpsi. or Fl., Cello & Harpsi. — C563

Les Langueurs-Tendres, Harpsi. — C564

Les Moissonneurs, Harpsi. — C565

Le Moucheron, Harpsi. — C566

Musette de Choisi, Harpsi. — C567

Musette de Taverni, Harpsi. — C568

La Nanète, Harpsi. — C569

Passacaille, Harpsi.
Theme A — C570

Theme B — C571

Les Petits Moulins à Vent
Harpsi. — C572

Le Rossignol en Amour, Harpsi — C573

Soeur Monique, Harpsi. — C574

Les Tambourins, Harpsi. — C575

Le Tic-Toc-Chic ou Les Maillotins, Harpsi. — C576

Les Vergers Fleuris, Harpsi. — C577

Messe Pour Les Convents, Organ
Offertoire Sur Les Grands Jeux — C578

Recit de Chromhorne — C579

Messe Pour Les Paroisses, Organ
Fugue on the Kyrie — C580

Récit de Chromhorne — C581

Offertoire Sur
Les Grands Jeux   1st Theme — C582

2nd Theme — C583

CUI César (1835-1918)

Orientale, Op. 50, No.9, Vn. & Pft.
Copyright renewal assigned 1945
to G. Schirmer, Inc. — C584

Tarantella, Op. 12, Orch.   1st Theme — C585
By permission of Associated
Music Publishers, Inc.

2nd Theme — C586

3rd Theme — C587

4th Theme — C588

DAQUIN, Louis Claude (1694-1772)

Le Coucou, Harpsi.   1st Theme — D1

2nd Theme — D2

La Guitarre, Harpsi. ... D3

L'Hirondelle, Harpsi. ... D4

Musette Et Tambourin Harpsi. 1st Theme Musette ... D5

2nd Theme Tambourin ... D6

Noël No. 9, (Sur Les Flutes), Organ ... D7

Noël No. 10, Organ ... D8

DARGOMIJSKY, Alexander Sergeivich (1813-1869)

Roussalka, Opera Danse Slave ... D9

Gypsy Dance ... D10

Dance of the Nymphs 1st Theme ... D11

2nd Theme ... D12

DEBUSSY, Claude (1862-1918)

Prélude A L'Après-Midi D'Un Faune (Afternoon of A Faun) Orch.
Permission for reprint granted by Jean Jobert, Paris. Elkan-Vogel Co. Inc., Philadelphia, Copyright Owners
1st Theme ... D13

2nd Theme ... D14

Arabesque No. 1, in E, Pft.
Permission for reprint granted by Durand & Cie, Paris. Elkan-Vogel Co.,Inc., Philadelphia, Copyright Owners
1st Theme, A ... D15

1st Theme, B ... D16

2nd Theme ... D17

Arabesque No. 2, in G, Pft.
Permission for reprint granted by Durand & Cie, Paris. Elkan-Vogel Co., Inc., Philadelphia, Copyright Owners.
1st Theme ... D18

2nd Theme ... D19

Ballade, Pft.
Permission for reprint granted by Jean Jobert, Paris. Elkan-Vogel Co., Philadelphia,Inc. Copyright Owners.
1st Theme ... D20

DEBUSSY

2nd Theme — D21

Children's Corner
Suite, Pft.
Permission for reprint
granted by Durand
& Cie, Paris.
Elkan-Vogel Co., Inc.,
Philadelphia, Copyright
Owners.

Doctor Gradus Ad
Parnassum — D22

Jimbo's Lullaby — D23

Serenade of the Doll — D24

The Little Shepherd
1st Theme — D25

2nd Theme — D26

Golliwogg's Cake Walk
1st Theme — D27

2nd Theme — D28

3rd Theme
(Parody on Tristan) — D29

Danses, Harp
Permission for reprint
granted by Durand
& Cie, Paris.
Elkan-Vogel Co., Inc.,
Philadelphia,
Copyright Owners.

I Danse Sacrée — D30

II Danse Profane — D31

Danse (Tarantelle
Styrienne), Pft.
Permission for reprint
granted by Jean Jobert,
Paris. Elkan-Vogel Co., Inc.
Philadelphia,
Copyright Owners.

1st Theme — D32

2nd Theme — D33

Estampes, Pft.
Permission for reprint granted
by Durand & Cie, Paris.
Elkan-Vogel Co.
Inc.Philadelphia.
Copyright Owners.

Pagodes — D34

La Soirée dans Grenade
1st Theme — D35

2nd Theme — D36

3rd Theme — D37

Jardins Sous La Pluie
(Gardens in the Rain)
1st Theme — D38

2nd Theme — D39

L'Isle Joyeuse, Pft.
Permission for reprint granted
by Durand & Cie, Paris.
Elkan-Vogel Co., Inc., Philadelphia,
Copyright Owners.

Intro. — D40

1st Theme D41

2nd Theme D42

3rd Theme D43

Gigues, from Images, Orch., No. 1
Permission for reprint granted by Durand & Cie, Paris. Elkan-Vogel Co., Inc. Philadelphia, Copyright Owners.

1st Theme D44

2nd Theme D45

3rd Theme D46

Iberia, from Images, Orch., No. 2

Par Les Rues et Par Les Chemins (Along the Streets and Roads)
Permission for reprint granted by Durand & Cie, Paris. Elkan-Vogel Co., Inc. Philadelphia, Copyright Owners.

1st Movement 1st Theme D47

1st Movement 2nd Theme D48

1st Movement 3rd Theme D49

1st Movement 4th Theme D50

1st Movement 5th Theme D51

1st Movement 6th Theme D52

Les Parfums de La Nuit (Perfumes of the Night)

2nd Movement Intro. D53

2nd Movement 1st Theme D54

2nd Movement 2nd Theme D55

2nd Movement 3rd Theme D56

2nd Movement 4th Theme D57

2nd Movement 5th Theme D58

2nd Movement 6th Theme D59

Le Matin D'Un Jour De Fête (The Morning of a Holiday)

3rd Movement 1st Theme D60

I Reflets Dans L'Eau
from Images—1st Series, Pft.
Permission for reprint granted
by Durand & Cie, Paris.
Elkan-Vogel Co., Inc.
Philadelphia, Copyright Owners.

II Hommage à Rameau
from Images—1st Series, Pft.
Permission for reprint granted
by Durand & Cie, Paris.
Elkan-Vogel Co., Inc.
Philadelphia, Copyright Owners.

Poissons D'Or (Goldfish)
from Images—2nd Series, Pft.
Permission for reprint granted by Durand
& Cie, Paris. Elkan-Vogel Co., Inc.
Philadelphia, Copyright Owners.

Mazurka, Pft.
Permission for reprint granted by Jean
Jobert, Paris. Elkan-Vogel Co., Inc.
Philadelphia, Copyright Owners.

La Mer, Orch.
De L'Aube A
Midi Sur La Mer
(From Dawn to
Noon on the Sea)

Permission for reprint
granted by Durand & Cie,
Paris. Elkan-Vogel Co., Inc.
Philadelphia, Copyright
Owners,

Jeux De Vagues
(Play of the Waves)

Dialogue du Vent
et de la Mer
(Dialogue of the
Wind and the Sea)

Nocturnes, Orch.
Permission for reprint
granted by Jean Jobert, Paris.
Elkan-Vogel Co., Inc. Philadelphia,
Copyright Owners.

2nd Theme — D81

3rd Theme — D82

Fêtes
1st Theme — D83

2nd Theme — D84

3rd Theme — D85

4th Theme — D86

Sirènes
1st Theme — D87

2nd Theme — D88

Petite Suite, 2 Pianos
Permission for reprint granted
by Durand & Cie, Paris.
Elkan-Vogel Co., Inc.
Philadelphia, Copyright
Owners,

En Bateau
1st Theme — D89

2nd Theme — D90

Cortège
1st Theme — D91

2nd Theme — D92

Menuet
1st Theme — D93

2nd Theme — D94

Ballet
1st Theme — D95

2nd Theme — D96

Pour le Piano, Suite
Permission for reprint
granted by Durand & Cie, Paris.
Elkan-Vogel Co., Inc.
Philadelphia, Copyright
Owners,

Prélude
1st Theme — D97

2nd Theme — D98

Sarabande — D99

Toccata — D100

La Plus Que Lente, Waltz, Pft.
1st Theme   D101

Permission for reprint granted by Durand & Cie, Paris. Elkan-Vogel Co., Inc. Philadelphia, Copyright Owners.

2nd Theme   D102

Préludes, Book 1, Pft. Permission for reprint
No. 1 granted by Durand & Cie, Paris.
Elkan-Vogel Co., Inc. Philadelphia,
Danseuses De Delphes Copyright Owners,   D103

No. 2
Voiles (Veils)   1st Theme   D104

2nd Theme   D105

No. 5
Les Collines D'Anacapri
(The Hills of Anacapri)   D106

No. 8
La Fille Aux Cheveux De Lin
(The Girl With the Flaxen Hair)   D107

No. 10
La Cathédrale Engloutie   1st Theme   D108
(The Sunken Cathedral)

2nd Theme   D109

No. 11
La Danse De Puck   D110

No. 12
Minstrels   D111

Préludes, Book II, Pft. Permission for reprint
No. 3 granted by Durand & Cie, Paris.
Elkan-Vogel Co., Inc. Philadelphia,
La Puerta Del Vino Copyright Owners,   D112

No. 5
Bruyères (Heather)   D113

No. 6
General Lavine-Eccentric   D114

No. 9, Hommage à
S. Pickwick, Esq., P.P.M.P.C.
(Parody on God Save the King)   D115

Printemps
Symphonic Suite, Orch.
1st Movement
1st Theme   D116

Permission for reprint granted by Durand & Cie. Paris. Elkan-Vogel Co., Inc. Philadelphia, Copyright Owners.

1st Movement
2nd Theme   D117

2nd Movement
1st Theme   D118

2nd Movement
2nd Theme   D119

Quartet in G Minor,
Str.
1st Movement
1st Theme   D120

Permission for reprint granted by Durand & Cie, Paris. Elkan-Vogel Co., Inc. Philadelphia, Copyright Owners.

Suite Bergamasque, Pft.
Permission for reprint granted
by Jean Jobert, Paris.
Elkan-Vogel Co., Inc.
Philadelphia, Copyright Owners.

Valse Romantique, Pft.
Permission for reprint granted
by Jean Jobert, Paris.
Elkan-Vogel Co., Inc.
Philadelphia, Copyright Owners,

Prelude — D141
Menuet 1st Theme — D142
2nd Theme — D143
Clair de Lune 1st Theme — D144
2nd Theme — D145
Passepied 1st Theme — D146
2nd Theme — D147
— D148

DELIBES, Clement Philibert Leo (1836-1891)

Coppelia, Ballet
Act I

Prelude 1st Theme — D149
2nd Theme — D150
3rd Theme (Also Mazurka Theme) — D151
Waltz — D152
Scene — D153
Thème Slave — D154
Czardas 1st Theme — D155
2nd Theme — D156

Act II   Musique des Automates — D157
Valse de la Poupée — D158

Act III   Marche de la Cloche 1st Theme — D159

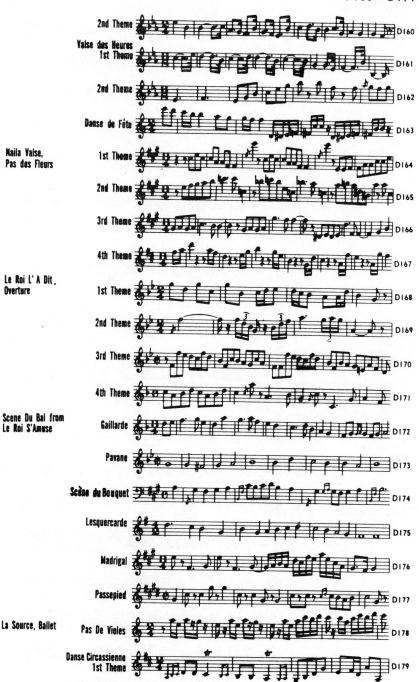

DELIUS, Frederick (1862-1934)

Eventyr "Once Upon a Time", Orch.
By permission of Augener, Ltd., London

1st Theme — D199

2nd Theme — D200

3rd Theme — D201

Hassan, Suite for Orch.
By permission of the copyright owner, Boosey and Hawkes, Inc.

Intermezzo — D202

Serenade — D203

In a Summer Garden, Orch.
By permission of Associated Music Publishers, Inc.

1st Theme, A — D204

1st Theme, B — D205

2nd Theme — D206

3rd Theme — D207

4th Theme — D208

Irmelin–Prelude, Orch.
By permission of the copyright owner, Boosey and Hawkes, Inc.

D209

Paris, Nocturne, Orch.
By permission of Associated Music Publishers, Inc.

1st Theme — D210

2nd Theme — D211

3rd Theme — D212

4th Theme — D213

Sonata No. 2, Vn. & Pft.
By permission of the copyright owner, Boosey and Hawkes, Inc.

1st Theme — D214

2nd Theme — D215

3rd Theme — D216

4th Theme — D217

Two Pieces for Small Orchestra
No. 1, On Hearing the First Cuckoo in Spring — D218

Copyright by the Oxford University Press
Reproduced by permission.

No.11 Summer Night on the River — D219

The Walk to the Paradise Garden, from A Village Romeo & Juliet, Orch.
By permission of the copyright owner, Boosey and Hawkes, Inc.

1st Theme — D220

2nd Theme — D221

DETT, Robert Nathaniel (1882-1943)

Juba Dance, Pft.
from In the Bottoms
By permission of Clayton F. Summy Co., owners of the copyright.

1st Theme — D222

2nd Theme — D223

DIAMOND, David (1915-   )

Rounds,
Str. Orch.
Permission granted by Elkan-Vogel Co.,Inc. Philadelphia, Pa. Copyright 1946

1st Movement 1st Theme — D223a

1st Movement 2nd Theme — D223b

1st Movement 3rd Theme — D223c

2nd Movement — D223d

3rd Movement 1st Theme — D223e

3rd Movement 2nd Theme — D223f

DINICU, ARR. BY HEIFETZ

Hora Staccato, Vn. & Pft.
Copyright 1930 by Carl Fischer, Inc., N. Y.

1st Theme — D224

2nd Theme — D225

DITTERSDORF, Carl Ditters von (1739-1799)

Quartet, No. 5, in E Flat, Str.

1st Movement — D226

2nd Movement 1st Theme — D227

2nd Movement 2nd Theme — D228

3rd Movement — D229

Quartet, No. 6, in A, Str. — 1st Movement — D230

2nd Movement — D231

3rd Movement — D232

DOHNÁNYI, Ernö von (1877-1960)

Capriccio, Op. 28, Pft. — D233

Rhapsody, Op. 11, No. 3, Pft.
By permission of Associated Music Publishers, Inc. — 1st Theme — D234

2nd Theme — D235

Ruralia Hungarica, Op. 32a, No. 1 — D236

Ruralia Hungarica, Op. 32a, No. 2 — 1st Theme — D237

2nd Theme — D238

Ruralia Hungarica, Op. 32a, No. 7 — D239

Suite, Op. 19, Orch.
By permission of Associated Music Publishers, Inc. — Andante con Variazioni — D240

Scherzo 1st Theme — D241

2nd Theme — D242

Romance 1st Theme — D243

2nd Theme — D244

Rondo 1st Theme — D245

2nd Theme — D246

DONIZETTI, Gaetano (1797-1848)

Daughter of the Regiment Overture — 1st Theme — D247

2nd Theme — D248

3rd Theme — D249

4th Theme — D250

La Favorita Overture — 1st Theme — D251

2nd Theme — D252

Don Pasquale Overture — 1st Theme — D253

2nd Theme — D254

DOWLAND, John (1563-1626)

M. George Whitehead, His Almand Lute & Strings — D255

Mrs. Nichols' Almand Lute & Strings — D256

M. Henry Noël, His Galliard Lute & Strings — D257

M. Thomas Collier, His Galliard Lute & Strings — D258

M. John Langton's Pavan Lute & Strings — D259

The King of Denmark's Galliard Lute & Strings — D260

The Earl of Essex Galliard Lute & Strings — D261

DRDLA, Franz (1868-1944)

Souvenir, Vn. & Pft. — 1st Theme — D261a

2nd Theme — D261b

DRIGO, Riccardo (1846-1930)

Les Millions
d'Arlequin, Serenade
Vn. & Pft. — 1st Theme — D261c

2nd Theme — D261d

Valse Bluette, Vn. & Pft. — D261e

DUKAS, Paul (1865-1935)

L'Apprenti Sorcier
(The Sorcerer's Apprentice)
Scherzo for Orch. — Intro. — D262
Permission for reprint granted
by Durand & Cie, Paris.
Elkan-Vogel, Inc.
Philadelphia, Copyright Owners. — 1st Theme — D263

2nd Theme — D264

La Péri
Dance Poem for Orch. — 1st Theme — D265

Permission for reprint granted
by Durand & Cie, Paris.
Elkan-Vogel Co., Inc.
Philadelphia, Copyright Owners. — 2nd Theme — D266

3rd Theme — D267

4th Theme — D268

DVOŘÁK, Antonin (1841-1904)

Bagatelles, Op. 47,
Pft. & Str. — 1st Movement — D269
By permission of Associated
Music Publishers, Inc.

2nd Movement — D270

4th Movement — D271

5th Movement
1st Theme — D272

5th Movement
2nd Theme — D273

Carnaval Overture, Op. 92 — 1st Theme — D274
By permission of Associated
Music Publishers, Inc.

2nd Theme — D275

3rd Theme — D276

4th Theme — D277

Concerto in B Minor, Op.104, Cello & Orch.
Copyright 1930 by G. Schirmer, Inc.

1st Movement 1st Theme — D278

1st Movement 2nd Theme — D279

2nd Movement 1st Theme — D280

2nd Movement 2nd Theme — D281

3rd Movement 1st Theme — D282

3rd Movement 2nd Theme — D283

Concerto in A Minor, Op. 53, Vn. & Orch.
By permission of Associated Music Publishers, Inc.

1st Movement 1st Theme, A — D284

1st Movement 1st Theme, B — D285

1st Movement 2nd Theme — D286

2nd Movement 1st Theme — D287

2nd Movement 2nd Theme — D288

3rd Movement 1st Theme — D289

3rd Movement 2nd Theme — D290

3rd Movement 3rd Theme — D291

Humoresque, Op. 101, No. 7, Pft.
By permission of Associated Music Publishers, Inc.

1st Theme — D292

2nd Theme — D293

3rd Theme — D294

Quartet in D, Op. 23, Pft. & Str.
By permission of Associated Music Publishers, Inc.

1st Movement 1st Theme — D295

Quartet in E Flat, Op. 87, Pft. & Str.
By permission of Associated Music Publishers, Inc.

Quart., in F, Op. 96 Str.,"American"
By permission of Associated Music Publishers, Inc.

DVORAK

Quartet in
A Flat, Op. 105, Str.
By permission of
Associated Music
Publishers, Inc.

1st Movement 1st Theme — D316

1st Movement 2nd Theme — D317

2nd Movement 1st Theme — D318

2nd Movement 2nd Theme — D319

3rd Movement — D320

4th Movement 1st Theme — D321

4th Movement 2nd Theme — D322

4th Movement 3rd Theme — D323

Quartet in
G, Op. 106, Str.
By permission of
Associated Music
Publishers, Inc.

1st Movement 1st Theme — D324

1st Movement 2nd Theme — D325

2nd Movement — D326

3rd Movement 1st Theme — D327

3rd Movement 2nd Theme — D328

3rd Movement 3rd Theme — D329

4th Movement 1st Theme — D330

4th Movement 2nd Theme — D331

4th Movement 3rd Theme — D332

Quintet, Op. 81
Pft. & Str.

1st Movement 1st Theme — D332a

1st Movement 2nd Theme — D332b

2nd Movement Dumka 1st Theme, A — D332c

2nd Movement 1st Theme, B — D332d

2nd Movement 1st Theme, C — D332e

2nd Movement 2nd Theme — D332f

3rd Movement — D332g

4th Movement 1st Theme — D332h

4th Movement 2nd Theme — D332i

Quintet in E Flat, Op. 97, Str.
By permission of Associated Music Publishers, Inc.

1st Movement 1st Theme — D333

1st Movement 2nd Theme — D334

2nd Movement 1st Theme — D335

2nd Movement 2nd Theme — D336

3rd Movement — D337

4th Movement — D338

Scherzo Capriccioso, Op. 66, Orch.
By permission of Associated Music Publishers, Inc.

1st Theme — D339

2nd Theme — D340

3rd Theme — D341

4th Theme — D342

Serenade for Strings, in E, Op. 22
By permission of Associated Music Publishers, Inc.

1st Movement 1st Theme — D343

1st Movement 2nd Theme — D344

2nd Movement 1st Theme — D345

2nd Movement 2nd Theme — D346

3rd Movement — D347

4th Movement — D348

5th Movement — D349

Sextet, Op. 48, Str.
By permission of
Associated Music
Publishers, Inc.

1st Movement
1st Theme — D350

1st Movement
2nd Theme — D351

2nd Movement
Dumka
1st Theme
A — D352

2nd Movement
1st Theme,
B — D353

2nd Movement
2nd Theme — D354

3rd Movement — D355

4th Movement
(Theme for Variations) — D356

Slavonic Dances, Op. 46,
Orch.   No. 1

1st Theme — D357

2nd Theme — D358

No. 2

1st Theme — D359

2nd Theme — D360

No. 3

1st Theme — D361

2nd Theme — D362

No. 4

1st Theme — D363

2nd Theme — D364

No. 5

1st Theme — D365

2nd Theme — D366

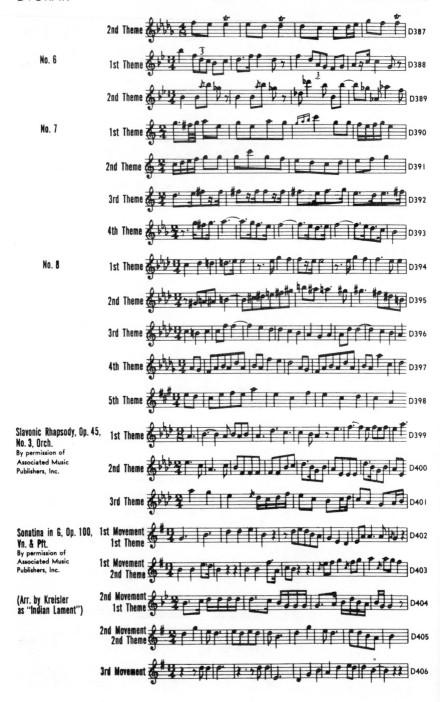

4th Movement 1st Theme D407

4th Movement 2nd Theme D408

4th Movement 3rd Theme D409

Symphony No. 1, in D.
Op. 60
By permission of
Associated Music
Publishers, Inc.

1st Movement 1st Theme D410

1st Movement 2nd Theme D411

2nd Movement D412

3rd Movement 1st Theme A D413

3rd Movement 1st Theme, B D414

3rd Movement 2nd Theme D415

4th Movement 1st Theme D416

4th Movement 2nd Theme D417

Symphony No. 2
in D Minor, Op. 70
By permission of
Associated Music
Publishers, Inc.

1st Movement 1st Theme D418

1st Movement 2nd Theme D419

2nd Movement D420

3rd Movement 1st Theme D421

3rd Movement 2nd Theme D422

4th Movement 1st Theme D423

4th Movement 2nd Theme D424

4th Movement 3rd Theme D425

Symphony No. 4
in G, Op. 88
By permission of
Novello & Co., Ltd.,
London

1st Movement 1st Theme D426

Symphony No. 5,
in E Minor, Op. 95
"From The New World"
Published and
Copyrighted 1928
by Oliver Ditson Co.

Trio in F Minor, Op. 65, 1st Movement
Vn., Pft. & Cello
By permission of Associated
Music Publishers, Inc.

1st Movement
2nd Theme — D447

2nd Movement — D448

3rd Movement — D449

4th Movement
1st Theme — D450

4th Movement
2nd Theme — D451

Trio, Op. 90 Vn. Pft. & Cello,"Dumky"
By permission of Associated Music Publishers, Inc.

1st Movement
Intro. — D452

1st Movement
1st Theme,
A — D453

1st Movement
1st Theme,
B — D454

1st Movement
2nd Theme — D455

1st Movement
3rd Theme — D456

2nd Movement — D457

3rd Movement
1st Theme — D458

3rd Movement
2nd Theme — D459

4th Movement
1st Theme — D460

4th Movement
2nd Theme — D461

5th Movement
Intro. — D462

5th Movement — D463

Wedding Dance From Die Waldtaube, Op. 110, Orch.
By permission of Associated Music Publishers, Inc.

1st Theme — D464

2nd Theme — D465

Waltzes, Op. 54, Pft. No. 1
By permission of Associated Music Publishers, Inc.

— D466

No. 3 1st Theme D467

2nd Theme D468

No. 6 D469

ELGAR, Sir Edward (1857-1934)

Chanson de Nuit, Op. 15, No. 1,
Orch.
By permission of Novello & Co., Ltd., London. E1

Cockaigne, In London Town 1st Theme E2
Op. 40, Concert Overture,
Orch.
By permission of the
copyright owner, 2nd Theme E3
Boosey and Hawkes, Inc.

3rd Theme E4

4th Theme E5

Concerto in E Minor, 1st Movement E6
Op. 85, Cello & Orch. Intro.
By permission of
Novello & Co., Ltd., 1st Movement E7
London. 1st Theme

1st Movement E8
2nd Theme

2nd Movement E9
1st Theme

2nd Movement E10
2nd Theme

3rd Movement E11

4th Movement E12

Concerto in B Minor, 1st Movement E13
Op. 61, Vn. & Orch. 1st Theme,
By permission of A
Novello & Co., Ltd., 1st Movement E14
London. 1st Theme,
B
1st Movement E15
2nd Theme

2nd Movement E16
1st Theme

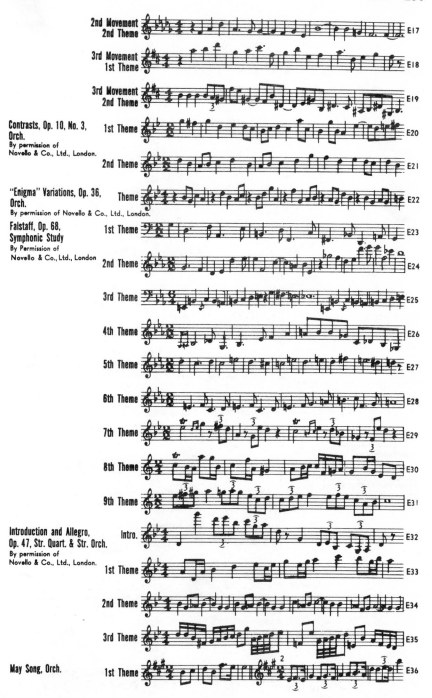

2nd Theme — E37

Pomp and Circumstance,
Military Marches, Op. 39
No. 1
By permission of the
copyright owner,
Boosey and Hawkes, Inc.

1st Theme — E38

2nd Theme — E39

No. 2

1st Theme — E40

2nd Theme — E41

3rd Theme — E42

No. 3

1st Theme — E43

2nd Theme — E44

3rd Theme
A — E45

3rd Theme
B — E46

No. 4

1st Theme — E47

2nd Theme — E48

Salut D'Amour, Op. 12, Orch.
By permission of Associated
Music Publishers, Inc.
— E49

Serenade, Op. 20.
Str. Orch.
By permission of Associated
Music Publishers, Inc.

1st Movement
1st Theme — E50

1st Movement
2nd Theme — E51

2nd Movement — E52

3rd Movement — E53

Sonata in E Minor,
Op. 82, Vn. & Pft.
By permission of
Novello & Co., Ltd.,
London.

1st Movement
1st Theme — E54

1st Movement
2nd Theme — E55

2nd Movement
Romance
1st Theme — E56

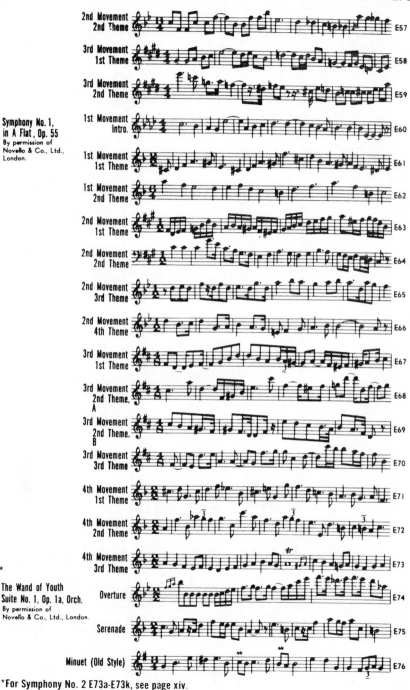

Symphony No. 1,
in A Flat, Op. 55
By permission of
Novello & Co., Ltd.,
London.

The Wand of Youth
Suite No. 1, Op. 1a, Orch.
By permission of
Novello & Co., Ltd., London.

*For Symphony No. 2 E73a-E73k, see page xiv.

Sun Dance — E77

Fairy Pipers — E78

Slumber Scene — E79

ENESCO, Georges (1881-1955)

Poème Roumain, Op. 1
Symphonic Suite
By permission of
M M Enoch & Cie.,
Music Publishers,
27 Boulevard
des Italiens, Paris

1st Movement 1st Theme — E80

1st Movement 2nd Theme — E81

1st Movement 3rd Theme — E82

2nd Movement 1st Theme — E83

2nd Movement 2nd Theme — E84

2nd Movement Roumanian Folk Song 3rd Theme — E85

2nd Movement 4th Theme — E86

2nd Movement 5th Theme — E87

2nd Movement Roumanian National Anthem — E88

Roumanian Rhapsody No. 1,
Op. 11, Orch.
By permission of
M M Enoch & Cie.,
Music Publishers,
27 Boulevard
des Italiens, Paris

1st Theme, A — E89

1st Theme, B — E90

2nd Theme — E91

3rd Theme, A — E92

3rd Theme, B — E93

4th Theme — E94

5th Theme — E95

6th Theme — E96

7th Theme — E97

8th Theme — E98

Roumanian Rhapsody No. 2
Op. 11, Orch.

By permission of
M M Enoch & Cie.
Music Publishers,
27 Boulevard
des Italiens, Paris.

1st Theme — E99

2nd Theme — E100

3rd Theme — E101

4th Theme — E102

5th Theme — E103

ERKEL, Franz (1810-1893)

Hunyadi László, Opera
Overture

1st Theme — E104

2nd Theme — E105

3rd Theme — E106

4th Theme — E107

FALLA, Manuel de (1876-1946)

El Amor Brujo,
Ballet
By permission of
the copyright holders,
J. & W. Chester, Ltd., 11
Great Marlborough
Street, London, W. I.

Introduction & Scene — F1

En La Cueva — F2

Canción del Amor Dolido — F3

Dance of Terror
1st Theme — F4

2nd Theme — F5

Ritual Fire Dance
1st Theme — F6

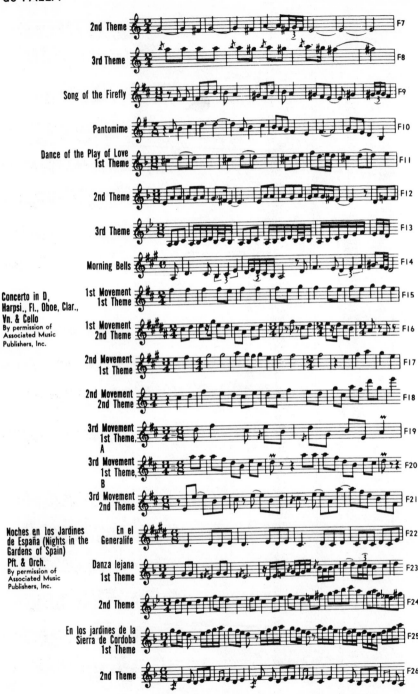

4 Pieces Espagñoles, Pft. — Aragonesa — F27
Permission for reprint granted by Durand & Cie, Paris. Elkan-Vogel Co., Inc. Philadelphia, Copyright Owners.

Cubana — F28

Montañesa 1st Theme — F29

2nd Theme — F30

Andaluza 1st Theme — F31

2nd Theme — F32

3 Dances from El Sombrero de Tres Picos (The Three Cornered Hat), Orch. — Dance of the Neighbors 1st Theme — F33
By permission of the copyright holders, J. & W. Chester, Ltd., 11 Great Marlborough Street, London, W. 1.

2nd Theme — F34

Danse du Corregidor (Mayor's Dance) 1st Theme — F35

2nd Theme — F36

Jota 1st Theme — F37

2nd Theme — F38

3rd Theme — F39

4th Theme — F40

Miller's Dance — F41

Suite Populaire Espagñole, Vn. & Pft. — El Pano Moruno — F42
By permission of the copyright holders, J. & W. Chester, Ltd., 11 Great Marlborough Street, London, W. 1.

Nana — F43

Canción — F44

Polo — F45

Asturiana — F46

Jota
1st Theme — F47

2nd Theme — F48

La Vida Breve
Orch.
By permission of Associated
Music Publishers, Inc.

Dance, No. 1
1st Theme — F49

2nd Theme — F50

Dance No. 2
1st Theme — F51

2nd Theme — F52

FARNABY, Giles (1560-1600)

His Conceit, Fitzwilliam Virginal
Book No. 273, Harpsi. — F53

His Dreame, Fitzwilliam Virginal
Book No. 260, Harpsi. — F54

His Humour, Fitzwilliam Virginal
Book No. 196, Harpsi. — F55

His Rest, Fitzwilliam Virginal
Book No. 195, Harpsi. — F56

Rosa Solis, Fitzwilliam Virginal
Book No. 143, Harpsi. — F57

Tower Hill, Fitzwilliam Virginal
Book No. 245, Harpsi. — F58

A Toye, Fitzwilliam Virginal
Book No. 270, Harpsi. — F59

FAURÉ, Gabriel (1845-1924)

Ballade, Op. 19, Pft. & Orch 1st Theme
By permission of
J. Hamelle Music
Publishers, Paris. — F60

2nd Theme — F61

3rd Theme — F62

4th Theme — F63

Barcarolle No. 5, Op. 66, Pft.
By permission of J. Hamelle
Music Publishers, Paris. — F64

Barcarolle No. 6, Op. 70, Pft.
By permission of
J. Hamelle Music
Publishers, Paris.

F65

**Dolly, Op. 56, Pft.,
4 Hands**
By permission of
J. Hamelle Music
Publishers, Paris.

Berceuse — F66

Mi-a-ou
1st Theme — F67

2nd Theme — F68

Le Jardin de Dolly — F69

Kitty-Valse
1st Theme — F70

2nd Theme — F71

Tendresse — F72

Le Pas Espagnol
1st Theme — F73

2nd Theme — F74

**Elégie, Op. 24,
Cello & Orch.**
By permission of
J. Hamelle Music
Publishers, Paris.

1st Theme — F75

2nd Theme — F76

**Impromptu, No. 2,
Op. 34, Pft.**
By permission of
International Music Co.

1st Theme — F76a

2nd Theme — F76b

**Impromptu, No.3,
Op. 34, Pft.**
By permission of
International Music Co.

1st Theme — F76c

2nd Theme — F76d

3rd Nocturne, Op. 33, No. 3, Pft.
By permission of
J. Hamelle Music
Publishers, Paris.

F77

4th Nocturne, Op. 36, Pft.
By permission of
J. Hamelle Music
Publishers, Paris.

F78

6th Nocturne, Op. 63, Pft.
By permission of
J. Hamelle Music
Publishers, Paris.

1st Theme — F79

2nd Theme — F80

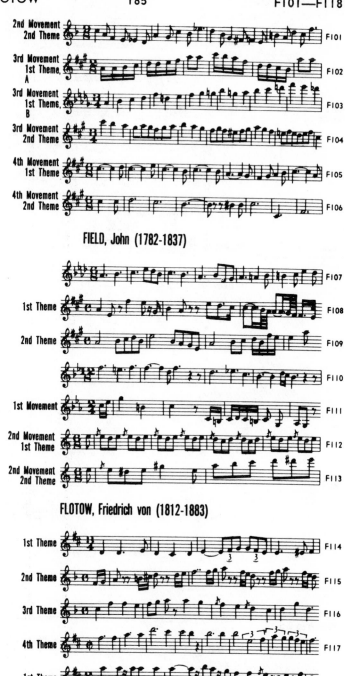

2nd Movement 2nd Theme — F101

3rd Movement 1st Theme, A — F102

3rd Movement 1st Theme, B — F103

3rd Movement 2nd Theme — F104

4th Movement 1st Theme — F105

4th Movement 2nd Theme — F106

FIELD, John (1782-1837)

Nocturne No. 3, Pft. — F107

Nocturne No. 4, Pft. — 1st Theme — F108

2nd Theme — F109

Nocturne No. 5, Pft. — F110

Sonata in C Minor, Op. 1, No. 3, Pft. — 1st Movement — F111

2nd Movement 1st Theme — F112

2nd Movement 2nd Theme — F113

FLOTOW, Friedrich von (1812-1883)

Alessandro Stradella Overture — 1st Theme — F114

2nd Theme — F115

3rd Theme — F116

4th Theme — F117

Fatme (Zilda) Overture — 1st Theme — F118

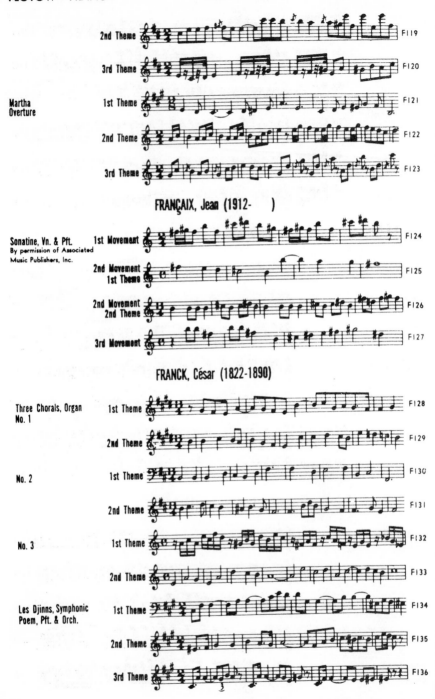

FLOTOW—FRANCK

2nd Theme — F119

3rd Theme — F120

Martha Overture

1st Theme — F121

2nd Theme — F122

3rd Theme — F123

FRANÇAIX, Jean (1912-   )

Sonatine, Vn. & Pft.
By permission of Associated Music Publishers, Inc.

1st Movement — F124

2nd Movement 1st Theme — F125

2nd Movement 2nd Theme — F126

3rd Movement — F127

FRANCK, César (1822-1890)

Three Chorals, Organ No. 1

1st Theme — F128

2nd Theme — F129

No. 2

1st Theme — F130

2nd Theme — F131

No. 3

1st Theme — F132

2nd Theme — F133

Les Djinns, Symphonic Poem, Pft. & Orch.

1st Theme — F134

2nd Theme — F135

3rd Theme — F136

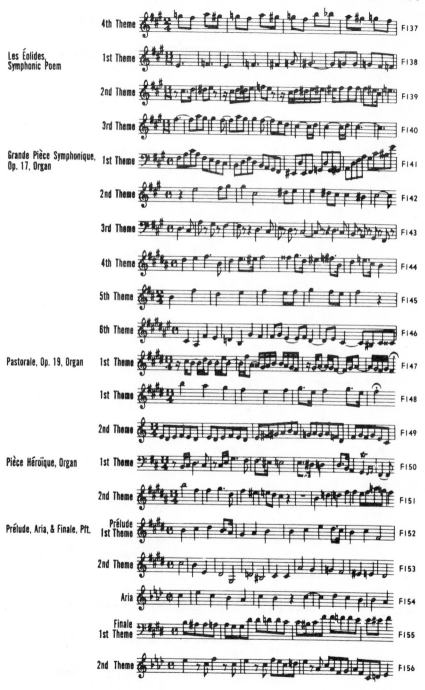

FRANCK

4th Theme — F137

Les Éolides,
Symphonic Poem — 1st Theme — F138

2nd Theme — F139

3rd Theme — F140

Grande Pièce Symphonique,
Op. 17, Organ — 1st Theme — F141

2nd Theme — F142

3rd Theme — F143

4th Theme — F144

5th Theme — F145

6th Theme — F146

Pastorale, Op. 19, Organ — 1st Theme — F147

1st Theme — F148

2nd Theme — F149

Pièce Héroïque, Organ — 1st Theme — F150

2nd Theme — F151

Prélude, Aria, & Finale, Pft. — Prélude 1st Theme — F152

2nd Theme — F153

Aria — F154

Finale 1st Theme — F155

2nd Theme — F156

Prélude, Chorale & Fugue, Pft.

Prélude 1st Theme — F157

2nd Theme — F158

Chorale 1st Theme — F159

2nd Theme — F160

Fugue — F161

Prélude, Fugue & Variations, Op. 18 Organ or Pft.

Prélude & Variations — F162

Fugue — F163

Quartet in D, Str.

1st Movement 1st Theme — F164

1st Movement 2nd Theme — F165

1st Movement 3rd Theme — F166

2nd Movement 1st Theme — F167

2nd Movement 2nd Theme — F168

3rd Movement 1st Theme — F169

3rd Movement 2nd Theme — F170

4th Movement 1st Theme — F171

4th Movement 2nd Theme — F172

4th Movement 3rd Theme — F173

Quintet in F Minor, Pft. & Str.

1st Movement Intro. A — F174

1st Movement Intro. B — F175

1st Movement 1st Theme — F176

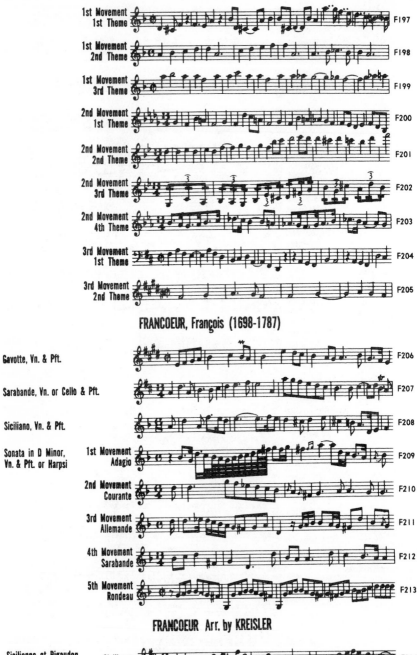

1st Movement 1st Theme — F197
1st Movement 2nd Theme — F198
1st Movement 3rd Theme — F199
2nd Movement 1st Theme — F200
2nd Movement 2nd Theme — F201
2nd Movement 3rd Theme — F202
2nd Movement 4th Theme — F203
3rd Movement 1st Theme — F204
3rd Movement 2nd Theme — F205

FRANCOEUR, François (1698-1787)

Gavotte, Vn. & Pft. — F206
Sarabande, Vn. or Cello & Pft. — F207
Siciliano, Vn. & Pft. — F208
Sonata in D Minor, Vn. & Pft. or Harpsi — 1st Movement Adagio — F209
2nd Movement Courante — F210
3rd Movement Allemande — F211
4th Movement Sarabande — F212
5th Movement Rondeau — F213

FRANCOEUR Arr. by KREISLER

Sicilienne et Rigaudon, Vn. & Pft. — Sicilienne — F214

Rigaudon  F215

FREDERICK II, King of Prussia (1712-1786)

Concerto No. 2, in
G, Flute & Str.

1st Movement
1st Theme  F216

1st Movement
2nd Theme F217

2nd Movement F218

3rd Movement F219

FRESCOBALDI, Girolamo (1583-1643)

Capriccio on the Cuckoo,
Harpsi.  F220

Capriccio on La Girolometa
Harpsi. F221

Capriccio on L'Aria di Ruggiero
Harpsi. F222

Capriccio: La Spagnoletta
Harpsi. F223

Fugue in G Minor, Organ & Str. F224

Ricercar Cromatico Post II Credo
Organ F225

Toccata, Spinet or Lute F226

FUCÎK, Julius (1872-1916)

Entry of the Gladiators,
March

1st Theme 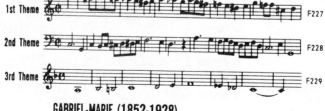 F227

2nd Theme F228

3rd Theme F229

GABRIEL-MARIE (1852-1928)

La Cinquantaine, Air Dans
Le Style Ancien, Pft.

1st Theme G1

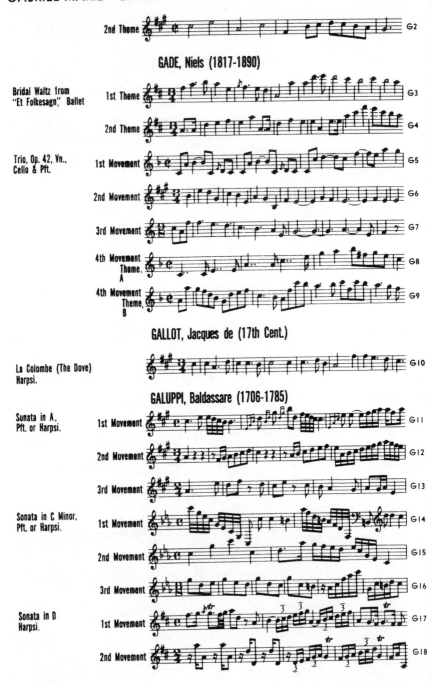

2nd Theme — G2

GADE, Niels (1817-1890)

Bridal Waltz from "Et Folkesagn," Ballet
1st Theme — G3
2nd Theme — G4

Trio, Op. 42, Vn., Cello & Pft.
1st Movement — G5
2nd Movement — G6
3rd Movement — G7
4th Movement Theme, A — G8
4th Movement Theme, B — G9

GALLOT, Jacques de (17th Cent.)

La Colombe (The Dove) Harpsi. — G10

GALUPPI, Baldassare (1706-1785)

Sonata in A, Pft. or Harpsi.
1st Movement — G11
2nd Movement — G12
3rd Movement — G13

Sonata in C Minor, Pft. or Harpsi.
1st Movement — G14
2nd Movement — G15
3rd Movement — G16

Sonata in D Harpsi.
1st Movement — G17
2nd Movement — G18

3rd Movement 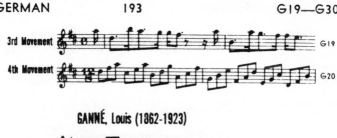 G19

4th Movement G20

GANNÉ, Louis (1862-1923)

La Czarina, Mazurka 1st Theme 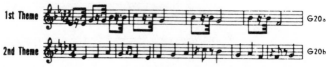 G20a

2nd Theme G20b

GAUTIER, Jean (1822-1878)

The Secret, Vn. & Pft. 1st Theme 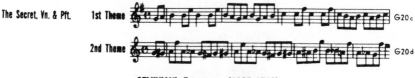 G20c

2nd Theme G20d

GEMINIANI, Francesco (1687-1762)

Sonata in C Minor, Vn. & Pft. 1st Movement 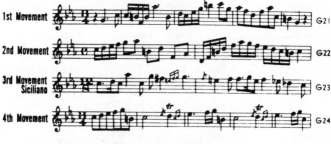 G21

2nd Movement G22

3rd Movement Siciliano G23

4th Movement G24

GERMAN, Sir Edward (1862-1936)

As You Like It
Incidental Music
By permission of
Novello & Co., Ltd.,
London. 1st Movement Woodland Dance 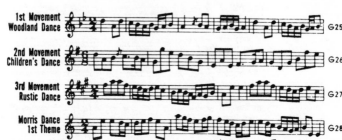 G25

2nd Movement Children's Dance G26

3rd Movement Rustic Dance G27

Henry VIII
Incidental Music
By permission of
Novello & Co., Ltd., London Morris Dance 1st Theme G28

2nd Theme G29

Shepherd's Dance G30

Torch Dance   G31

Romeo and Juliet
Incidental Music, Orch.
Pavane   G32
By permission of Novello & Co., Ltd., London.

Welsh Rhapsody, Orch.   1st Theme
By permission of   Loudly Proclaim   G33
Novello & Co., Ltd., London.

2nd Theme   G34

3rd Theme
Hunting the Hare   G35

4th Theme
Bells of Aberdovy   G36

5th Theme
David of the White Rock   G37

6th Theme
Men of Harlech   G38

GERSHWIN, George (1898-1937)

An American in Paris,
Orch.
1st Theme   G39
Copyright 1930 by
New World Music Corp.
2nd Theme   G40
Reprinted by
special permission.

3rd Theme
Blues Theme   G41

4th Theme   G42

Concerto in F,
Pft. & Orch.
1st Movement
1st Theme   G43
Copyright 1927
by Harms, Inc.
1st Movement
2nd Theme   G44
Reprinted by
special permission.

1st Movement
3rd Theme   G45

2nd Movement
1st Theme,
A   G46

2nd Movement
1st Theme,
B   G47

2nd Movement
2nd Theme   G48

2nd Movement
3rd Theme   G49

3rd Movement 1st Theme — G50

3rd Movement 2nd Theme — G51

Prelude No. 1, Pft.
Copyright 1927 by New
World Music Corp.
Reprinted by special permission.
— G52

Prelude No. 2, Pft.
Copyright 1927 by New
World Music Corp.
Reprinted by special permission.
1st Theme — G53

2nd Theme — G54

Prelude No. 3, Pft.
Copyright 1927 by New
World Music Corp.
Reprinted by special permission.
— G55

Rhapsody in Blue,
Pft. & Orch.
Copyright 1924 by
Harms, Inc.
Reprinted by special permission
1st Theme — G56

2nd Theme — G57

3rd Theme — G58

4th Theme — G59

5th Theme — G60

GIBBONS, Orlando (1583-1625)

The Lord of Salisbury, His Pavane,
Harpsi.
— G61

The Queen's Command, Harpsi.
— G62

GLAZUNOFF, Alexander (1865-1936)

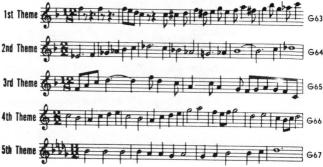

Carnaval, Overture,
Op. 45, Orch.
By permission of Associated
Music Publishers, Inc.
1st Theme — G63

2nd Theme — G64

3rd Theme — G65

4th Theme — G66

5th Theme — G67

GLAZUNOFF

G68—G79

Concerto in A Minor, Op. 82, Vn. & Orch.
By permission of Associated Music Publishers, Inc.

1st Theme — G68
2nd Theme — G69
3rd Theme — G70
4th Theme — G71
5th Theme — G72

Une Fête Slave, from Slav Str. Quartet Op. 26, No. 4, Orch.
By permission of Associated Music Publishers, Inc.

1st Theme — G73
2nd Theme — G74
3rd Theme — G75

Méditation, Op. 32, Vn. & Pft.
By permission of Associated Music Publishers, Inc.
— G76

Mélodie Arabe, Op. 20, No. 1, Cello & Pft.
By permission of Associated Music Publishers, Inc.

1st Theme — G77
2nd Theme — G78

Novelettes, Op. 15, Str. Quart.
By permission of Associated Music Publishers, Inc.

1st Movement Alla Spagnuola 1st Theme — G78a
1st Movement 2nd Theme — G78b
2nd Movement Orientale 1st Theme — G78c
2nd Movement 2nd Theme — G78d
3rd Movement Interludium in Modo Antico — G78e
4th Movement Waltz 1st Theme — G78f
4th Movement 2nd Theme — G78g
5th Movement All 'Ungherese — G78h

Ouverture Solennelle
By permission of Associated Music Publishers, Inc.

1st Theme — G79

2nd Theme — G80

3rd Theme — G81

4th Theme — G82

Rêverie, Op. 24
Fr. Horn & Pft.
By permission of Associated
Music Publishers, Inc. — G83

The Seasons (Ballet), Bacchanal
Op. 67
By permission of Associated
Music Publishers, Inc. — G84

Stenka Razin, Op. 13,
Symphonic Poem,
Orch.
By permission of Associated
Music Publishers, Inc.

1st Theme Volga Boat Song — G85

2nd Theme — G86

Valsa de Concert,
Op. 47, Orch.
By permission of Associated
Music Publishers, Inc.

1st Theme — G87

2nd Theme — G88

3rd Theme — G89

GLIÈRE, Reinhold (1875-1956)

Russian Sailors' Dance
from the Red Poppy, Ballet — G90

Symphony No. 3, Op. 42
"Ilia Mourometz"   Scherzo
1st Theme — G91

2nd Theme — G92

GLINKA, Michael (1804-1857)

Capriccio Brilliant on the
Jota Aragonesa, Orch.   1st Theme — G92a

2nd Theme — G93

Kamarinskaya, Orch.   1st Theme — G94

2nd Theme,
A — G95

2nd Theme,
B — G96

The Lark, (Arr. by Balakirev), Pft.

A Life for the Czar or
Ivan Soussanine, Overture — Intro.

1st Theme

2nd Theme

3rd Theme

4th Theme

Quartet in F, Str. — 1st Movement 1st Theme

1st Movement 2nd Theme

2nd Movement

3rd Movement 1st Theme

3rd Movement 2nd Theme

4th Movement

Romance, Pft., Vn. & Cello (Also as Song)

Russian and Ludmilla, Overture — 1st Theme

2nd Theme

Souvenir of a Night in Madrid, Orch. — 1st Theme Jota

2nd Theme Punto Muruno

3rd Theme Seguidillas Manchegas

4th Theme Seguidillas Manchegas

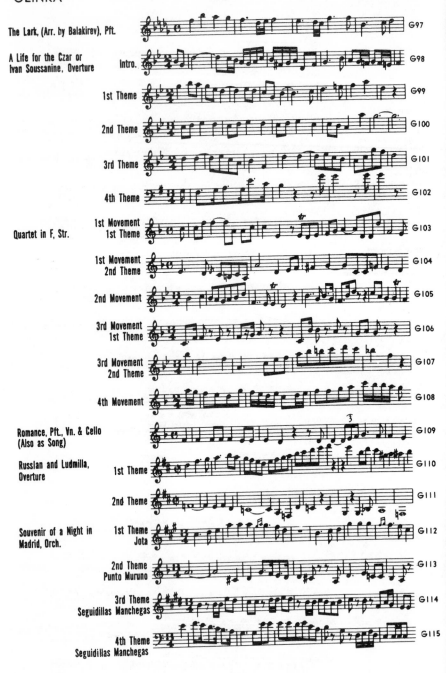

GLUCK, Christoph (1714-1787)

Alceste, Overture — 1st Theme — G116

2nd Theme — G117

3rd Theme — G118

Air de Ballet (also theme for Saint-Saëns Caprice for Pft.) — G119

Ballet, Act II — 1st Movement — G120

2nd Movement — G121

3rd Movement — G122

Ballet, Act IV — 1st Movement — G123

2nd Movement March — G124

3rd Movement — G125

4th Movement Minuet — G126

5th Movement Gavotte — G127

6th Movement Chaconne — G128

Armide, Musette from Ballet, Act IV — G129

Iphigenia in Aulis, Overture 1st Theme — G130

2nd Theme — G131

3rd Theme — G132

3rd Theme — G133

4th Theme — G134

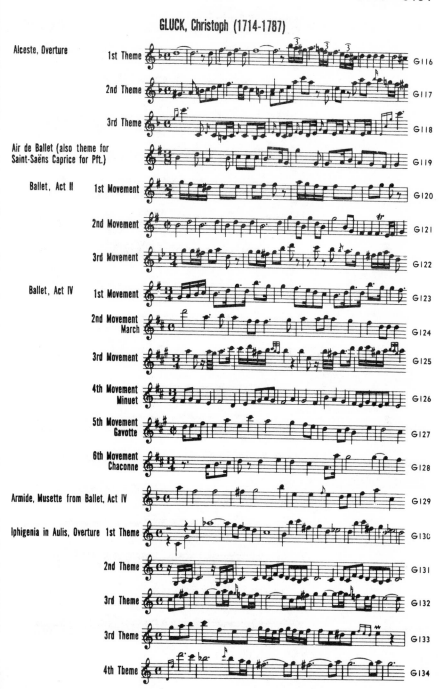

Act I   Air Gai  G135

Lento   G136

Act II   March   G137

(Theme used by Brahms)   Gavotte
1st Theme   G138

2nd Theme   G139

Act III   Danse des Esclaves   G140

(Also in Orpheus)   Chaconne   G141

Orpheus and Eurydice, Overture   G142

Dance of the Furies   G143

Dance of the Happy Spirits   G144

Melody   G145

GODARD, Benjamin (1849-1895)

Au Matin, Op. 83, Pft.   G146

Berceuse from Jocelyn   1st Theme, A
Published and Copyrighted
(renewal 1933) by Oliver
Ditson Co. Used by permission.   G147

1st Theme, B   G148

2nd Theme   G149

2nd Mazurka, Pft.   G150

GODOWSKY, Leopold (1870-1938)

Alt-Wien, Pft.
  G151

GOLDMARK, Karl (1830-1915)

Im Frühling, Op. 36,
Overture
By permission of Associated
Music Publishers, Inc.

1st Theme — G152

2nd Theme — G153

Sakuntala, Op. 13,
Overture
By permission of Associated
Music Publishers, Inc.

1st Theme — G154

2nd Theme — G155

3rd Theme — G156

4th Theme — G157

Symphony, Op. 26,
"Rustic Wedding"
By permission of
Associated Music
Publishers, Inc.

1st Movement
Wedding March — G158

2nd Movement
Bridal Song — G159

3rd Movement
Serenade
1st Theme — G160

3rd Movement
2nd Theme — G161

4th Movement
In the Garden
1st Theme — G162

4th Movement
2nd Theme — G163

5th Movement
Dance
1st Theme — G164

5th Movement
2nd Theme — G165

GOOSSENS, Eugene (1893-1962)

The Hurdy-Gurdy Man, Op. 18,
No. 3, Pft.
By permission of the copyright
holders, J. & W. Chester, Ltd.,
11 Great Marlborough Street,
London, W. 1.

G166

GOSSEC, François Joseph (1734-1829)

Gavotte in D, Vn. & Pft.

1st Theme — G167

2nd Theme — G168

Tambourin, Vn. & Pft. — G169

GOTTSCHALK, Louis (1829-1869)

The Dying Poet, Pft. — G169a

GOUNOD, Charles François (1818-1893)

Faust, Ballet Music, Act V — 1st Theme — G170
2nd Theme — G171
3rd Theme — G172
4th Theme — G173
5th Theme — G174
6th Theme — G175

Funeral March of a Marionette, Orch. — 1st Theme — G176
2nd Theme — G177

The Queen of Sheba — Cortège — G178

GRAENER, Paul (1872-1944)

Die Flöte von Sans-Souci, Op. 88, Orch. — Intro. 1st Theme — G179
Copyright by Eulenburg, Licensed by SESAC, Inc., N. Y. — Intro. 2nd Theme — G180
1st Movement Sarabande — G181
2nd Movement Gavotte — G182
3rd Movement Air — G183
4th Movement Rigaudon — G184

GRAINGER, Percy (1882-1961)

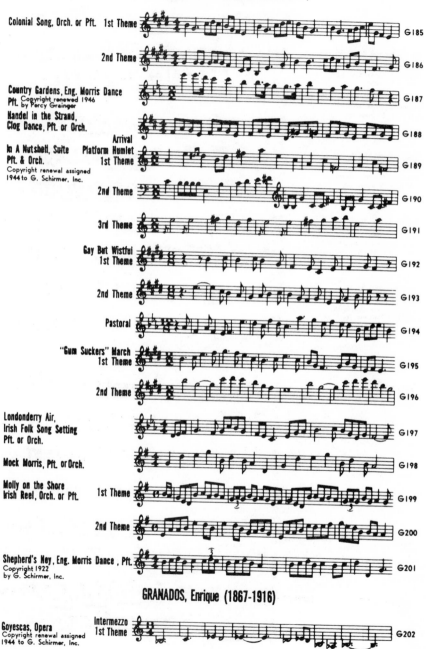

Colonial Song, Orch. or Pft. 1st Theme — G185

2nd Theme — G186

Country Gardens, Eng. Morris Dance
Pft. Copyright renewed 1946 by Percy Grainger — G187

Handel in the Strand,
Clog Dance, Pft. or Orch. — G188

In A Nutshell, Suite   Arrival
Pft. & Orch.   Platform Humlet
Copyright renewal assigned   1st Theme — G189
1944 to G. Schirmer, Inc.

2nd Theme — G190

3rd Theme — G191

Gay But Wistful
1st Theme — G192

2nd Theme — G193

Pastoral — G194

"Gum Suckers" March
1st Theme — G195

2nd Theme — G196

Londonderry Air,
Irish Folk Song Setting
Pft. or Orch. — G197

Mock Morris, Pft. or Orch. — G198

Molly on the Shore
Irish Reel, Orch. or Pft.   1st Theme — G199

2nd Theme — G200

Shepherd's Hey, Eng. Morris Dance , Pft. — G201
Copyright 1922
by G. Schirmer, Inc.

GRANADOS, Enrique (1867-1916)

Goyescas, Opera   Intermezzo
Copyright renewal assigned   1st Theme — G202
1944 to G. Schirmer, Inc.

2nd Theme — G203

3rd Theme — G204

**The Maiden and the Nightingale,
Goyescas No. 4, Pft.**
Copyright renewal assigned
1944 to G. Schirmer, Inc. — G205

Spanish Dance, No. 2, Pft.
Copyright renewal assigned
1943 to G. Schirmer, Inc.
1st Theme — G206

2nd Theme — G207

**Spanish Dance, No. 4,
Villanesca, Pft.**
Copyright renewal assigned
1943 to G. Schirmer, Inc.
1st Theme — G208

2nd Theme — G209

**Spanish Dance, No. 5,
Playera -Andaluza, Pft.**
Copyright renewal assigned
1943 to G. Schirmer, Inc.
1st Theme — G210

2nd Theme — G211

**Spanish Dance, No. 6,
Rondalla Aragonesa**
Copyright renewal assigned
1943 to G. Schirmer, Inc.
1st Theme — G212

2nd Theme — G213

GRETRY, André (1741-1813)

**Ballet Suite from
Cephale et Procris**
Gavotte — G214

Tambourin
1st Theme,
A — G215

1st Theme,
B — G216

2nd Theme — G217

Minuet
Nymphes de Diane — G218

Gigue — G219

**Colinette à la Cour
Opera**
Tambourin — G220

Gavotte — G221

GRIEG, Edvard (1843-1907)

Richard Coeur-de-Lion Opera — Rustic Dance — G222

La Rosière de Salency Opera — 1st Entr'acte 1st Theme — G223

2nd Theme — G224

2nd Entr'acte — G225

Ballet Suite from La Rosière Républicaine — Danse Légère — G226

Gavotte Gracieuse — G227

Contre Danse — G228

Romance — G229

Danse Générale — G230

Carmagnole — G231

Ballet Suite From Zémire et Azor — 1st Movement Air — G232

2nd Movement Pantomime — G233

3rd Movement Passepied — G234

Album Leaf, Op. 12, No. 7, Pft. — G235

Ballade, Op. 24, Pft.
By Permission of C. F. Peters,
Clayton F. Summy Co., Chicago, Agents in the U. S. — G236

Concerto, Op. 16, Pft. & Orch. — 1st Movement Intro. — G237

1st Movement 1st Theme, A — G238

1st Movement 1st Theme, B — G239

1st Movement 2nd Theme — G240

1st Movement 3rd Theme, A — G241

1st Movement 3rd Theme B — G242

2nd Movement 1st Theme — G243

2nd Movement 2nd Theme — G244

3rd Movement 1st Theme — G245

3rd Movement 2nd Theme — G246

Cradle Song, Op. 68, No. 5, Pft.
By Permission of C. F. Peters, Clayton F. Summy Co., Chicago, Agents in the U. S. — G247

Dance Caprice, Op. 28, No. 3, Pft. 1st Theme — G248

2nd Theme — G249

Elfin Dance, Op. 12, No. 4, Pft. — G250

Erotic, Op. 43, No. 5, Pft.
By Permission of C. F. Peters, Clayton F. Summy Co., Chicago, Agents in the U. S. — G251

French Serenade, Op. 62, No. 3, Pft.
By Permission of C. F. Peters, Clayton F. Summy Co., Chicago, Agents in the U. S. — G252

Holberg Suite, Op. 40, Str. Orch. 1st Movement Prelude — G253

2nd Movement Sarabande — G254

3rd Movement 1st Theme Gavotte — G255

3rd Movement 2nd Theme Musette — G256

4th Movement Air — G257

5th Movement Rigaudon — G258

In Der Heimat, Op. 43, No. 3, Pft. — G259

Little Bird, Op. 43, No. 4, Pft. — G260

The Lonely Wanderer, Op. 43, No. 2, Pft. — G261

Lyric Suite, Op. 54, Pft. Shepherd Boy — G262
By Permission of C. F. Peters,
Clayton F. Summy Co., Chicago,
Agents in the U. S.
Norwegian Rustic March — G263

March of the Dwarfs
1st Theme — G264

2nd Theme — G265

Nocturne — G266

Melancholy, Op. 65, No. 3, Pft. — G267
By Permission of C. F. Peters,
Clayton F. Summy Co., Chicago,
Agents in the U. S.
Mélodie, Op. 47, No. 3, Pft. — G268
By Permission of C. F. Peters, Clayton F.
Summy Co., Chicago, Agents in the U. S.
Norwegian Bridal Procession,
Op. 19, No. 2, Pft. — G269
By Permission of C. F. Peters, Clayton F.
Summy Co., Chicago, Agents in the U. S.
Norwegian Dances, No. 1
Op. 35, Pft. or Str. Orch. 1st Theme — G270
By Permission of C. F. Peters,
Clayton F. Summy Co., Chicago,
Agents in the U. S.

2nd Theme — G271

No. 2
1st Theme — G272

2nd Theme — G273

No. 3 — G274

No. 4
1st Theme — G275

2nd Theme — G276

Norwegian Melody, Op. 12,
No. 7, Pft. 1st Theme — G277
Copyright 1899
by G. Schirmer, Inc.

2nd Theme — G278

Norwegian Melodies, 1st Movement
Op. 63, Str. Orch. Popular Song — G279
By Permission of C. F.
Peters, Clayton F. Summy 2nd Movement
Co., Chicago, 1st Theme — G280
Agents in the U. S. Cow Keeper's Tune

2nd Movement
2nd Theme
Peasant Dance   G281

Papillon (Butterfly), Op. 43, No. 1, Pft.   G282

Peer Gynt, Suite No. 1, Op. 46, Orch.   1st Movement Morning Mood   G283

2nd Movement Ase's Death   G284

3rd Movement Anitra's Dance 1st Theme   G285

3rd Movement 2nd Theme   G286

4th Movement In the Hall of the Mountain King   G287

Peer Gynt, Suite No. 2, Op. 55 Orch.
Copyright 1899 by G. Schirmer, Inc.

1st Movement Ingrid's Complaint 1st Theme   G288

1st Movement 2nd Theme   G289

2nd Movement Arabian Dance 1st Theme   G290

2nd Movement 2nd Theme   G291

3rd Movement Peer Gynt's Return Home   G292

4th Movement Solvejg's Song Intro.   G293

4th Movement 1st Theme   G294

4th Movement 2nd Theme   G295

Puck, Op. 71, No. 3, Pft.
By Permission of C. F. Peters, Clayton F. Summy Co., Chicago, Agents in the U. S.   G296

Quartet in G Minor, Op. 27, Str.
By permission of International Music Co.

1st Movement 1st Theme   G297

1st Movement 2nd Theme   G298

2nd Movement Romanze 1st Theme   G298a

2nd Movement 2nd Theme   G299

3rd Movement
Intermezzo
1st Theme — G300

3rd Movement
2nd Theme — G301

4th Movement
1st Theme — G302

4th Movement
2nd Theme — G303

Scherzo-Impromptu, Op. 73, No. 2, Pft.
By Permission of C. F. Peters, Clayton
F. Summy Co., Chicago, Agents in the U. S. — G304

Sigurd Jorsalfar, Orch. 1st Movement
Op. 56, In the King's Hall (Prelude)
(Incidental Music), — G305

By Permission of C. F.
Peters, Clayton F. Summy 1st Movement
Co., Chicago, 2nd Theme — G306
Agents in the U. S.

2nd Movement
Borghild's Dream (Intermezzo) — G307

3rd Movement
Triumphal March
1st Theme — G308

3rd Movement
2nd Theme — G309

Sonata in A Minor, 1st Movement
Op. 36, Cello & Pft. 1st Theme — G310
By Permission of
C. F. Peters, Clayton
F. Summy Co., Chicago, 1st Movement
Agents in the U. S. 2nd Theme — G311

2nd Movement — G312

3rd Movement
1st Theme — G313

3rd Movement
2nd Theme — G314

3rd Movement
3rd Theme — G315

Sonata in E Minor, 1st Movement
Op. 7, Pft. 1st Theme — G316
Published and Copyrighted
(renewal 1936) 1st Movement
by Oliver Ditson Co. 2nd Theme — G317
Used by permission.

1st Movement
3rd Theme — G318

2nd Movement — G319

GRIEG

3rd Movement — G320

4th Movement — G321

Sonata in G, Op. 13, No. 2, Vn. & Pft.
1st Movement Intro. — G322

1st Movement 1st Theme — G323

1st Movement 2nd Theme — G324

1st Movement 3rd Theme — G325

2nd Movement — G326

3rd Movement 1st Theme — G327

3rd Movement 2nd Theme — G328

Sonata in C Minor, Op. 45, No. 3, Vn. & Pft.
Copyright 1917 by Carl Fischer, Inc., N. Y.
1st Movement Intro. — G329

1st Movement 1st Theme — G330

1st Movement 2nd Theme — G331

2nd Movement 1st Theme — G332

2nd Movement 2nd Theme — G333

3rd Movement 1st Theme — G334

3rd Movement 2nd Theme — G335

Summer's Eve, Op. 71, No. 2, Pft.
By Permission of C. F. Peters, Clayton F. Summy Co., Chicago, Agents in the U. S. — G336

Symphonic Dances, Op. 64, Orch.
By Permission of C. F. Peters, Clayton F. Summy Co., Chicago, Agents in the U. S.
No. 1 — G337

No. 2 1st Theme, A — G338

1st Theme, B — G339

2nd Theme — G340

No. 3 — G341

No. 4
1st Theme — G342

2nd Theme — G343

To Spring, Op. 43, No. 6, Pft. — G344

Two Elegaic Melodies,
Op. 34, Str. Orch.
By Permission of C. F.
Peters, Clayton F. Summy Co.,
Chicago, Agents in the U. S.
No. 1
Heart Wounds — G345

No. 2
Springtime — G346

Two Melodies, Op. 53,
Str. Orch.
By Permission of C. F.
Peters, Clayton F. Summy Co.,
Chicago, Agents
in the U. S.
No. 1
Norwegian — G347

No. 2
The First Meeting — G348

Waltz, Op. 12, No. 2, Pft.
By Permission of C. F.
Peters, Clayton F. Summy Co.,
Chicago, Agents in the U. S.
1st Theme — G349

2nd Theme — G350

Wedding Day at Troldhaugen,
Op. 65, No. 6, Pft.
By Permission of C. F.
Peters, Clayton F. Summy Co.,
Chicago, Agents in the U. S. — G351

GRIFFES, Charles Tomlinson (1884-1920)

The Pleasure Dome of
Kubla Khan, Orch.
Copyright 1920
by G. Schirmer, Inc.
1st Theme — G352

2nd Theme — G353

3rd Theme — G354

4th Theme — G355

Two Sketches (Based on
Indian Themes),
Str. Quart.
Copyright 1922
by G. Schirmer, Inc.
1st Movement
Farewell Song of
Chippewa Indians — G356

2nd Movement
1st Theme — G357

2nd Movement
2nd Theme — G358

2nd Movement 3rd Theme — G359

The White Peacock, Op. 7, No. 1, Pft.
Copyright renewal assigned
1945 to G. Schirmer, Inc.
— G362

GROFÉ, Ferde (1892-1972)

Grand Canyon Suite, Orch.
Copyright 1932 Robbins Music Corp.
Used by special permission Copyright Proprietor.

1st Movement Sunrise — G361

2nd Movement Painted Desert — G362

3rd Movement On the Trail 1st Theme — G363

3rd Movement 2nd Theme — G364

Mississippi Suite, Orch.
Copyright 1926 Leo Feist, Inc.
Used by Special Permission Copyright Proprietor.

1st Movement Father of Waters — G365

2nd Movement Huckleberry Finn — G366

3rd Movement Old Creole Days — G367

4th Movement Mardi Gras 1st Theme — G368

4th Movement 2nd Theme — G369

HALVORSEN, Johan (1864-1935)

Andante Religioso Vn. & Orch.
By permission of Associated Music Publishers, Inc.

1st Theme — H1

2nd Theme — H2

Triumphal Entry of the Boyars Orch.
By permission of Associated Music Publishers, Inc.

1st Theme — H3

2nd Theme — H4

HANDEL, George Frideric (1685-1759)

Concerto No. 1 in B Flat, Oboe & Orch.

1st Movement — H5

2nd Movement Fugue — H6

3rd Movement — H7

4th Movement — H8

Concerto No. 3 in G Minor, Oboe & Orch. — 1st Movement — H9

2nd Movement — H10

3rd Movement — H11

4th Movement — H12

Concerto No. 1 in G Minor, Organ & Orch., Op. 4, No. 1 — 1st Movement 1st Theme — H13

1st Movement 2nd Theme — H14

2nd Movement 1st Theme — H15

2nd Movement 2nd Theme — H16

3rd Movement — H17

Concerto No. 2 in B Flat, Organ & Orch., Op. 4, No. 2 — 1st Movement — H18

2nd Movement — H19

3rd Movement — H20

4th Movement — H21

Concerto No. 4 in F Organ & Orch., Op. 4, No. 4 — 1st Movement — H22

2nd Movement — H23

3rd Movement — H24

4th Movement 1st Theme — H25

4th Movement 2nd Theme — H26

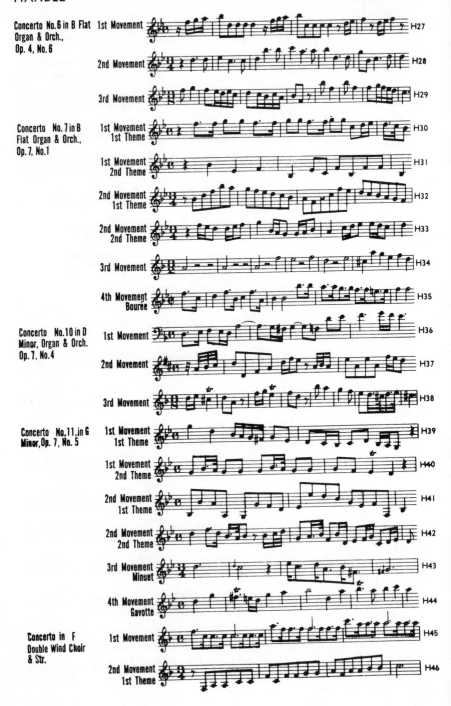

Concerto No.6 in B Flat Organ & Orch., Op. 4, No. 6 — 1st Movement H27

2nd Movement H28

3rd Movement H29

Concerto No.7 in B Flat Organ & Orch., Op. 7, No. 1 — 1st Movement 1st Theme H30

1st Movement 2nd Theme H31

2nd Movement 1st Theme H32

2nd Movement 2nd Theme H33

3rd Movement H34

4th Movement Bourée H35

Concerto No.10 in D Minor, Organ & Orch. Op. 7, No. 4 — 1st Movement H36

2nd Movement H37

3rd Movement H38

Concerto No.11, in G Minor, Op. 7, No. 5 — 1st Movement 1st Theme H39

1st Movement 2nd Theme H40

2nd Movement 1st Theme H41

2nd Movement 2nd Theme H42

3rd Movement Minuet H43

4th Movement Gavotte H44

Concerto in F Double Wind Choir & Str. — 1st Movement H45

2nd Movement 1st Theme H46

Concerto Grosso in A Minor, Op. 6, No. 4 Str. Orch. — 1st Movement H67

2nd Movement H68

3rd Movement H69

4th Movement 1st Theme H70

4th Movement 2nd Theme H71

Concerto Grosso in D, Op. 6, No. 5 Str. Orch. — 1st Movement H72

2nd Movement H73

3rd Movement H74

4th Movement H75

5th Movement 1st Theme H76

5th Movement 2nd Theme H77

6th Movement H78

Concerto Grosso in G Minor Op. 6, No. 6 Str. Orch. — 1st Movement H79

2nd Movement H80

3rd Movement 1st Theme H81

3rd Movement 2nd Theme H82

4th Movement H83

5th Movement H84

Concerto Grosso in B flat Op. 6, No. 7 Str. Orch. — 1st Movement H85

2nd Movement H86

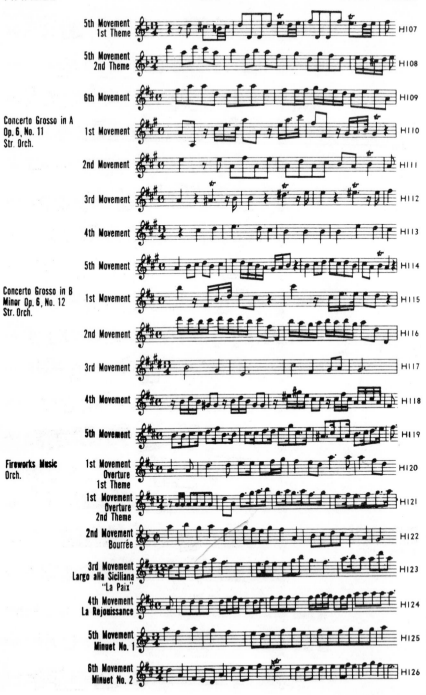

Alcina, Opera — Overture 1st Theme — H127
Overture 2nd Theme — H128
Musette — H129
Minuet — H130
Gavotte From Ballet — H131
Sarabande From Ballet — H132
Minuet From Ballet — H133
Gavotte No. 2 From Ballet — H134
Tamburino — H135

Oratorios — March from Joseph — H136
March from Judas Maccabeus — H137
Dead March from Saul — H138

Messiah — Overture 1st Theme — H139
2nd Theme — H140
Pt. 1 (Pastoral Symphony) — H141

Sonata in G, Flute & Fig. Bass Op. 1, No. 5 — 1st Movement — H142
2nd Movement — H143
3rd Movement — H144
4th Movement — H145
5th Movement — H146

Sonata in C,
Flute & Fig. Bass
Op. 1 , No. 7

1st Movement

2nd Movement

3rd Movement

4th Movement

5th Movement

Sonata in B Minor,
Flute & Fig. Bass
Op. 1 , No. 9

1st Movement

2nd Movement

3rd Movement

4th Movement

5th Movement

6th Movement

7th Movement

Sonata in F,
Flute & Fig. Bass
Op. 1 , No. 11

1st Movement

2nd Movement

3rd Movement

4th Movement

Sonata in C Minor,
Fl., Vn., & Fig. Bass
Op. 2 , No. 1

1st Movement

2nd Movement

3rd Movement

4th Movement

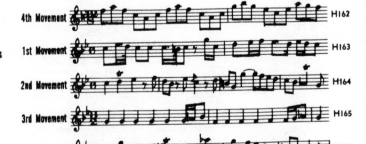

H147

H148

H149

H150

H151

H152

H153

H154

H155

H156

H157

H158

H159

H160

H161

H162

H163

H164

H165

H166

Sonata, G Minor,
2 Fls. or 2 Vns.
& Fig. Bass, Op. 2, No. 2

1st Movement — H167

2nd Movement — H168

3rd Movement — H169

4th Movement — H170

Sonata in G Minor,
Oboe & Fig. Bass
Op. 1, No. 6

1st Movement — H171

2nd Movement — H172

3rd Movement — H173

4th Movement — H174

Sonata in E,
Oboe or Vn. & Fig. Bass
Op. 1, No. 15

1st Movement — H175

2nd Movement — H176

3rd Movement — H177

4th Movement — H178

Sonata in E Flat
2 Vns. or 2 Oboes
& Fig. Bass

1st Movement — H179

2nd Movement — H180

3rd Movement — H181

4th Movement — H182

Sonata in A
Op. 1, No. 3
Vn. & Fig. Bass

1st Movement — H183

2nd Movement — H184

3rd Movement — H185

4th Movement — H186

20th Movement
Coro — H267

HANSON, Howard (1896-   )

Merry Mount Suite
Copyright 1933 by Harms, Inc.

Reprinted by special permission.

Overture — H268

Children's Dance
1st Theme — H269

2nd Theme — H270

Prelude to Act II
& Maypole Dances
1st Theme — H271

2nd Theme — H272

3rd Theme — H273

Chorale for Strings, Op. 3
Copyright 1932 by
Eastman School of Music,
Rochester, N. Y.

1st Movement
Intro. — H274

Sonata Op. 1, Pft.
Copyright 1931
Cos Cob Press, Inc.

1st Movement
1st Theme — H275

1st Movement
2nd Theme — H276

1st Movement
3rd Theme,
A — H277

1st Movement
3rd Theme,
B — H278

2nd Movement — H279

3rd Movement
1st Theme — H280

3rd Movement
2nd Theme — H281

HARRIS, Roy (1898-   )

Symphony No. 2
"Romantic"
Copyright 1934 by
Harold Flammer, Inc.
Used by permission.

— H282

1st Movement
Prelude — H283

2nd Movement
Andante Ostinato — H284

Concerto in D
Pft. & Orch.

3rd Movement
2nd Theme — H304

1st Movement — H305

2nd Movement
1st Theme — H306

2nd Movement
2nd Theme — H307

3rd Movement
1st Theme — H308

3rd Movement
2nd Theme — H309

Concerto in E Flat
Trumpet & Orch.

1st Movement
1st Theme — H310

1st Movement
2nd Theme — H311

2nd Movement — H312

3rd Movement — H314

Quartet in B Flat
Op. 1, No. 1, Str.
"La Chasse"

1st Movement — H315

2nd Movement — H316

3rd Movement — H317

4th Movement — H318

5th Movement — H319

Quartet in C
Op. 1, No. 6 Str.

1st Movement — H320

2nd Movement — H321

3rd Movement — H322

4th Movement
1st Theme — H323

4th Movement
2nd Theme — H324

5th Movement — H325

Quartet in B Flat
Op.3, No. 4, Str.

1st Movement
1st Theme — H326

1st Movement
2nd Theme — H327

2nd Movement
1st Theme — H328

2nd Movement
2nd Theme — H329

Quartet in F
Op.3, No.5, Str.

1st Movement
1st Theme — H330

1st Movement
2nd Theme — H331

2nd Movement — H332

3rd Movement
1st Theme — H333

3rd Movement
2nd Theme — H334

4th Movement — H335

Quartet in E Flat
Op.20, No. 1, Str.

1st Movement — H336

2nd Movement — H337

3rd Movement — H338

4th Movement — H339

Quartet in C
Op.20, No. 2, Str.

1st Movement — H340

2nd Movement
1st Theme — H341

2nd Movement
2nd Theme — H342

3rd Movement — H343

4th Movement — H344

Quartet in D
Op. 20, No. 4, Str.
"The Rose of Venice"

1st Movement — H345

2nd Movement — H346

3rd Movement — H347

4th Movement — H348

Quartet in F Minor
Op. 20, No. 5, Str.

1st Movement — H349

2nd Movement — H350

3rd Movement
1st Theme — H351

3rd Movement
2nd Theme — H352

4th Movement
1st Fugue Theme — H353

4th Movement
2nd Fugue theme — H354

Quartet in E Flat
Op. 33, No. 2, Str.
"The Joke"

1st Movement — H355

2nd Movement — H356

3rd Movement — H357

4th Movement — H358

Quartet in C
Op. 33, No. 3, Str.
"The Bird"

1st Movement
1st Theme — H359

1st Movement
2nd Theme — H360

2nd Movement
1st Theme — H361

2nd Movement
2nd Theme — H362

3rd Movement — H363

4th Movement
1st Theme — H364

4th Movement
2nd Theme — H365

Quartet in D
Op. 33, No. 6, Str.
1st Movement — H366

2nd Movement — H367

3rd Movement — H368

4th Movement — H369

Quartet in E Flat
Op. 50, No. 3, Str.
1st Movement — H370

2nd Movement — H371

3rd Movement — H372

4th Movement — H373

Quartet in D
Op. 50, No. 6, Str.
"The Frog"
1st Movement — H374

2nd Movement — H375

3rd Movement
1st Theme — H376

3rd Movement
2nd Theme — H377

4th Movement
1st Theme — H378

4th Movement
2nd Theme — H379

Quartet in G
Op. 54, No. 1, Str.
1st Movement — H380

2nd Movement — H381

3rd Movement — H382

4th Movement — H383

Quartet in C
Op. 54, No. 2, Str.
1st Movement
1st Theme — H384

HAYDN

232

H385—H404

Quartet in B Flat
Op. 64, No. 3, Str.

1st Movement / 1st Theme — H405

1st Movement / 2nd Theme — H406

2nd Movement — H407

3rd Movement / 1st Theme — H408

3rd Movement / 2nd Theme — H409

4th Movement / 1st Theme — H410

4th Movement / 2nd Theme — H411

Quartet in G
Op. 64, No. 4, Str.

1st Movement / 1st Theme — H412

1st Movement / 2nd Theme — H413

1st Movement / 3rd Theme — H414

2nd Movement — H415

3rd Movement — H416

4th Movement — H417

Quartet in D
Op. 64 No. 5, Str.
"The Lark"

1st Movement / 1st Theme — H418

1st Movement / 2nd Theme — H419

1st Movement / 3rd Theme — H420

2nd Movement — H421

3rd Movement / 1st Theme — H422

3rd Movement / 2nd Theme — H423

4th Movement — H424

3rd Movement
2nd Theme — H444a

4th Movement
1st Theme — H445

4th Movement
2nd Theme — H446

Quartet in G Minor
Op.74, No. 3, Str.
"Horseman"

1st Movement
1st Theme — H447

1st Movement
2nd Theme — H448

2nd Movement
1st Theme — H449

2nd Movement
2nd Theme — H450

3rd Movement
1st Theme — H451

3rd Movement
2nd Theme — H452

4th Movement
1st Theme — H453

4th Movement
2nd Theme — H454

Quartet in G
Op. 76, No.1, Str.

1st Movement
1st Theme — H455

1st Movement
2nd Theme — H456

2nd Movement — H457

3rd Movement
1st Theme — H458

3rd Movement
2nd Theme — H459

4th Movement — H460

Quartet in D
Op. 76, No. 2, Str.
"Quinten"

1st Movement — H461

2nd Movement
1st Theme — H462

2nd Movement
2nd Theme — H463

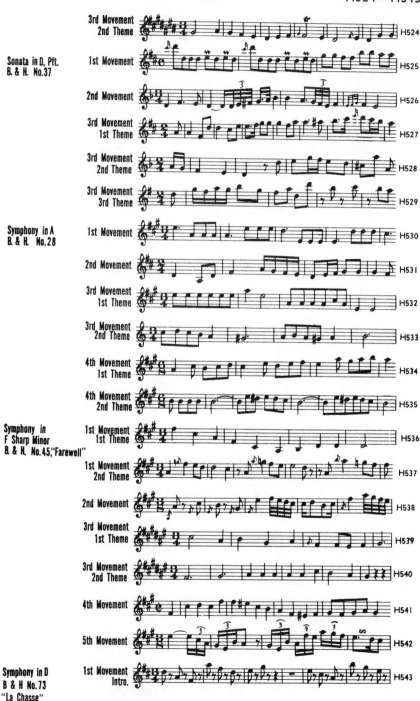

3rd Movement 2nd Theme — H524

Sonata in D, Pft. B. & H. No.37 — 1st Movement — H525

2nd Movement — H526

3rd Movement 1st Theme — H527

3rd Movement 2nd Theme — H528

3rd Movement 3rd Theme — H529

Symphony in A B. & H. No.28 — 1st Movement — H530

2nd Movement — H531

3rd Movement 1st Theme — H532

3rd Movement 2nd Theme — H533

4th Movement 1st Theme — H534

4th Movement 2nd Theme — H535

Symphony in F Sharp Minor B. & H. No.45,"Farewell" — 1st Movement 1st Theme — H536

1st Movement 2nd Theme — H537

2nd Movement — H538

3rd Movement 1st Theme — H539

3rd Movement 2nd Theme — H540

4th Movement — H541

5th Movement — H542

Symphony in D B. & H No.73 "La Chasse" — 1st Movement Intro. — H543

HAYDN

240

H544—H563

1st Movement 1st Theme — H544

1st Movement 2nd Theme — H545

2nd Movement — H546

3rd Movement 1st Theme — H547

3rd Movement 2nd Theme — H548

4th Movement 1st Theme — H549

4th Movement 2nd Theme — H550

Symphony in C
B. & H. No.82
"L'Ours"

1st Movement 1st Theme — H551

1st Movement 2nd Theme — H552

2nd Movement — H553

3rd Movement 1st Theme — H554

3rd Movement 2nd Theme — H555

4th Movement 1st Theme, A — H556

4th Movement 1st Theme, B — H557

4th Movement 2nd Theme — H558

Symphony in D
B. & H. No. 86

1st Movement Intro. — H559

1st Movement 1st Theme — H560

1st Movement 2nd Theme — H561

2nd Movement 1st Theme — H562

2nd Movement 2nd Theme — H563

1st Movement / 2nd Theme — H584

2nd Movement — H585

3rd Movement / 1st Theme — H586

3rd Movement / 2nd Theme — H587

4th Movement / 1st Theme — H588

4th Movement / 2nd Theme — H589

Symphony in D
B. & H. No. 93
London 2

1st Movement / Intro. — H590

1st Movement / 1st Theme — H591

1st Movement / 2nd Theme — H592

2nd Movement — H593

3rd Movement / 1st Theme — H594

3rd Movement / 2nd Theme, A — H595

3rd Movement / 2nd Theme, B — H596

4th Movement / 1st Theme — H597

4th Movement / 2nd Theme — H598

Symphony in G
B. & H. No. 94
"Surprise"

1st Movement / Intro. — H599

1st Movement / 1st Theme — H600

1st Movement / 2nd Theme — H601

2nd Movement — H602

3rd Movement / 1st Theme — H603

Symphony in E Flat
B. & H. No.99
London 10
"Imperial"

Symphony in G
B. & H. No.100
"Military"

2nd Movement — H644

3rd Movement 1st Theme — H645

3rd Movement 2nd Theme — H646

4th Movement 1st Theme — H647

4th Movement 2nd Theme — H648

**Symphony in D
B. & H. No. 101
"Clock"**

1st Movement 1st Theme — H649

1st Movement 2nd Theme — H650

2nd Movement — H651

3rd Movement 1st Theme — H652

3rd Movement 2nd Theme — H653

4th Movement 1st Theme — H654

4th Movement 2nd Theme — H655

4th Movement 3rd Theme — H656

**Symphony in B Flat
B. & H. No.102
London 9**

1st Movement Intro. — H657

1st Movement 1st Theme — H658

1st Movement 2nd Theme — H659

1st Movement 3rd Theme — H660

2nd Movement — H661

3rd Movement 1st Theme — H662

3rd Movement 2nd Theme — H663

Symphony in E Flat
B. & H. No.103
"Drum Roll"

Symphony in D
B. & H. No 104
"London"

Symphony in C
"Toy Symphony"

4th Movement 1st Theme — H664
4th Movement 2nd Theme — H665
1st Movement Intro. — H666
1st Movement 1st Theme — H667
1st Movement 2nd Theme — H668
2nd Movement 1st Theme — H669
2nd Movement 2nd Theme — H670
3rd Movement 1st Theme — H671
3rd Movement 2nd Theme — H672
4th Movement — H673
1st Movement Intro. — H674
1st Movement 1st Theme — H675
1st Movement 2nd Theme — H676
2nd Movement — H677
3rd Movement 1st Theme — H678
3rd Movement 2nd Theme — H679
4th Movement 1st Theme — H680
4th Movement 2nd Theme — H681
1st Movement 1st Theme — H682
1st Movement 2nd Theme — H683

HAYDN

247

H684—H703

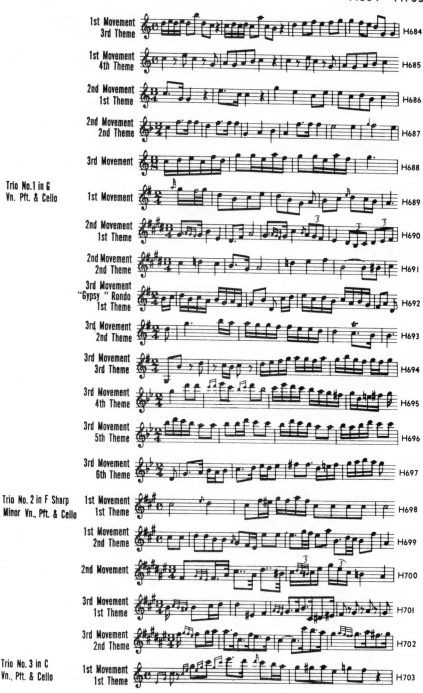

1st Movement 2nd Theme H704

2nd Movement H705

3rd Movement H706

Trio No. 5 in E Flat
Vn., Pft. & Cello — 1st Movement H707

2nd Movement H708

3rd Movement H709

Trio No. 1 in C
2 Flutes and Cello
"London" — 1st Movement 1st Theme H710

1st Movement 2nd Theme H711

2nd Movement H712

3rd Movement H713

Trio No. 2 in G
2 Flutes and Cello
"London" — 1st Movement H714

2nd Movement H715

3rd Movement H716

HERBERT, Victor (1859-1924)

Babes in Toyland, Orch.
Copyright 1903 by
M. Witmark & Sons
Copyright renewed.
Reprinted by
special permission. — March 1st Theme H717

2nd Theme H718

Natoma,
Opera
Copyright renewal assigned
1938 to G. Schirmer, Inc. — Dagger Dance H719

Habañera H720

HEROLD, Louis (1791-1833)

Zampa
Overture — 1st Theme H721

2nd Theme

HINDEMITH, Paul (1895-1963)

Kleine Kammermusik
Op.24 No.2
Ob., Fl., Cl., Hn., Fag.
By permission of
Associated Music
Publishers, Inc.

1st Movement
1st Theme

1st Movement
2nd Theme

2nd Movement
Waltz
1st Theme

2nd Movement
2nd Theme

2nd Movement
3rd Theme

3rd Movement
1st Theme

3rd Movement
2nd Theme

4th Movement

5th Movement
1st Theme

5th Movement
2nd Theme

5th Movement
3rd Theme

5th Movement
4th Theme

Mathis der Mahler
Symphony
By permission of
Associated Music
Publishers, Inc.

1st Movement
Concert of Angels
Intro.

1st Movement
1st Theme,
A

1st Movement
1st Theme,
B

1st Movement
2nd Theme

1st Movement
3rd Theme

1st Movement
4th Theme

2nd Movement Entombment 1st Theme — H741
2nd Movement 2nd Theme — H742
3rd Movement Temptation of St. Anthony Intro. — H743
3rd Movement 1st Theme — H744
3rd Movement 2nd Theme — H745
3rd Movement 3rd Theme — H746
3rd Movement 4th Theme — H747
3rd Movement 5th Theme — H748
3rd Movement 6th Theme — H749

Quartet
Op. 22, No. 3, Str.
By permission of
Associated Music
Publishers, Inc.

1st Movement — H750
2nd Movement 1st Theme — H751
2nd Movement 2nd Theme — H752
3rd Movement 1st Theme — H753
3rd Movement 2nd Theme — H754
4th Movement — H755
5th Movement 1st Theme — H756
5th Movement 2nd Theme — H757
5th Movement 3rd Theme — H758

Der Schwanendreher
Concerto, Vla. & Orch.
On Old Folk Tunes
By permission
of Associated Music
Publishers, Inc.

1st Movement "Zwischen Berg und Tiefem Tal" 1st Theme — H759
1st Movement 2nd Theme — H760

2nd Movement 1st Theme — H761

2nd Movement 2nd Theme — H762

2nd Movement 3rd Theme (theme for Fugato) "Der Gutzgauch Auf Dem Zaune Sass" — H763

3rd Movement Theme for Variations "Seid Ihr Der Schwanendreher" — H764

Sonata No. 2 Pft.
By permission of Associated Music Publishers, Inc.

1st Movement 1st Theme — H765

1st Movement 2nd Theme — H766

2nd Movement 1st Theme — H767

2nd Movement 2nd Theme — H768

3rd Movement — H769

3rd Movement 2nd Theme Rondo — H770

Sonata No. 3 Pft.
By permission of Associated Music Publishers, Inc.

1st Movement 1st Theme — H771

1st Movement 2nd Theme — H772

2nd Movement — H773

3rd Movement — H774

4th Movement Fugue theme — H775

Sonata Pft., 4 Hands
By permission of Associated Music Publishers, Inc.

1st Movement 1st Theme — H776

1st Movement 2nd Theme — H777

2nd Movement 1st Theme — H778

2nd Movement 2nd Theme — H779

3rd Movement — H780

Trauermusik, Orch.
(Funeral Music)
For George V of England
1st Movement — H781

By permission of Associated
Music Publishers, Inc.
2nd Movement — H782

3rd Movement — H783

4th Movement
Choral
Für deinen
Thron Tret'Ich Hiermit — H784

Trio No.2
Vn., Viola, Cello
By permission of
Associated Music Publishers, Inc.
1st Movement
1st Theme — H785

1st Movement
2nd Theme — H786

2nd Movement
1st Theme — H787

2nd Movement
2nd Theme — H788

3rd Movement
1st Theme — H789

3rd Movement
2nd Theme — H790

3rd Movement
3rd Theme — H791

HOLBROOKE, Josef (1878-1958)

Bronwen
Overture
Copyright by Lienau,
Licensed by
SESAC, Inc., N. Y.
1st Theme — H792

2nd Theme — H793

3rd Theme — H794

Quintet, Op. 27, No. 1
Cl. & Str.
By Permission of
Novello & Co., Ltd.,
London
1st Movement
Cavatina — H795

2nd Movement
Variations — H796

HOLST, Gustav Theodore (1874-1934)

The Planets, Op. 32
Orch.
   Mars, the Bringer
      of War
Copyright 1921 by
Goodwin & Tabb,
Ltd., London.
1st Movement
1st Theme — H797

1st Movement
2nd Theme — H798

HOLST

	1st Movement 3rd Theme	H799
Venus, the Bringer of Peace	2nd Movement 1st Theme	H800
	2nd Movement 2nd Theme	H801
Mercury, the Winged Messenger	3rd Movement 1st Theme	H802
	3rd Movement 2nd Theme	H803
Jupiter, the Bringer of Jollity	4th Movement 1st Theme	H804
	4th Movement 2nd Theme	H805
	4th Movement 3rd Theme	H806
	4th Movement 4th Theme	H807
Saturn, the Bringer of Old Age	5th Movement	H808
Uranus, the Magician	6th Movement 1st Theme	H809
	6th Movement 2nd Theme	H810
	6th Movement 3rd Theme	H811
	6th Movement 4th Theme	H812
Neptune, the Mystic	7th Movement 1st Theme	H813
	7th Movement 2nd Theme	H814
St. Paul's Suite St. Orch. Copyright 1922 by Goodwin & Tabb. Ltd., London.	1st Movement Jig 1st Theme, A	H815
	1st Movement 1st Theme, B	H816
	2nd Movement Ostinato	H817
	3rd Movement Intermezzo 1st Theme	H818

3rd Movement / 2nd Theme — H819

4th Movement / The Dargason / Finale — H820

Two Songs without Words / Op. 22, Orch.
Copyright 1925 / by E.C. Schirmer, Boston.

I Country Song / 1st Theme — H821

2nd Theme — H822

II Marching Song / 1st Theme — H823

2nd Theme — H824

3rd Theme — H825

HONEGGER, Arthur (1892-1955)

Chant de Nigamon / Orch.
Copyright by Editions Salabert
Editions Salabert, / 22 Rue Chaucat, Paris
Salabert, Inc., / I East 57 St., N. Y.

1st Theme — H826

2nd Theme — H827

3rd Theme — H828

4th Theme — H829

Concertino / Pft. & Orch.
Copyright by Editions / Salabert Editions Salabert, / 22 Rue Chaucat, Paris / Salabert, Inc., / I East 57 St., N. Y.

1st Movement / 1st Theme — H830

1st Movement / 2nd Theme — H831

1st Movement / 3rd Theme — H832

2nd Movement — H833

3rd Movement / 1st Theme — H834

3rd Movement / 2nd Theme — H835

King David / Symphonic Psalm

1st Movement / Intro. — H836

Cortège
By permission of / Novello & Co., / Ltd., London.

1st Theme — H837

2nd Theme — H838

March of the Philistines — H839

March of the Israelites — H840

Pastorale D'Été
Orch.
Copyright by Editions Salabert
Editions Salabert,
22 Rue Chaucat, Paris
Salabert, Inc.,
I East 57 St., N. Y.

1st Theme — H841

2nd Theme — H842

3rd Theme — H843

4th Theme — H844

Rugby,
Orch.
Copyright by Editions Salabert
Editions Salabert,
22 Rue Chaucat, Paris
Salabert, Inc.,
I East 57 St., N. Y.

1st Theme — H845

2nd Theme — H846

HOWELLS, Herbert (1892-   )

Puck's Minuet, Op. 20,
No. 1, Orch.
Copyright 1919 by
Goodwin & Tabb.
Ltd., London.

1st Theme — H847

2nd Theme — H848

HUBAY, Jeno (1858-1937)

Hejre Kati, Op.32, No.4,
Vn. & Orch., from
Hungarian Czardas Scenes
Copyright 1901
by Carl Fischer, Inc., N. Y.

1st Theme — H849

2nd Theme — H850

3rd Theme — H851

Poème Hongrois, Op. 27, No. 1
Vn. & Orch. — H852

Poème Hongrois, Op. 27,
No. 9 Vn. & Orch.
By permission of J. Hamelle
Music Publishers, Paris.

1st Theme — H853

2nd Theme — H854

HUMMEL, Johann (1778-1837)

Rondo in E Flat, Op.11  H855

HUMPERDINCK, Engelbert (1854-1921)

Hansel & Gretel, Opera
Prelude to Act 1   1st Theme   H856

Copyright 1895
by B. Schott's Söhne

2nd Theme   H857

Prelude to Act 2 "Witch's Ride"   H858

Pantomine   H859

Prelude "The Gingerbread House"
to Act 3   1st Theme   H860

2nd Theme   H861

"Gingerbread Waltz"   H862

Königskinder, Opera
Prelude   1st Theme, A   H863

1st Theme, B   H864

Prelude
to Act 2   "Children's Rounds"
1st Theme   H865

2nd Theme   H866

3rd Theme   H867

IBERT, Jacques (1890-1962)

Concerto, Alto Sax
& Small Orch.   1st Movement
1st Theme   I1

Copyright by A. Leduc
Music Publishers, Paris

1st Movement
2nd Theme   I2

2nd Movement   I3

3rd Movement
1st Theme   I4

IBERT

3rd Movement
2nd Theme — i5

Divertissement, Chamber Orch.
Permission for reprint granted by Durand & Cie. Paris. Elkan-Vogel Co., Inc. Philadelphia, Copyright Owners.

1st Movement
Intro. — i6

2nd Movement
Cortège
1st Theme — i7

2nd Movement
2nd Theme — i8

3rd Movement
Nocturne — i9

4th Movement
Waltz
1st Theme — i10

4th Movement
2nd Theme — i11

5th Movement
Parade
1st Theme — i12

5th Movement
2nd Theme — i13

6th Movement
Finale — i14

Entr'Acte, Flute & Guitar
Copyright by A. Leduc Music Publishers, Paris

1st Theme — i15

2nd Theme — i16

Escales (Ports of Call), Orch.
Copyright by A. Leduc Music Publishers, Paris

1st Movement
Rome—Palerme
1st Theme — i17

1st Movement
2nd Theme — i18

2nd Movement
Tunis—Nefta — i19

3rd Movement
Valencia
1st Theme — i20

3rd Movement
2nd Theme — i21

Histoires, Pft.
ight by A. Leduc Publishers, Paris

No. 1
La Meneuse de Tortues D'Or
(The Keeper of the Golden Tortoises) — i22

No. 2
Le Petit Ane Blanc
(The Little White Donkey) — i23

No. 3
Le Vieux Mendicant
(The Old Beggar) — i24

Pièce, flute alone
Copyright by A. Leduc
Music Publishers, Paris

ILYINSKY, Alexander (1859-1919)

Berceuse, Pft.

D'INDY, Vincent (1851-1931)

Le Camp de Wallenstein,
Op. 12, Orch.
Permission for reprint
granted by Durand & Cie,
Paris. Elkan-Vogel Co. Inc.
Philadelphia, Copyright
Owners.

Istar, Op. 42,
Symphonic Variations
Permission for reprint granted
by Durand & Cie, Paris.
Elkan-Vogel Co., Philadelphia,
Inc. Copyright Owners.

Sonata in C,
Op. 59, Vn. &, Pft.
Permission for reprint
granted by Durand & Cie,
Paris. Elkan-Vogel Co., Inc.
Philadelphia, Copyright
Owners.

2nd Movement 1st Theme — 143

2nd Movement 2nd Theme — 144

3rd Movement 1st Theme, A — 145

3rd Movement 1st Theme, B — 146

3rd Movement 2nd Theme — 147

4th Movement — 148

Suite en Parties, Op. 91, 1st Movement
FL., Vn., Viola, Cello, Entrée en Sonate — 149
Harp

By permission of the copyright owner, Heugel Ltd., London.

2nd Movement Air Désuet — 150

3rd Movement Sarabande 1st Theme — 151

3rd Movement 2nd Theme — 152

3rd Movement 3rd Theme — 153

4th Movement Farandole — 154

Symphony on a French Mountain Theme, Op. 25 1st Movement 1st Theme — 155

By permission of J. Hamelle Music Publishers, Paris.

1st Movement 2nd Theme — 156

2nd Movement — 157

3rd Movement 1st Theme — 158

3rd Movement 2nd Theme — 159

INFANTE, Manuel (1883-)

Pochades Andalouses, No. 1
Pft. Canto Flamenco — 160

No. 2 Danse Gitane — 161

No. 3
Aniers sur la Route de Seville
162

No. 4
Tientos
163

INGHELBRECHT, D. E. (1880-1965)

Four Fanfares, Brass
Copyright by Editions
Salabert Editions Salabert,
22 Rue Chaucat, Paris
Salabert, Inc.,
1 East 57 St., N. Y.

No. 1
Pour une Fête
164

No. 2
Pour le Président
165

No. 3
Funèbre Pour des Mineurs Ensevelis
166

No. 4
Dédicatoire
167

Nurseries (3rd Set),
Orch.
Copyright by A. Leduc
Music Publishers, Paris

No. 1
Nous N'irons Plus au Bois
168

No. 2
Le Tour Prends Garde!
169

No. 3
Bon Voyage Monsieur Dumollet
170

No. 4
Sur le Pont d'Avignon
171

No. 5
Où est la Marguerite?
172

No. 6
Arlequin marie sa Fille
173

IPPOLITOFF-IVANOFF, Michael (1859-1935)

Caucasian Sketches,
Op. 10, Orch.
By permission of
International Music Co.

1st Movement
In the Mountain Pass
1st Theme
174

1st Movement
2nd Theme
175

1st Movement
3rd Theme
176

2nd Movement
In the Village
Intro.
177

2nd Movement
1st Theme
178

2nd Movement
2nd Theme
179

3rd Movement
In the Mosque 180

4th Movement
Procession of the Sardar
1st Theme 181

4th Movement
2nd Theme 182

Quartet, Op. 13, Str.

1st Movement
Intro. 183

1st Movement
1st Theme 184

1st Movement
2nd Theme 185

2nd Movement
(Humoresca—Scherzando)
1st Theme 186

2nd Movement
2nd Theme 187

3rd Movement
Intermezzo 188

4th Movement
1st Theme 189

4th Movement
2nd Theme 190

4th Movement
3rd Theme 191

IRELAND, John (1879-1962)

April, Pft. 192

Concertino Pastorale,
Str. Orch.
By permission of the
copyright owner, Boosey
and Hawkes, Inc.

1st Movement
Eclogue
1st Theme 193

1st Movement
2nd Theme 194

2nd Movement
Threnody 195

Concerto in E Flat
Pft. & Orch.
By permission of the
copyright holders,
J. & W. Chester, Ltd.,
11 Great Marlborough
Street, London, W. 1.

1st Movement
1st Theme 196

1st Movement
2nd Theme 197

2nd Movement
1st Theme 198

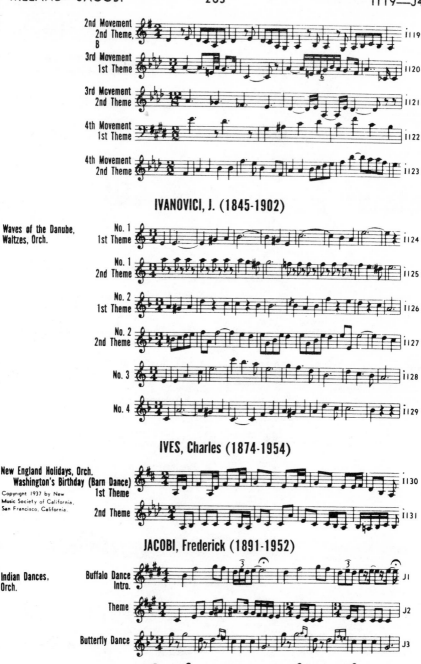

2nd Movement 2nd Theme, B — I119

3rd Movement 1st Theme — I120

3rd Movement 2nd Theme — I121

4th Movement 1st Theme — I122

4th Movement 2nd Theme — I123

IVANOVICI, J. (1845-1902)

Waves of the Danube, Waltzes, Orch.

No. 1 1st Theme — I124

No. 1 2nd Theme — I125

No. 2 1st Theme — I126

No. 2 2nd Theme — I127

No. 3 — I128

No. 4 — I129

IVES, Charles (1874-1954)

New England Holidays, Orch. Washington's Birthday (Barn Dance) 1st Theme — I130

2nd Theme — I131

JACOBI, Frederick (1891-1952)

Indian Dances, Orch.

Buffalo Dance Intro. — J1

Theme — J2

Butterfly Dance — J3

War Dance 1st Theme — J4

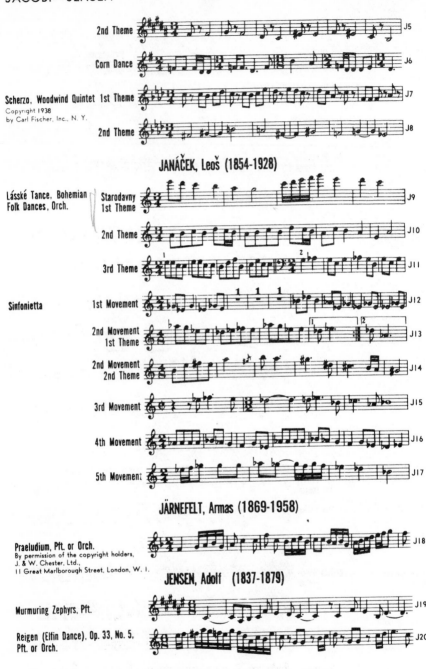

2nd Theme — J5

Corn Dance — J6

Scherzo, Woodwind Quintet 1st Theme — J7
Copyright 1938
by Carl Fischer, Inc., N. Y.

2nd Theme — J8

JANÁČEK, Leoš (1854-1928)

Lásské Tance, Bohemian
Folk Dances, Orch.

Starodavny
1st Theme — J9

2nd Theme — J10

3rd Theme — J11

Sinfonietta

1st Movement — J12

2nd Movement
1st Theme — J13

2nd Movement
2nd Theme — J14

3rd Movement — J15

4th Movement — J16

5th Movement — J17

JÄRNEFELT, Armas (1869-1958)

Praeludium, Pft. or Orch.
By permission of the copyright holders,
J. & W. Chester, Ltd.,
11 Great Marlborough Street, London, W. 1.

— J18

JENSEN, Adolf (1837-1879)

Murmuring Zephyrs, Pft. — J19

Reigen (Elfin Dance), Op. 33, No. 5,
Pft. or Orch. — J20

JONGEN, Joseph (1873-1953)

Légende Naïve, Op. 59, No. 1,
Vn. & Pft.
By permission of the copyright holders,
J. & W. Chester, Ltd., 11 Great Marlborough
Street, London, W. 1.

Petite Suite, Pft.

1st Movement
Petite Marche
Militaire

2nd Movement
Conte Plaisant

3rd Movement
Nostalgie

4th Movement
Valse Gracieuse

5th Movement
Tambourin
1st Theme

5th Movement
2nd Theme

JUON, Paul (1872-1940)

Arva (Valse Mignonne),
Op. 52, No. 2, Vn. & Pft.
Copyright by Lienau, Licensed
by SESAC, Inc., N. Y.

1st Theme

2nd Theme

Berceuse, Op. 28, No. 3, Vn. & Pft.
Copyright by Lienau, Licensed
by SESAC, Inc., N. Y.

Chamber Symphony in
B Flat, Op. 27
Copyright by Lienau, Licensed
by SESAC, Inc., N. Y.

1st Movement
1st Theme

1st Movement
2nd Theme

2nd Movement

3rd Movement
1st Theme,
A

3rd Movement
1st Theme,
B

3rd Movement
2nd Theme

4th Movement

KABALEVSKY, Dmitri (1904-)

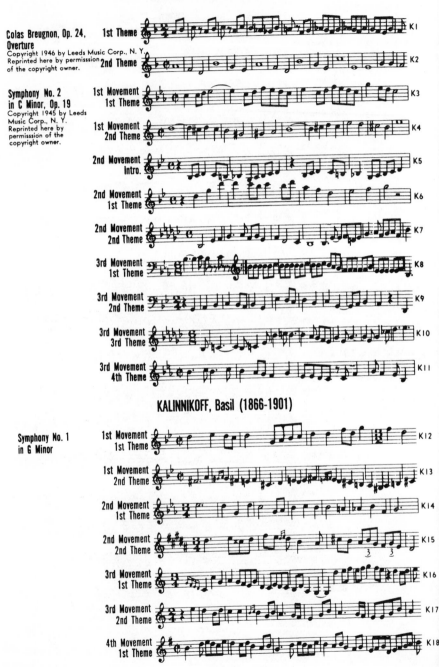

Colas Breugnon, Op. 24, **1st Theme**   K1
Overture
Copyright 1946 by Leeds Music Corp., N. Y.
Reprinted here by permission **2nd Theme**   K2
of the copyright owner.

Symphony No. 2 **1st Movement** **1st Theme**   K3
in C Minor, Op. 19
Copyright 1945 by Leeds **1st Movement** **2nd Theme**   K4
Music Corp., N. Y.
Reprinted here by
permisssion of the **2nd Movement** **Intro.**   K5
copyright owner.

2nd Movement **1st Theme**   K6

2nd Movement **2nd Theme**   K7

3rd Movement **1st Theme**   K8

3rd Movement **2nd Theme**   K9

3rd Movement **3rd Theme**   K10

3rd Movement **4th Theme**   K11

KALINNIKOFF, Basil (1866-1901)

Symphony No. 1 **1st Movement** **1st Theme**   K12
in G Minor
1st Movement **2nd Theme**   K13

2nd Movement **1st Theme**   K14

2nd Movement **2nd Theme**   K15

3rd Movement **1st Theme**   K16

3rd Movement **2nd Theme**   K17

4th Movement **1st Theme**   K18

KETELBEY, Albert W. (1880-1959)

In a Persian Market, Pft. or Orch.

By permission of Balwin, Inc., Sole Selling Agents for the copyright owner, Bosworth & Co., Ltd., Copyright 1923.

In a Monastery Garden, Pft. or Orch.

Copyright 1915 by J.H. Larway.

Copyright renewed and assigned to Harms, Inc. N.Y.

In a Chinese Temple Garden, Pft. or Orch.

By permission of Balwin, Inc., Sole Selling Agents for the copyright owner, Bosworth & Co., Ltd., Copyright 1920 renewal copyright secured.

KHACHATURIAN, Aram (1903-   )

Concerto, Pft. & Orch. Copyright 1945 by Leeds Music Corp., N.Y. Reprinted here by permission of the copyright owner.

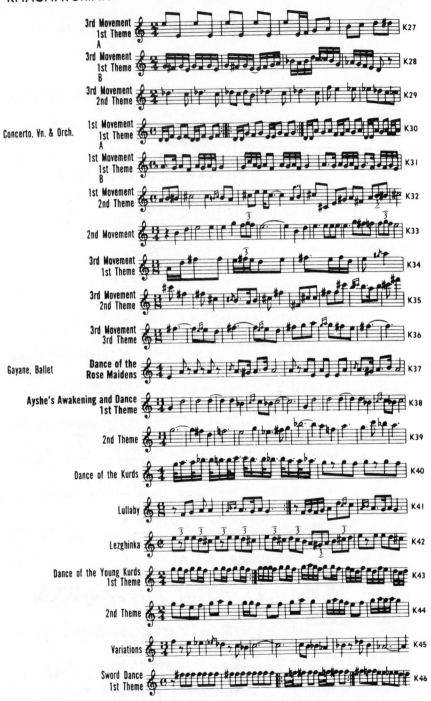

2nd Theme — K47

Masquerade
Suite for Orch.

1st Movement
Waltz
1st Theme — K48

1st Movement
2nd Theme — K49

2nd Movement
Nocturne — K50

3rd Movement
Mazurka — K51

4th Movement
Romance — K52

5th Movement
Galop — K53

Toccata, Pft.

1st Theme — K54

2nd Theme — K55

KHRENNIKOFF, Tikhon (1913-   )

Symphony No. 1, Op. 4
Copyright 1945 by Leeds
Music Corp., N. Y.
Reprinted here by
permisssion of the
copyright owner.

1st Movement
1st Theme — K56

1st Movement
2nd Theme — K57

1st Movement
3rd Theme — K58

2nd Movement
1st Theme — K59

2nd Movement
2nd Theme — K60

3rd Movement
1st Theme — K61

3rd Movement
2nd Theme — K62

KODÁLY, Zoltán (1882-1967)

Galanta Dances
Orch.
By permission of the copyright owner,
Boosey and Hawkes, Inc.

Intro. — K63

1st Movement — K64

2nd Movement — K65

3rd Movement — K66

4th Movement
1st Theme — K67

4th Movement
2nd Theme — K68

5th Movement
1st Theme — K69

5th Movement
2nd Theme — K70

Háry János, Op. 15,
Suite from Opera
By permission of the
copyright owner,
Boosey and Hawkes, Inc.

Kezdodik a Mese
(The Fairy Tale
Begins) — K71

Bécsi Harangjáték
(Viennese Musical Clock) — K72

Dal (Song) — K73

(Battle and Defeat of Napoleon)
1st Theme
Franciak Indulója — K74

2nd Theme
Napoleon Bevonulása — K75

3rd Theme
Gyászinduló — K76

Kőzjáték
1st Theme — K77

2nd Theme — K78

3rd Theme — K79

Piros Alma — K80

Bordal-Ó Melysok Hal — K81

Hogyan Tudtal Rozsám — K82

Hej Két Tikom — K83

Toborzó
1st Theme — K84

2nd Theme — K85

A Császári Udvar Bevonulása 1st Theme — K86

2nd Theme — K87

Szegény Vagyok — K88

Felszantóm A Császár Udvarát — K89

KORNGOLD, Erich Wolfgang (1897-1957)

Much Ado About Nothing,
Suite, Op. 11
Vn. & Pft.
By permission of
Associated Music
Publishers, Inc.

1st Movement
Mädchen im
Brautgemach
1st Theme — K90

1st Movement
2nd Theme — K91

2nd Movement
Holzapfel und Schlehwein
1st Theme — K92

2nd Movement
2nd Theme — K93

3rd Movement
Mummenschantz — K94

KREISLER, Fritz (1875-1962)

Andantino, (Style of Padre Martini)
Vn. & Pft.
Copyright by Charles Foley, New York — K95

Caprice Viennois, Op. 2,
Vn. & Pft.
Copyright by
Charles Foley, New York

1st Theme,
A — K96

1st Theme,
B — K97

2nd Theme — K98

Chanson Louis XIII et
Pavane, (Style of
Couperin), Vn. & Pft.
Copyright by Charles Foley,
New York

1st Theme
Chanson — K99

2nd Theme
Pavane — K100

La Chasse, Caprice (Style of
Jean-Baptiste Cartier), Vn. & Pft.
Copyright by Charles Foley, New York — K101

Liebesfreud,
Old Viennese Song
Vn. & Pft.
Copyright by Charles Foley, New York

1st Theme — K102

2nd Theme — K103

3rd Theme — K104

Liebeslied,
Old Viennese Song
Vn. & Pft.
Copyright by Charles Foley,
New York

1st Theme — K105

2nd Theme — K106

The Old Refrain
Viennese Popular Song
Vn. & Pft.
Copyright by Charles Foley, New York

— K107

Polichinelle, Serenade
Vn. & Pft.
Copyright by Charles Foley, New York

— K108

Praeludium and Allegro
(Style of Pugnani)
Vn. & Pft.
Copyright by Charles Foley, New York

Praeludium — K109

Allegro — K110

La Précieuse
(Style of Couperin)
Vn. & Pft.
Copyright by Charles Foley,
New York

1st Theme — K111

2nd Theme — K112

Rondino on a Theme by Beethoven
Vn. & Pft.
Copyright by Charles Foley, New York

— K113

Schön Rosmarin
Vn. & Pft.
Copyright by Charles Foley, New York

1st Theme — K114

2nd Theme — K115

Tambourin Chinois, Op. 3
Vn. & Pft.
Copyright by Charles Foley, New York

1st Theme — K116

2nd Theme — K117

Tempo di Minuetto
(Style of Pugnani), Vn. & Pft.
Copyright by Charles Foley, New York

— K118

KREUTZER, Conradin (1780-1849)

Das Nachtlager in Granada, 1st Theme
Overture

— K119

2nd Theme — K120

3rd Theme — K121

KUHNAU, Johann (1660-1722)

Sonata, The Combat Between David and Goliath, Pft.
1st Theme — The Bravado of Goliath — K122

2nd Theme — The Prayer of the Israelites — K123

3rd Theme — The Courage of David — K124

4th Theme — The Contest — K125

5th Theme — Joy of the Israelites Over the Victory — K126

LACK, Théodore (1846-1921)

Idilio, Op. 134, Pft. — L1

Arlequin, Vn. & Orch.
1st Theme — L2

2nd Theme — L3

LALO, Edouard (1823-1892)

Concerto in D Minor, Vcl. & Orch.
1st Movement 1st Theme — L4

1st Movement 2nd Theme — L5

2nd Movement Intermezzo 1st Theme — L6

2nd Movement 2nd Theme — L7

3rd Movement — L8

Concerto Russe, Op. 29, Vn. & Orch.
1st Movement Intro. — L9

1st Movement 1st Theme — L10

1st Movement 2nd Theme — L11

2nd Movement Chant Russe — L12

2nd Theme — L33

Symphonie Espagnole, Op. 21, Vn. & Orch.

1st Movement 1st Theme, A — L34

1st Movement 1st Theme, B — L35

1st Movement 2nd Theme — L36

2nd Movement 1st Theme — L37

2nd Movement 2nd Theme — L38

3rd Movement Intermezzo Intro. — L39

3rd Movement Intermezzo 1st Theme — L40

3rd Movement 2nd Theme — L41

4th Movement Intro. — L42

4th Movement — L43

5th Movement Intro. — L44

5th Movement 1st Theme — L45

5th Movement 2nd Theme — L46

LANGE, Gustav (1830-1889)

Flower Song, Pft. — L47

LASSEN, Eduard (1830-1904)

Fest-Overtüre Op. 51, Orch.
By permission of Associated Music Publishers, Inc.

Intro. — L48

1st Theme — L49

2nd Theme — L50

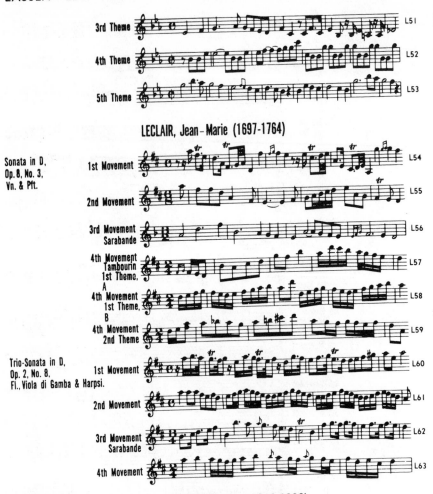

3rd Theme — L51
4th Theme — L52
5th Theme — L53

LECLAIR, Jean – Marie (1697-1764)

Sonata in D,
Op. 8, No. 3,
Vn. & Pft.

1st Movement — L54
2nd Movement — L55
3rd Movement Sarabande — L56
4th Movement Tambourin 1st Theme, A — L57
4th Movement 1st Theme, B — L58
4th Movement 2nd Theme — L59

Trio-Sonata in D,
Op. 2, No. 8,
Fl., Viola di Gamba & Harpsi.

1st Movement — L60
2nd Movement — L61
3rd Movement Sarabande — L62
4th Movement — L63

LECUONA, Ernesto (1896-1963)

Andalucia 1st Theme — L64
2nd Theme — L65
Gitanerias 1st Theme — L66
2nd Theme — L67
Malaguena 1st Theme — L68

2nd Theme ... L69

3rd Theme ... L70

LEKEU, Guillaume (1870-1894)

Adagio, Op. 3, Str. Orch.   1st Theme ... L75

2nd Theme ... L76

Quartet in B Minor,   1st Movement
(Unfinished), Pft. & Str.   1st Theme ... L77

1st Movement
2nd Theme ... L78

2nd Movement
1st Theme ... L79

2nd Movement
2nd Theme ... L80

Sonata in G,   1st Movement
Vn. & Pft.   1st Theme ... L81

1st Movement
2nd Theme ... L82

2nd Movement
1st Theme ... L83

2nd Movement
2nd Theme ... L84

3rd Movement
1st Theme ... L85

3rd Movement
2nd Theme ... L86

LIADOFF, Anatol (1855-1914)

Baba Yaga, Op. 56, Orch.
By permission of Associated
Music Publishers, Inc. ... L87

The Enchanted Lake
Op. 62, Orch.   1st Theme ... L88
By permission of Associated
Music Publishers, Inc.

2nd Theme ... L89

Kikimora, Op. 63, Orch.
By permission of Associated Music Publishers, Inc.
1st Theme, A — L90

1st Theme, B — L91

2nd Theme — L92

3rd Theme — L93

The Music Box, Op. 32, Pft. (or The Musical Snuff Box)
By permission of Associated Music Publishers, Inc.
1st Theme — L94

2nd Theme — L95

3rd Theme — L96

Russian Folk Dances, Op. 58, Orch.
By permission of Associated Music Publishers, Inc.
Legend of the Birds — L97

I Danced With a Mosquito — L98

Cradle Song — L99

Village Dance — L100

LISZT, Franz (1811-1886)

Ballade No. 2, in B Minor, Pft.
1st Theme — L101

2nd Theme — L102

Bénédiction de Dieu Dans la Solitude Pft. — L103

Berceuse, Pft. — L104

Concerto No. 1 in E Flat Pft. & Orch.
1st Theme — L105

2nd Theme — L106

3rd Theme — L107

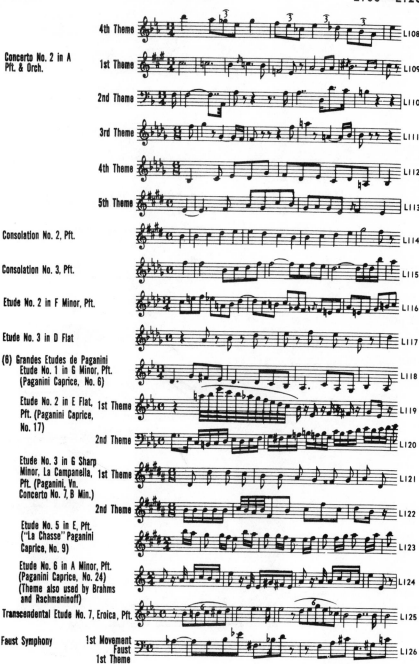

LISZT

4th Theme — L108

Concerto No. 2 in A
Pft. & Orch.

1st Theme — L109

2nd Theme — L110

3rd Theme — L111

4th Theme — L112

5th Theme — L113

Consolation No. 2, Pft. — L114

Consolation No. 3, Pft. — L115

Etude No. 2 in F Minor, Pft. — L116

Etude No. 3 in D Flat — L117

(6) Grandes Etudes de Paganini
Etude No. 1 in G Minor, Pft.
(Paganini Caprice, No. 6) — L118

Etude No. 2 in E Flat,
Pft. (Paganini Caprice,
No. 17)   1st Theme — L119

2nd Theme — L120

Etude No. 3 in G Sharp
Minor, La Campanella,
Pft. (Paganini, Vn.
Concerto No. 7, B Min.)   1st Theme — L121

2nd Theme — L122

Etude No. 5 in E, Pft.
("La Chasse" Paganini
Caprice, No. 9) — L123

Etude No. 6 in A Minor, Pft.
(Paganini Caprice, No. 24)
(Theme also used by Brahms
and Rachmaninoff) — L124

Transcendental Etude No. 7, Eroica, Pft. — L125

Faust Symphony   1st Movement
Faust
1st Theme — L126

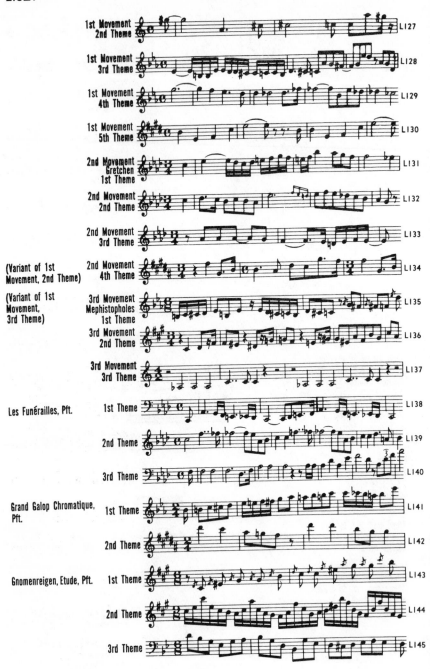

Hungarian Rhapsody No. 8
in F Sharp Minor, Pft. — L165

Hungarian Rhapsody No. 9
in E Flat, Pft.
"Carnival in Pesth" — 1st Theme L166

2nd Theme — L167

3rd Theme — L168

4th Theme — L169

Hungarian Rhapsody No. 10
in E, Pft. — 1st Theme L170

2nd Theme — L171

Hungarian Rhapsody No. 12
in C Sharp Minor, Pft. — 1st Theme L172

2nd Theme — L173

3rd Theme — L174

4th Theme — L175

5th Theme — L176

Hungarian Rhapsody No. 13
in A Minor, Pft. — 1st Theme L177

2nd Theme — L178

3rd Theme — L179

Hungarian Rhapsody No. 14
in F Minor (same material
as for Hungarian Fantasie,
Pft. & Orch.) — 1st Theme L180

2nd Theme — L181

3rd Theme — L182

4th Theme — L183

Hungarian Rhapsody No. 15
in A Minor, Pft.
"Rakóczy March" — 1st Theme L184

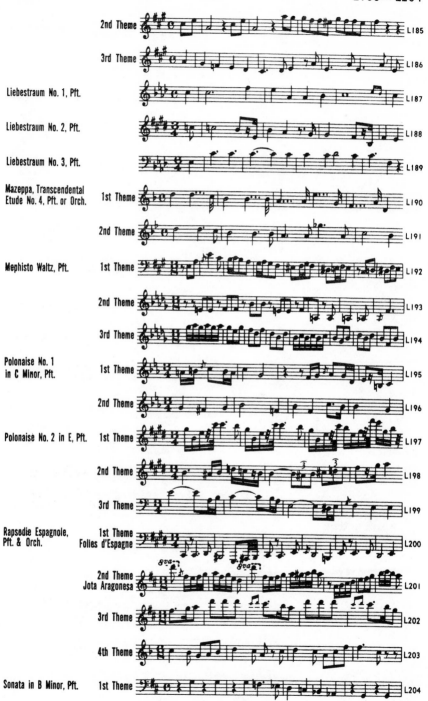

2nd Theme — L185

3rd Theme — L186

Liebestraum No. 1, Pft. — L187

Liebestraum No. 2, Pft. — L188

Liebestraum No. 3, Pft. — L189

Mazeppa, Transcendental Etude No. 4, Pft. or Orch. — 1st Theme L190

2nd Theme — L191

Mephisto Waltz, Pft. — 1st Theme L192

2nd Theme — L193

3rd Theme — L194

Polonaise No. 1 in C Minor, Pft. — 1st Theme L195

2nd Theme — L196

Polonaise No. 2 in E, Pft. — 1st Theme L197

2nd Theme — L198

3rd Theme — L199

Rapsodie Espagnole, Pft. & Orch. — 1st Theme Folies d'Espagne L200

2nd Theme Jota Aragonesa — L201

3rd Theme — L202

4th Theme — L203

Sonata in B Minor, Pft. — 1st Theme L204

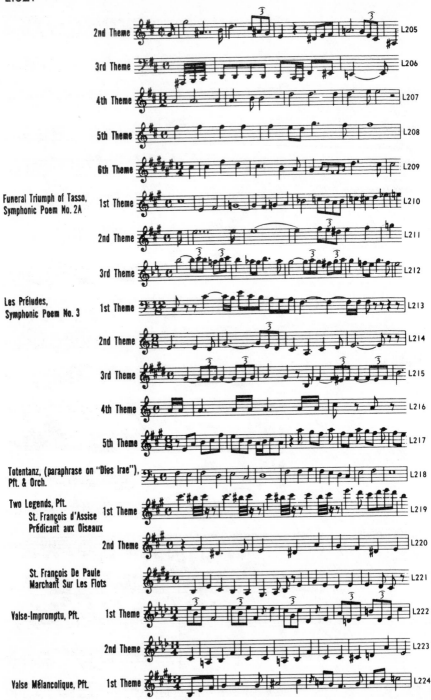

2nd Theme ... L205

3rd Theme ... L206

4th Theme ... L207

5th Theme ... L208

6th Theme ... L209

Funeral Triumph of Tasso,
Symphonic Poem No. 2A   1st Theme ... L210

2nd Theme ... L211

3rd Theme ... L212

Les Préludes,
Symphonic Poem No. 3   1st Theme ... L213

2nd Theme ... L214

3rd Theme ... L215

4th Theme ... L216

5th Theme ... L217

Totentanz, (paraphrase on "Dies Irae"),
Pft. & Orch. ... L218

Two Legends, Pft.
    St. François d'Assise   1st Theme ... L219
    Prédicant aux Oiseaux

2nd Theme ... L220

    St. François De Paule
    Marchant Sur Les Flots ... L221

Valse-Impromptu, Pft.   1st Theme ... L222

2nd Theme ... L223

Valse Mélancolique, Pft.   1st Theme ... L224

LOCATELLI, Pietro (1695-1764)

4th Movement  L244

5th Movement L245

LOEFFLER, Charles Martin (1861-1935)

La Mort de Tintagiles,
Op. 6, Orch.
Copyright renewal assigned
1933 to G. Schirmer, Inc.

1st Theme, A  L246

1st Theme, B L247

2nd Theme L248

3rd Theme L249

4th Theme L250

5th Theme L251

A Pagan Poem (after Virgil),
Op. 14, Pft. & Orch.
Copyright renewal assigned
1937 to G. Schirmer, Inc.

Intro. L252

1st Theme L253

2nd Theme L254

3rd Theme L255

4th Theme L256

5th Theme L257

Quintet, Str.
(In One Movement)
Copyright 1938
by G. Schirmer, Inc.

1st Theme  L258

2nd Theme L259

3rd Theme L260

4th Theme L261

5th Theme L262

Two Rhapsodies,
Oboe, Vla. & Pft.   L'Étang,(The Pool)   L263
Copyright renewal assigned
1932 to G. Schirmer, Inc.

La Cornemuse,(The Bagpipe)
1st Theme   L264

2nd Theme   L265

LOEILLET, Jean Baptiste (1653-1728)

Sonata No. 7 in
F, Fl. & Pft.   1st Movement   L266

2nd Movement   L267

3rd Movement   L268

4th Movement
Gavotte   L269

5th Movement
Aria   L270

6th Movement   L271

Suita No. 1 in
G Minor, Harpsi.   1st Movement
Allemande   L272

2nd Movement
Minuet   L273

3rd Movement
Sarabande   L274

4th Movement   L275

LORTZING, Gustav Albert (1801-1851)

Czar und Zimmerman,
Overture   1st Theme   L276

2nd Theme   L277

3rd Theme   L278

4th Theme, A
Clog Dance   L279

4th Theme,
B   L280

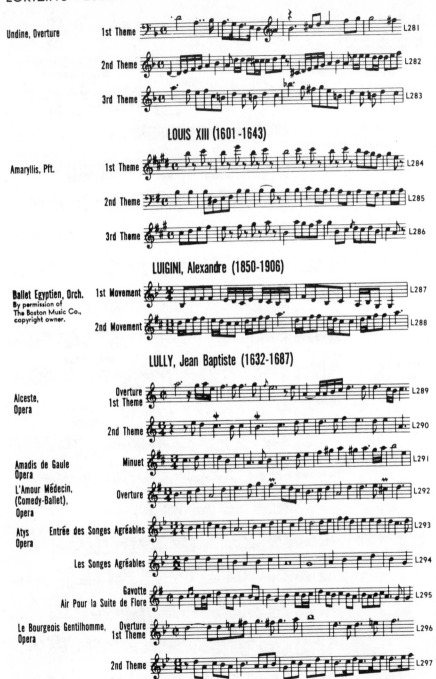

Undine, Overture — 1st Theme — L281
2nd Theme — L282
3rd Theme — L283

LOUIS XIII (1601-1643)

Amaryllis, Pft. — 1st Theme — L284
2nd Theme — L285
3rd Theme — L286

LUIGINI, Alexandre (1850-1906)

Ballet Egyptien, Orch.
By permission of
The Boston Music Co.,
copyright owner. — 1st Movement — L287
2nd Movement — L288

LULLY, Jean Baptiste (1632-1687)

Alceste,
Opera — Overture 1st Theme — L289
2nd Theme — L290

Amadis de Gaule
Opera — Minuet — L291

L'Amour Médecin,
(Comedy-Ballet),
Opera — Overture — L292

Atys
Opera — Entrée des Songes Agréables — L293
Les Songes Agréables — L294

Gavotte
Air Pour la Suite de Flore — L295

Le Bourgeois Gentilhomme,
Opera — Overture 1st Theme — L296
2nd Theme — L297

Ballet, Act 1 / 1st Theme — L298

2nd Theme / Sarabande — L299

3rd Theme / Gaillarde — L300

4th Theme — L301

Act IV / Cérémonie Turque — L302

Proserpine, Menuet des Ombres Heureuses / Opera — 1st Movement — L303

2nd Movement — L304

Le Temple de la Paix / Orch. — Intro. 1st Theme — L305

Intro. 2nd Theme — L306

Minuet 1st Theme — L307

2nd Theme — L308

Thésée / Opera — Overture 1st Theme — L309

2nd Theme — L310

Marche des Sacrificateurs — L311

Le Triomphe de L'Amour, / Ballet — Nocturne — L312

MacDOWELL, Edward (1861-1908)

Concerto No. 1, in A Minor, Op. 15, Pft. & Orch.
By permission of Associated Music Publishers, Inc. — 1st Movement 1st Theme — M1

1st Movement 2nd Theme — M2

2nd Movement — M3

3rd Movement 1st Theme — M4

3rd Movement 2nd Theme — M5

3rd Movement 3rd Theme — M6

3rd Movement 4th Theme — M7

Concerto No. 2. in D Minor, Op. 23, Pft. & Orch.
Copyright 1922 by G. Schirmer, Inc.

1st Movement 1st Theme — M8

1st Movement 2nd Theme — M9

2nd Movement 1st Theme — M10

2nd Movement 2nd Theme — M11

2nd Movement 3rd Theme — M12

3rd Movement 1st Theme — M13

3rd Movement 2nd Theme — M14

Marionettes, Pft. Witch, Op. 38. No. 4
Revised and Augmented Edition, Copyright 1929 by The Arthur P. Schmidt Co. Used by Permission. — M15

Clown, Op. 38, No. 5
Revised and Augmented Edition, Copyright 1929 by The Arthur P. Schmidt Co. Used by Permission. — M16

Villain, Op. 38, No. 6
Revised and Augmented Edition, Copyright 1929 by The Arthur P. Schmidt Co. Used by Permission — M17

Of Br'er Rabbit, Op. 61, No. 2, Pft.
Copyright 1930 by The Arthur P. Schmidt Co. Used by Permission — M18

Of a Tailor and a Bear, Pft.
Copyright 1925 and 1942 by The Arthur P. Schmidt Co. Used by Permission. — M19

An Old Garden. Op. 62. No. 1. Pft.,
Copyright 1930 by The Arthur P. Schmidt Co. Used by Permission. — M20

Polonaise, Op. 46, No. 12, Pft. — M21

Scotch Poem, Op. 31, No. 2, Pft.
Revised Edition, Copyright 1923 by The Arthur P. Schmidt Co. Used by Permission — M22

Sea Pieces, Pft.
To the Sea. Op. 55. No. 1
Copyright 1926 by The Arthur P. Schmidt Co. Used by Permission. — M23

A. D. 1620, Op. 55, No. 3 — M24
Copyright 1926 by The Arthur P. Schmidt Co. Used by Permission.

Starlight, Op. 55, No. 4
M25

Nautilus, Op. 55, No. 7
M26

Suite No. 2, (Indian) Orch.
I. Legend, Intro.
M27

1st Theme M28

2nd Theme M29

II. Love Song 1st Theme M30

2nd Theme M31

III. In War-Time M32

IV. Elegy M33

V. Village Festival 1st Theme M34

2nd Theme M35

Witches' Dance, Op. 17, No. 2, Pft.
M36

Woodland Sketches, Pft. To a Wild Rose, Op. 51, No. 1
M37

Will O'the Wisp, Op. 51, No. 2
M38

In Autumn, Op. 51, No. 4
M39

From an Indian Lodge, Op. 51, No. 5 1st Theme
M40

2nd Theme M41

To a Water Lily, Op. 51, No. 6 1st Theme
M42

2nd Theme M43

From Uncle Remus, Op. 51, No. 7
M44

Op. 51, No. 8   M45

MAHLER, Gustav (1860-1911)

Symphony No. 1
in D

1st Movement
Intro.   M46

1st Movement
1st Theme   M47

1st Movement
2nd Theme   M48

1st Movement
3rd Theme   M49

2nd Movement
1st Theme   M50

2nd Movement
2nd Theme   M51

3rd Movement
1st Theme   M52

3rd Movement
2nd Theme   M53

4th Movement
1st Theme,
A   M54

4th Movement
1st Theme,
B   M55

4th Movement
2nd Theme   M56

Symphony No. 2
in C Minor
"Resurrection"

1st Movement
1st Theme,
A   M57

1st Movement
1st Theme,
B   M58

1st Movement
2nd Theme   M59

1st Movement
3rd Theme   M60

2nd Movement
1st Theme   M61

2nd Movement
2nd Theme   M62

2nd Movement
3rd Theme   M63

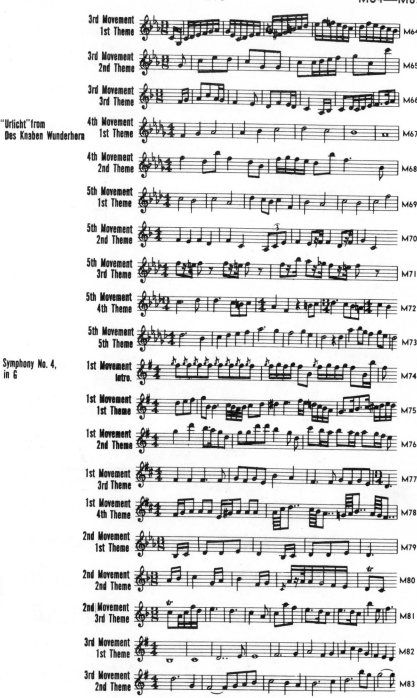

Symphony No. 5
By Permission of C. F. Peters,
Clayton F. Summy Co., Chicago, Agents in the U. S.

Symphony No.9
in D
By permission of the
copyright owner,
Boosey and Hawkes, Inc.

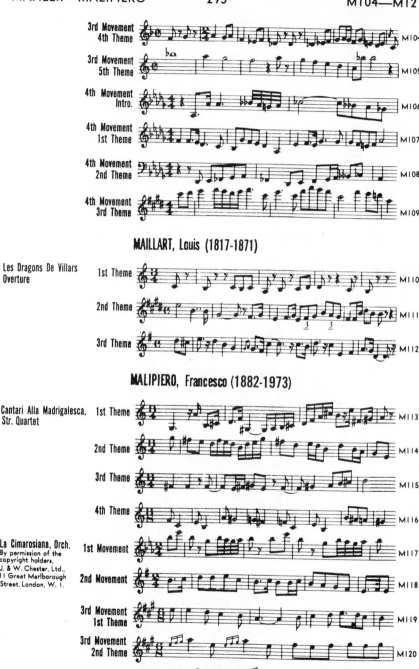

3rd Movement 4th Theme — M104

3rd Movement 5th Theme — M105

4th Movement Intro. — M106

4th Movement 1st Theme — M107

4th Movement 2nd Theme — M108

4th Movement 3rd Theme — M109

MAILLART, Louis (1817-1871)

Les Dragons De Villars Overture

1st Theme — M110

2nd Theme — M111

3rd Theme — M112

MALIPIERO, Francesco (1882-1973)

Cantari Alla Madrigalesca, Str. Quartet

1st Theme — M113

2nd Theme — M114

3rd Theme — M115

4th Theme — M116

La Cimarosiana, Orch.
By permission of the copyright holders,
J. & W. Chester, Ltd.,
11 Great Marlborough Street, London, W. 1.

1st Movement — M117

2nd Movement — M118

3rd Movement 1st Theme — M119

3rd Movement 2nd Theme — M120

4th Movement 1st Theme — M121

4th Movement
2nd Theme — M122

5th Movement — M123

Impressioni Dal Vero
Orch.
By permission of the copyright
holders, J. & W. Chester, Ltd.,
11 Great Marlborough Street,
London, W. 1.

Il Capinero
1st Theme — M124

2nd Theme — M125

Il Picchio
1st Theme — M126

2nd Theme — M127

Il Chiù — M128

Rispetti E Strambotti
Quartet, Str.
By permission of the copyright
holders, J. & W. Chester, Ltd.,
11 Great Marlborough Street,
London, W. 1.

1st Theme — M129

2nd Theme — M130

3rd Theme — M131

MARGIS, Alfred (1874-   )

Valse Bleue,
Vn. & Pft.

1st Theme — M131a

2nd Theme — M131b

MARIE, Gabriel, see GABRIEL-MARIE

MARSHNER, Heinrich August (1795-1861)

Hans Heiling
Overture

1st Theme — M132

2nd Theme — M133

3rd Theme — M134

MARTUCCI, Giuseppe (1856-1909)

Notturno, Orch.
Copyright 1922 by G. Ricordi & Co., Inc.

— M135

MASCAGNI, Pietro (1863-1945)

Cavalleria Rusticana,
Opera

Prelude
1st Theme — M136

MASSENET, Jules (1842-1912)

Le Cid, Ballet
By permission of
the copyright owner,
Heugel Ltd., London.

Les Erinnyes
(Incidental Music)
Orch.
By permission of the
copyright owner,
Heugel Ltd., London.

2nd Theme — M137

Intermezzo 1st Theme — M138

2nd Theme — M139

1st Movement Castillane — M140

2nd Movement Andalouse — M141

3rd Movement Aragonaise — M142

4th Movement Aubade — M143

5th Movement Catalane 1st Theme — M144

5th Movement 2nd Theme — M145

6th Movement Madrilène 1st Theme — M146

6th Movement 2nd Theme — M147

7th Movement Navarraise — M148

Prelude — M149

Danse Grecque 1st Theme — M150

2nd Theme — M151

Entr'acte — M152

Scène Religieuse — M153

Invocation, Elegy — M154

Finale, Saturnales 1st Theme — M155

Meditation from Opera Thais
By permission of the copyright owner, Heugel Ltd., London.

Phèdre Overture
By permission of the copyright owner, Heugel Ltd., London.

Le Roi De Lahore Overture
By permission of the copyright owner, Heugel Ltd., London.

Scènes Alsaciennes, Suite No. 7,
By permission of the copyright owner, Heugel Ltd., London.

Scènes Pittoresques, Suite No. 4,
By permission of the copyright owner, Heugel Ltd., London.

2nd Theme — M156
1st Theme — M157
2nd Theme — M158
1st Theme — M159
2nd Theme — M160
3rd Theme — M161
1st Theme — M162
2nd Theme — M163
I--Sunday Morning 1st Theme — M164
2nd Theme — M165
II--Cabaret 1st Theme — M166
2nd Theme — M167
3rd Theme — M168
III--Under the Lindens — M169
IV--Sunday Evening 1st Theme — M170
2nd Theme Alsatian Folk Tune — M171
3rd Theme Alsatian Tune — M172
I--March 1st Theme — M173
2nd Theme — M174
3rd Theme — M175

4th Theme — M176

H--Air De Ballet
1st Theme — M177

2nd Theme — M178

HI--Angelus
1st Theme — M179

2nd Theme — M180

IV--Fête Bohême
1st Theme — M181

2nd Theme — M182

McDONALD, Harl (1899-1955)

Rhumba, from
Symphony No. 2
Permission granted by
Elkan-Vogel Co., Inc.,
Philadelphia, Pa.
Copyright 1936

1st Theme — M183

2nd Theme — M184

3rd Theme — M185

4th Theme — M186

MEDTNER, Nicolas (1880-1951)

Arabesque, "Tragedie-Fragment",
Op. 7, No. 3, Pft.
By permission of International Music Co. — M187

Fairy Tales, Pft.
Op. 14, No. 2
By permission of International Music Co.
1st Theme — M188

2nd Theme — M189

Op. 20, No. 1 — M190

Op. 26, No. 3 — M191

Op. 34, No. 2 — M192

Op. 51, No. 1 — M193

Op. 51, No. 2 — M194

Novelette, Op. 17, No. 1, Pft.
By permission of International Music Co. — M195

MENDELSSOHN, Felix (1809-1847)

Capriccio Brilliant,
Op. 22, Pft. & Orch. — 1st Theme Intro. — M196

2nd Theme — M197

3rd Theme — M198

4th Theme — M199

Concerto No. 1,
in G Minor, Op. 25,
Pft. & Orch. — 1st Movement Intro. — M200

1st Movement 1st Theme — M201

1st Movement 2nd Theme — M202

1st Movement 3rd Theme — M203

2nd Movement — M204

3rd Movement — M205

Concerto No. 2,
in D Minor, Op. 40,
Pft. & Orch. — 1st Movement Intro. — M206

1st Movement 1st Theme — M207

1st Movement 2nd Theme — M208

2nd Movement — M209

3rd Movement — M210

Concerto in E Minor,
Op. 64, Vn. & Orch. — 1st Movement 1st Theme — M211

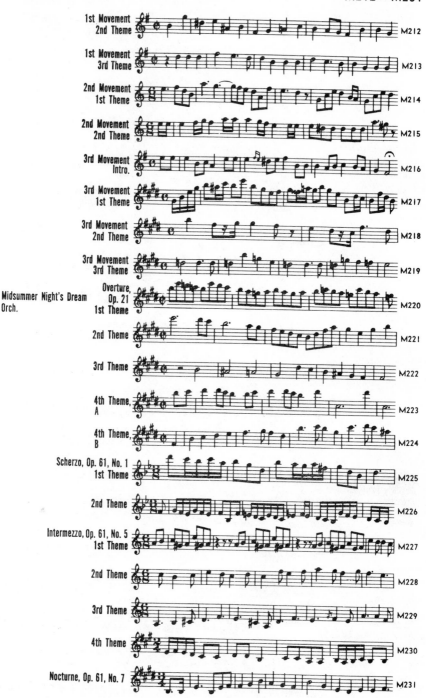

1st Movement 2nd Theme — M212

1st Movement 3rd Theme — M213

2nd Movement 1st Theme — M214

2nd Movement 2nd Theme — M215

3rd Movement Intro. — M216

3rd Movement 1st Theme — M217

3rd Movement 2nd Theme — M218

3rd Movement 3rd Theme — M219

Midsummer Night's Dream Orch.

Overture, Op. 21 1st Theme — M220

2nd Theme — M221

3rd Theme — M222

4th Theme, A — M223

4th Theme, B — M224

Scherzo, Op. 61, No. 1 1st Theme — M225

2nd Theme — M226

Intermezzo, Op. 61, No. 5 1st Theme — M227

2nd Theme — M228

3rd Theme — M229

4th Theme — M230

Nocturne, Op. 61, No. 7 — M231

Wedding March, Op. 61, No. 9, 1st Theme — M232

2nd Theme — M233

3rd Theme — M234

4th Theme — M235

Octet, in E Flat, Op. 20, Str.

1st Movement 1st Theme — M236

1st Movement 2nd Theme — M237

2nd Movement 1st Theme — M238

2nd Movement 2nd Theme — M239

3rd Movement 1st Theme — M240

3rd Movement 2nd Theme — M241

3rd Movement 3rd Theme — M242

4th Movement 1st Theme — M243

4th Movement 2nd Theme — M244

Meeresstille und Glückliche Fahrt, Op. 27 Overture, (Calm Sea and Prosperous Voyage)

Meeresstille — M245

Glückliche Fahrt 1st Theme — M246

2nd Theme — M247

3rd Theme — M248

Fingal's Cave (or The Hebrides), Op. 26 Overture

1st Theme — M249

2nd Theme — M250

3rd Theme — M251

Ruy Blas, Overture, Op. 95 — Intro. — M252
1st Theme — M253
2nd Theme, A — M254
2nd Theme, B — M255
3rd Theme — M256

Quartet No. 1, in E Flat, Op. 12, Str. — 1st Movement Intro. — M257
1st Movement 1st Theme — M258
1st Movement 2nd Theme — M259
1st Movement 3rd Theme — M260
2nd Movement — M261
3rd Movement — M262
4th Movement 1st Theme — M263
4th Movement 2nd Theme — M264

Quartet, No. 3 in D, Op. 44, No. 1, Str. — 1st Movement 1st Theme — M265
1st Movement 2nd Theme — M266
1st Movement 3rd Theme — M267
2nd Movement 1st Theme — M268
2nd Movement 2nd Theme — M269
3rd Movement 1st Theme, A — M270
3rd Movement 1st Theme, B — M271

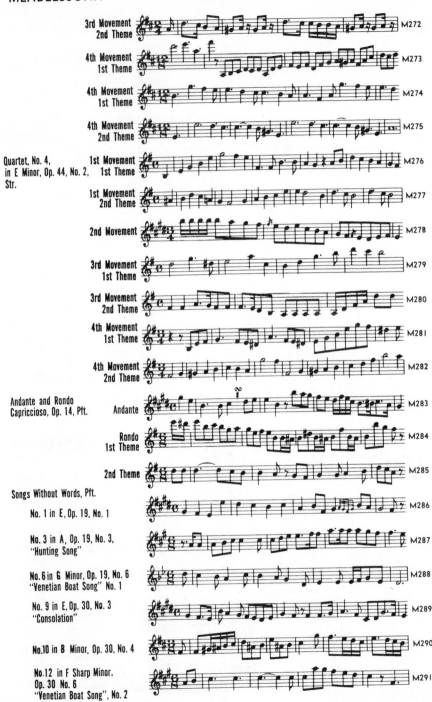

MENDELSSOHN

3rd Movement
2nd Theme — M272

4th Movement
1st Theme — M273

4th Movement
1st Theme — M274

4th Movement
2nd Theme — M275

Quartet, No. 4,
in E Minor, Op. 44, No. 2,
Str.

1st Movement
1st Theme — M276

1st Movement
2nd Theme — M277

2nd Movement — M278

3rd Movement
1st Theme — M279

3rd Movement
2nd Theme — M280

4th Movement
1st Theme — M281

4th Movement
2nd Theme — M282

Andante and Rondo
Capriccioso, Op. 14, Pft.

Andante — M283

Rondo
1st Theme — M284

2nd Theme — M285

Songs Without Words, Pft.

No. 1 in E, Op. 19, No. 1 — M286

No. 3 in A, Op. 19, No. 3,
"Hunting Song" — M287

No. 6 in G Minor, Op. 19, No. 6
"Venetian Boat Song" No. 1 — M288

No. 9 in E, Op. 30, No. 3
"Consolation" — M289

No. 10 in B Minor, Op. 30, No. 4 — M290

No. 12 in F Sharp Minor,
Op. 30 No. 6
"Venetian Boat Song", No. 2 — M291

No.14 in C Minor, Op. 38, No. 2, "Lost Happiness" — M292

No.18 in A Flat, Op. 38, No. 6, "Duet" — M293

No.20 in E Flat, Op. 53, No. 2, "The Fleecy Cloud" — M294

No.22 in F, Op. 53, No. 4, "Sadness of Soul" — M295

No.23 in A, Op. 53, No. 5, "Folk Song" 1st Theme — M296

2nd Theme — M297

No.25 in G, Op. 62, No. 1, "May Breezes" — M298

No. 27, in E Minor Op. 62, No. 3, "Funeral March" — M299

No.28, in G Op. 62, No. 4, "Morning Song" — M300

No.29, in A Minor, Op.62, No. 5 "Venetian Boat Song", No. 3 — M301

No. 30, in A, Op.62, No. 6 "Spring Song" — M302

No.34, in C, Op.67, No.4 "Spinning Song" — M303

No.35, in B Minor, Op.67, No. 5 "Song of the Heather" — M304

No.45, in C, "Tarantella" — M305

No.47, in A, Op.102 No. 5 "The Joyous Peasant" — M306

No.48, in C, Op. 102, No. 6 "Faith" — M307

No. 49, in A, Op.102, No. 7 "Boat-Song" — M308

Scherzo, Op. 16, No. 2, Pft. 1st Theme — M309

2nd Theme — M310

Symphony No. 3, in A Minor, Op.56 "Scotch" 1st Movement Intro. — M311

Symphony No. 4, in A, Op. 90, "Italian"

3rd Movement 2nd Theme — M332

4th Movement 1st Theme — M333

4th Movement 2nd Theme — M334

4th Movement 3rd Theme — M335

4th Movement 4th Theme — M336

Symphony No. 5, in D, Op. 107, "Reformation"

1st Movement Intro. — M337

1st Movement 1st Theme — M338

1st Movement 2nd Theme — M339

2nd Movement 1st Theme — M340

2nd Movement 2nd Theme — M341

3rd Movement 1st Theme — M342

Chorale, Eine Feste Burg ist unser Gott!

3rd Movement 2nd Theme — M343

3rd Movement 3rd Theme — M344

3rd Movement 4th Theme — M345

3rd Movement 5th Theme — M346

3rd Movement 6th Theme — M347

Trio No. 1, in D Minor, Op. 49, Vn, Cello, Pft.

1st Movement 1st Theme A — M348

1st Movement 1st Theme B — M349

2nd Movement 1st Theme — M350

2nd Movement 2nd Theme — M351

3rd Movement   M352

4th Movement
1st Theme   M353

4th Movement
2nd Theme   M354

Trio No. 2, in C Minor,
Op. 66, Vn, Cello, Pft.   1st Movement
1st Theme   M355

1st Movement
2nd Theme   M356

1st Movement
3rd Theme   M357

2nd Movement
1st Theme   M358

2nd Movement
2nd Theme   M359

3rd Movement
1st Theme   M360

3rd Movement
2nd Theme   M361

4th Movement
1st Theme   M362

4th Movement
2nd Theme   M363

Variations Serieuses, Op. 54,
Pft.   Theme   M364

MEYERBEER, Giacomo (1791-1864)

Le Prophète
Opera   Coronation March
1st Theme   M365

2nd Theme   M366

MIASKOVSKY, Nicolas (1881-1950)

Sinfonietta in B Minor,
Op. 32, No. 2, Str. Orch.   1st Movement
1st Theme   M367

1st Movement
2nd Theme   M368

2nd Movement
Theme for Variations   M369

3rd Movement
1st Theme — M370

3rd Movement
2nd Theme — M371

3rd Movement
3rd Theme — M372

Symphony No. 21,
in F Sharp Minor, Op. 51

1st Theme — M372a

2nd Theme — M372b

3rd Theme — M372c

4th Theme — M372d

5th Theme — M372e

6th Theme
(Variant of 4th Theme
Used as Fugue Theme) — M372 f

MILHAUD, Darius (1892-1974)

Le Boeuf Sur Le Toit,(The Nothing
Doing Bar), Ballet
based on South
American Tunes
Copyright by
Editions Salabert
Editions Salabert,
22 Rue Chaucat,
Paris Salabert, Inc.,
I East 57 St., N. Y.

1st Theme
Barman Theme — M373

2nd Theme
Entry of the Negroes — M374

3rd Theme
Entry of the Women,
A — M375

3rd Theme,
B — M376

4th Theme
Entry of the Men — M377

5th Theme
Dance of the
Bookmakers — M378

6th Theme
Tango — M379

7th Theme
Dance of the Policemen — M380

8th Theme
Dance of the Negro — M381

Concerto, Pft. & Orch.
Copyright by Editions
Salabert Editions Salabert,
22 Rue Chaucat, Paris
Salabert, Inc.,
I East 57 St., N. Y.

1st Movement
1st Theme — M382

1st Movement 2nd Theme — M383

1st Movement 3rd Theme — M384

2nd Movement — M385

3rd Movement 1st Theme — M386

3rd Movement 2nd Theme — M387

Création Du Monde, Ballet
By permission of Associated Music Publishers, Inc.

Prelude — M388

1st Movement — M389

2nd Movement — M390

3rd Movement — M391

4th Movement 1st Theme — M392

4th Movement 2nd Theme — M393

Pastorale
for Oboe, Cl., Bassoon
By permission of Associated Music Publishers, Inc.

1st Theme — M394

2nd Theme — M395

Saudades Do Brazil, Pft.
Copyright by Editions Salabert Editions Salabert, 22 Rue Chaucat. Paris Salabert, Inc., 1 East 57 St., N. Y.

I Sorocaba — M396

VII Corcovado — M397

VIII Tijuca — M398

IX Sumare — M399

XII Paysandu — M400

MONIUSZKO, Stanislaw (1819-1872)

Halka
Overture

Intro. — M401

1st Theme — M402

2nd Theme — M403

3rd Theme — M404

4th Theme — M405

MORGENSTERN, Sam (1907-   )

Toccata Guatemala, Pft.
Copyright 1947 by Carl
Fischer, Inc., N. Y.
Reprinted by permisssion.

1st Theme — M405a

2nd Theme — M405b

MOSZKOWSKI, Moritz (1854-1925)

Caprice Espagnol,
Op. 37, Pft.

1st Theme — M406

2nd Theme — M407

3rd Theme — M408

Étincelles (Sparks),
Op. 36, No. 6, Pft. — M409

Guitarre, Op. 45, No. 2,
Pft.
Copyright 1920 by Carl
Fischer, Inc., N. Y.

1st Theme — M410

2nd Theme — M411

Malagueña, from opera Boabdil,
Op. 49
By Permission of C. F. Peters, Clayton F. Summy Co.,
Chicago, Agents in the U. S. — M412

Serenata, Op. 15, No. 1, Pft. — M413

Spanish Dances, Pft.
Op. 12, No. 1

1st Theme — M414

2nd Theme — M415

3rd Theme — M416

Op. 12, No. 2

1st Theme — M417

MOZART, Wolfgang Amadeus (1756-1791)

Concerto in A,
K 414, Pft. & Orch.

1st Movement 1st Theme — M454

1st Movement 2nd Theme — M455

2nd Movement — M456

3rd Movement 1st Theme — M457

3rd Movement 2nd Theme — M458

Concerto in E Flat,
K 449, Pft. & Orch.

1st Movement — M459

2nd Movement — M460

3rd Movement — M461

Concerto in B Flat
K 450, Pft. & Orch.

1st Movement 1st Theme — M462

1st Movement 2nd Theme — M463

2nd Movement — M464

3rd Movement — M465

Concerto in G
K 453, Pft. & Orch.

1st Movement 1st Theme — M466

1st Movement 2nd Theme — M467

2nd Movement — M468

3rd Movement — M469

Concerto in F
K 459, Pft. & Orch.

1st Movement — M470

2nd Movement — M471

3rd Movement 1st Theme — M472

3rd Movement 2nd Theme — M473

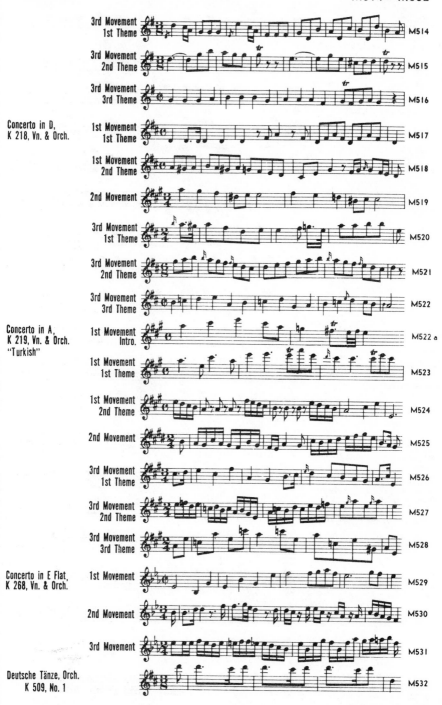

3rd Movement 1st Theme — M514
3rd Movement 2nd Theme — M515
3rd Movement 3rd Theme — M516

Concerto in D, K 218, Vn. & Orch.
1st Movement 1st Theme — M517
1st Movement 2nd Theme — M518
2nd Movement — M519
3rd Movement 1st Theme — M520
3rd Movement 2nd Theme — M521
3rd Movement 3rd Theme — M522

Concerto in A, K 219, Vn. & Orch. "Turkish"
1st Movement Intro. — M522 a
1st Movement 1st Theme — M523
1st Movement 2nd Theme — M524
2nd Movement — M525
3rd Movement 1st Theme — M526
3rd Movement 2nd Theme — M527
3rd Movement 3rd Theme — M528

Concerto in E Flat, K 268, Vn. & Orch.
1st Movement — M529
2nd Movement — M530
3rd Movement — M531

Deutsche Tänze, Orch. K 509, No. 1 — M532

K 509, No. 2 — M533
K 509, No. 4 — M534
K 509, No. 5 — M535
K 509, No. 6 — M536
K 571, No. 4 — M537
K 571, No. 6 — M538
K 600, No. 1 — M539
K 600, No. 2 — M540
K 600, No. 3 — M541
K 600, No. 4 — M542
K 600, No. 5 · 1st Theme — M543
2nd Theme (Der Kanarienvogel) — M544
K 600, No. 6 — M545
K 602, No. 3 · 1st Theme — M546
2nd Theme (Der Leiermann) — M547
K 605, No. 1 — M548
K 605, No. 2 — M549
K 605, No. 3 · 1st Theme — M550
2nd Theme (Die Schlitten Fahrt) — M551
Divertimento in D, K 136 · 2 Vns., Viola & Bass · 1st Movement — M552

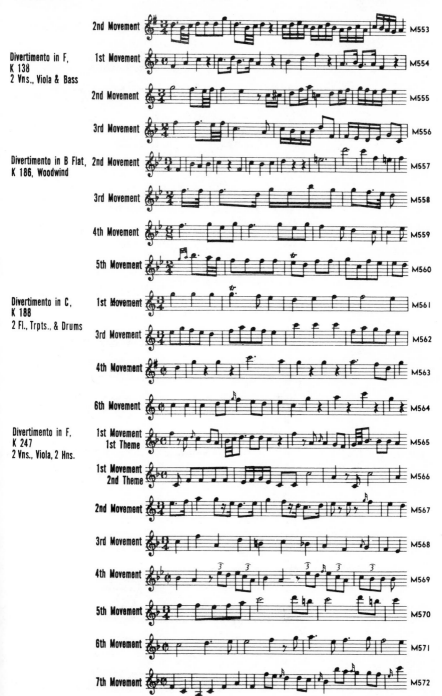

Divertimento in B Flat, K 287, 2 Vns., Viola, Bass, 2 Horns

1st Movement — M573
2nd Movement — M574
3rd Movement — M575
4th Movement — M576
5th Movement — M577
6th Movement — M578

Divertimento in D, K 334, 2 Vns., Viola, Bass, 2 Horns

1st Movement — M579
2nd Movement — M580
3rd Movement — M581
4th Movement — M582
5th Movement — M583
6th Movement — M584

Fantasia in F Minor, K 608, Mechanical Organ

1st Theme — M585
2nd Theme — M586
3rd Theme — M587

Fantasia in D Minor, K 397, Pft.

1st Theme — M588
2nd Theme — M589

Minuet, K 1, Pft. — M590

Minuet in F, K 2, Pft. — M591

Minuet in D, K 355, Pft. — M592

Quartet in D,
K 285, Fl. & Str.
1st Movement — M612
2nd Movement — M613
3rd Movement — M614

Quartet in A,
K 298, Fl. & Str.
1st Movement — M615
2nd Movement 1st Theme — M616
2nd Movement 2nd Theme — M617
3rd Movement — M618

Quartet in F,
K 370, Oboe & Str.
1st Movement — M619
2nd Movement — M620
3rd Movement — M621

Quartet in G Minor
K 4, Pft. & Str.
1st Movement 1st Theme — M622
1st Movement 2nd Theme — M623
2nd Movement — M624
3rd Movement 1st Theme — M625
3rd Movement 2nd Theme — M626

Quartet in E Flat
K 493, Pft. & Str.
1st Movement 1st Theme — M627
1st Movement 2nd Theme — M628
2nd Movement — M629
3rd Movement — M630

Quartet in G
K 80, Str.
1st Movement — M631

2nd Movement — M632

3rd Movement 1st Theme — M633

3rd Movement 2nd Theme — M634

4th Movement — M635

Quartet in G K 387, Str.

1st Movement — M636

2nd Movement 1st Theme — M637

2nd Movement 2nd Theme — M638

3rd Movement — M639

4th Movement — M640

Quartet in D Minor, K 421, Str.

1st Movement — M641

2nd Movement — M642

3rd Movement 1st Theme — M643

3rd Movement 2nd Theme — M644

4th Movement — M645

Quartet in E Flat, K 428, Str.

1st Movement — M646

2nd Movement — M647

3rd Movement — M648

4th Movement — M649

Quartet in B Flat, K 458, Str. "Hunting"

1st Movement — M650

2nd Movement 1st Theme — M651

2nd Movement 2nd Theme — M652

3rd Movement — M653

4th Movement — M654

Quartet in A, K 464, Str.

1st Movement — M655

2nd Movement — M656

3rd Movement — M657

4th Movement — M658

Quartet in C, K 465, Str. "Dissonant"

1st Movement Intro. — M659

1st Movement — M660

2nd Movement — M661

3rd Movement 1st Theme — M662

3rd Movement 2nd Theme — M663

4th Movement — M664

Quartet in D K 499, Str.

1st Movement — M665

2nd Movement 1st Theme — M666

2nd Movement 2nd Theme — M667

3rd Movement — M668

4th Movement — M669

Quartet in D K 575, Str.

1st Movement — M670

2nd Movement — M671

MOZART

326 · M692—M711

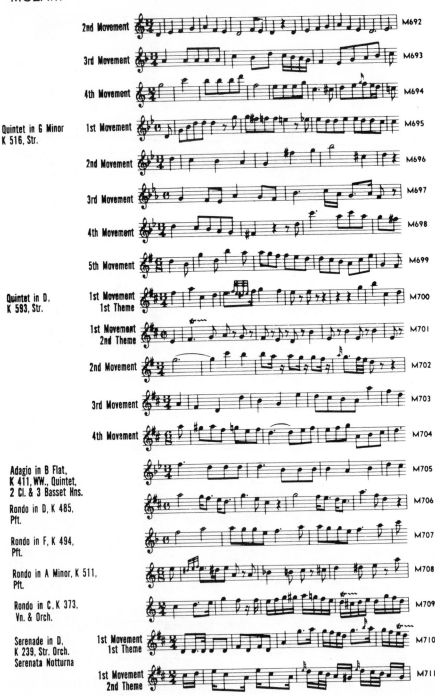

MOZART 326 M692—M711

2nd Movement — M692
3rd Movement — M693
4th Movement — M694

Quintet in G Minor
K 516, Str.
1st Movement — M695
2nd Movement — M696
3rd Movement — M697
4th Movement — M698
5th Movement — M699

Quintet in D,
K 593, Str.
1st Movement
1st Theme — M700
1st Movement
2nd Theme — M701
2nd Movement — M702
3rd Movement — M703
4th Movement — M704

Adagio in B Flat,
K 411, WW., Quintet,
2 Cl. & 3 Basset Hns. — M705

Rondo in D, K 485,
Pft. — M706

Rondo in F, K 494,
Pft. — M707

Rondo in A Minor, K 511,
Pft. — M708

Rondo in C, K 373,
Vn. & Orch. — M709

Serenade in D,
K 239, Str. Orch.
Serenata Notturna
1st Movement
1st Theme — M710

1st Movement
2nd Theme — M711

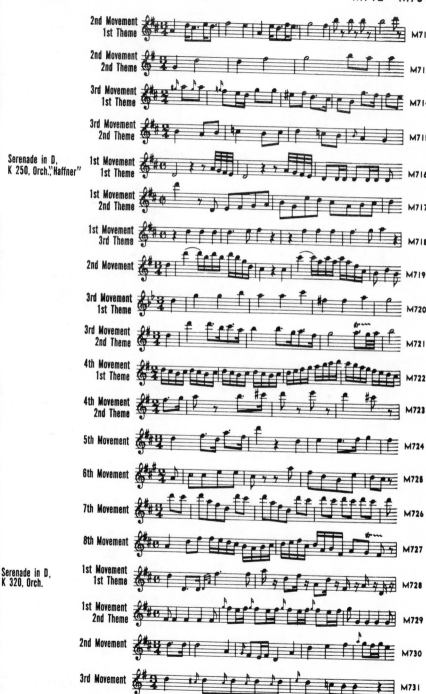

Serenade in D,
K 250, Orch.,"Haffner"

Serenade in D,
K 320, Orch.

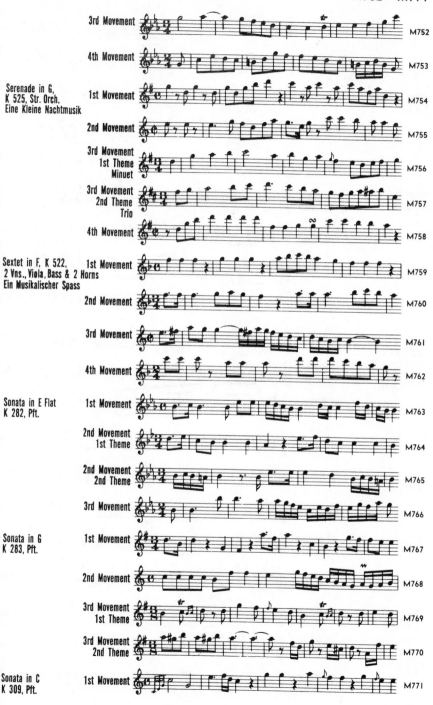

3rd Movement — M752
4th Movement — M753

Serenade in G,
K 525, Str. Orch.
Eine Kleine Nachtmusik
1st Movement — M754
2nd Movement — M755
3rd Movement
1st Theme
Minuet — M756
3rd Movement
2nd Theme
Trio — M757
4th Movement — M758

Sextet in F, K 522,
2 Vns., Viola, Bass & 2 Horns
Ein Musikalischer Spass
1st Movement — M759
2nd Movement — M760
3rd Movement — M761
4th Movement — M762

Sonata in E Flat
K 282, Pft.
1st Movement — M763
2nd Movement
1st Theme — M764
2nd Movement
2nd Theme — M765
3rd Movement — M766

Sonata in G
K 283, Pft.
1st Movement — M767
2nd Movement — M768
3rd Movement
1st Theme — M769
3rd Movement
2nd Theme — M770

Sonata in C
K 309, Pft.
1st Movement — M771

2nd Movement — M772

3rd Movement — M773

Sonata in A Minor
K 310, Pft.

1st Movement — M774

2nd Movement — M775

3rd Movement — M776

Sonata in D
K 311, Pft.

1st Movement
1st Theme — M777

1st Movement
2nd Theme — M778

2nd Movement — M779

3rd Movement — M780

Sonata in C
K 330, Pft.

1st Movement — M781

2nd Movement
1st Theme — M782

2nd Movement
2nd Theme — M783

3rd Movement — M784

Sonata in A
K 331, Pft.

1st Movement — M785

2nd Movement — M786

3rd Movement
1st Theme — M787

3rd Movement
2nd Theme — M788

Sonata in F
K 332, Pft.

1st Movement
1st Theme — M789

1st Movement
2nd Theme — M790

1st Movement
3rd Theme — M791

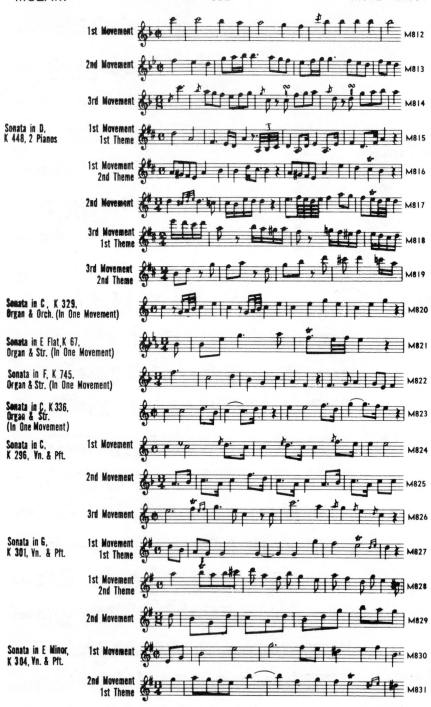

MOZART

2nd Movement 2nd Theme — M832

Sonata in F, K 376, Vn. & Pft.
1st Movement 1st Theme — M833
1st Movement 2nd Theme — M834
2nd Movement — M835
3rd Movement — M836

Sonata in F, K 377, Vn. & Pft.
1st Movement — M837
2nd Movement — M838
3rd Movement — M839

Sonata in B Flat, K 378, Vn. & Pft.
1st Movement — M840
2nd Movement — M841
3rd Movement — M842

Sonata in G, K 379, Vn. & Pft.
1st Movement 1st Theme — M843
1st Movement 2nd Theme — M844
2nd Movement — M845

Sonata in E Flat, K 380, Vn. & Pft.
1st Movement — M846
2nd Movement — M847
3rd Movement — M848

Sonata in C, K 404, Vn. & Pft.
1st Movement — M849
2nd Movement — M850

Sonata in E Flat, K 481, Vn. & Pft.
1st Movement 1st Theme — M851

1st Movement 2nd Theme   M852

2nd Movement   M853

3rd Movement   M854

Sonata in A, K 526, Vn. & Pft.   1st Movement 1st Theme   M855

1st Movement 2nd Theme   M856

3rd Movement   M857

Symphony No. 1, in E Flat, K 16   1st Movement 1st Theme   M858

1st Movement 2nd Theme   M859

2nd Movement   M860

3rd Movement 1st Theme   M861

3rd Movement 2nd Theme   M862

Symphony No. 12 in G, K 110   1st Movement 1st Theme   M863

1st Movement 2nd Theme   M864

2nd Movement 1st Theme   M865

2nd Movement 2nd Theme   M866

3rd Movement 1st Theme   M867

3rd Movement 2nd Theme   M868

4th Movement 1st Theme   M869

4th Movement 2nd Theme   M870

Symphony No. 13 in F, K 112   1st Movement 1st Theme   M871

1st Movement 2nd Theme — M872

2nd Movement — M873

3rd Movement 1st Theme — M874

3rd Movement 2nd Theme — M875

4th Movement 1st Theme — M876

4th Movement 2nd Theme — M877

Symphony No. 25 in G Minor, K 183

1st Movement 1st Theme — M878

1st Movement 2nd Theme — M879

1st Movement 3rd Theme — M880

2nd Movement — M881

3rd Movement 1st Theme — M882

3rd Movement 2nd Theme — M883

4th Movement 1st Theme — M884

4th Movement 2nd Theme — M885

Symphony No. 28 in C, K 200

1st Movement 1st Theme — M886

1st Movement 2nd Theme — M887

2nd Movement 1st Theme — M888

2nd Movement 2nd Theme — M889

3rd Movement 1st Theme — M890

3rd Movement 2nd Theme — M891

3rd Movement 1st Theme — M932

3rd Movement 2nd Theme — M933

4th Movement 1st Theme — M934

4th Movement 2nd Theme — M935

Symphony No. 36, in C, K 425 "Linz"

1st Movement Intro. — M936

1st Movement 1st Theme — M937

1st Movement 2nd Theme — M938

1st Movement 3rd Theme — M939

2nd Movement 1st Theme — M940

2nd Movement 2nd Theme — M941

3rd Movement 1st Theme — M942

3rd Movement 2nd Theme — M943

4th Movement 1st Theme — M944

4th Movement 2nd Theme — M945

4th Movement 3rd Theme — M946

Symphony No. 37 in G, K 444

1st Movement Intro. — M947

1st Movement 1st Theme — M948

1st Movement 2nd Theme — M949

2nd Movement 1st Theme — M950

2nd Movement 2nd Theme — M951

Symphony No. 40 in G Minor, K 550

1st Movement 1st Theme — M972
1st Movement 2nd Theme — M973
2nd Movement 1st Theme — M974
2nd Movement 2nd Theme — M975
2nd Movement 3rd Theme — M976
3rd Movement 1st Theme — M977
3rd Movement 2nd Theme — M978
4th Movement 1st Theme — M979
4th Movement 2nd Theme — M980

Symphony No. 41, in C K 551, "Jupiter"

1st Movement 1st Theme — M981
1st Movement 2nd Theme — M982
1st Movement 3rd Theme — M983
2nd Movement 1st Theme — M984
2nd Movement 2nd Theme — M985
3rd Movement 1st Theme — M986
3rd Movement 2nd Theme — M987
4th Movement 1st Theme — M988
4th Movement 2nd Theme — M989
4th Movement 3rd Theme — M990

Symphonie Concertante in E Flat, K 364, Vn., Viola & Orch.

1st Movement 1st Theme — M991

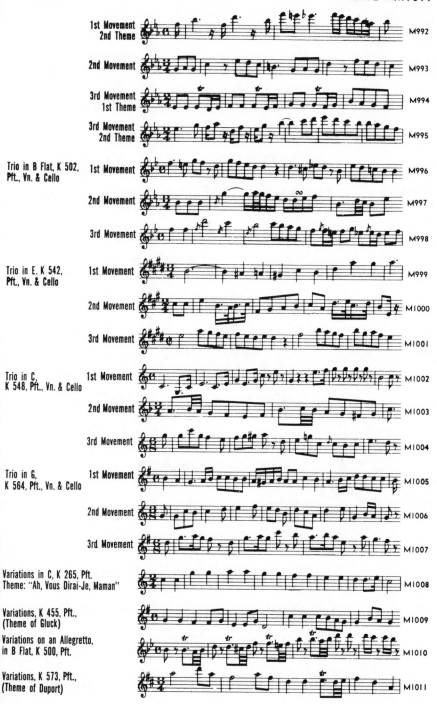

1st Movement 2nd Theme — M992

2nd Movement — M993

3rd Movement 1st Theme — M994

3rd Movement 2nd Theme — M995

Trio in B Flat, K 502, Pft., Vn. & Cello — 1st Movement — M996

2nd Movement — M997

3rd Movement — M998

Trio in E. K 542, Pft., Vn. & Cello — 1st Movement — M999

2nd Movement — M1000

3rd Movement — M1001

Trio in C, K 548, Pft., Vn. & Cello — 1st Movement — M1002

2nd Movement — M1003

3rd Movement — M1004

Trio in G, K 564, Pft., Vn. & Cello — 1st Movement — M1005

2nd Movement — M1006

3rd Movement — M1007

Variations in C, K 265, Pft. Theme: "Ah, Vous Dirai-Je, Maman" — M1008

Variations, K 455, Pft., (Theme of Gluck) — M1009

Variations on an Allegretto, in B Flat, K 500, Pft. — M1010

Variations, K 573, Pft., (Theme of Duport) — M1011

MUSSORGSKY, Modest Petrovich (1839-1881)

Boris Godunov
Opera — Prelude — M1012

Coronation Scene
1st Theme — M1013

2nd Theme — M1014

The Fair at Sorochinsk
Opera — Hopak — M1015

Khovantstchina
Opera — I Prelude
1st Theme — M1016

2nd Theme — M1017

II Persian Dance
1st Theme — M1018

2nd Theme — M1019

A Night on Bald Mountain,
Orch. — 1st Theme — M1020

2nd Theme — M1021

3rd Theme — M1022

4th Theme — M1023

5th Theme — M1024

Pictures From an
Exposition, Pft. or Orch. — Intro.
Promenade — M1025

The Gnome
1st Theme — M1026

2nd Theme — M1027

3rd Theme — M1028

II The Old Castle — M1029

III Tuileries,
(Children Quarreling at Play) — M1030

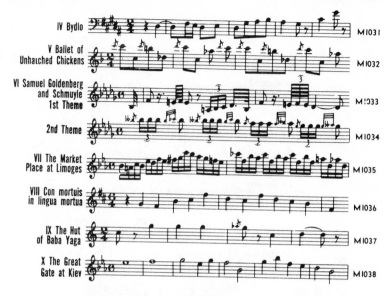

IV Bydlo   M1031

V Ballet of Unhatched Chickens   M1032

VI Samuel Goldenberg and Schmuyle 1st Theme   M1033

2nd Theme   M1034

VII The Market Place at Limoges   M1035

VIII Con mortuis in lingua mortua   M1036

IX The Hut of Baba Yaga   M1037

X The Great Gate at Kiev   M1038

NARDINI, Pietro (1722-1793)

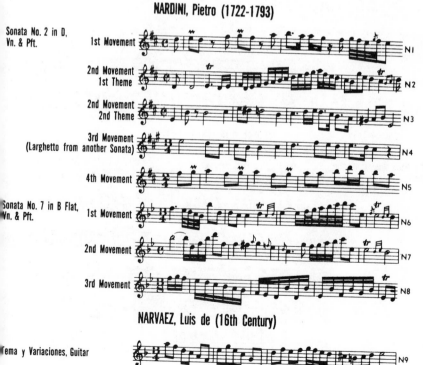

Sonata No. 2 in D, Vn. & Pft.   1st Movement   N1

2nd Movement 1st Theme   N2

2nd Movement 2nd Theme   N3

3rd Movement (Larghetto from another Sonata)   N4

4th Movement   N5

Sonata No. 7 in B Flat, Vn. & Pft.   1st Movement   N6

2nd Movement   N7

3rd Movement   N8

NARVAEZ, Luis de (16th Century)

Tema y Variaciones, Guitar   N9

NEVIN, Ethelbert (1862-1901)

Barchetta, Op. 21, No. 3, Pft.
By permission of The Boston Music Co.,
copyright owner.

N10

A Day in Venice,
Op. 25, Pft.
Published and copyrighted (1898)
by The John Church Co.
Used by permission.

1st Movement
Dawn
Intro.

N11

Theme

N12

2nd Movement
Gondolieri

N13

3rd Movement
Venetian Love Song
1st Theme

N14

2nd Theme

N15

4th Movement
Good Night

N16

Lullaby, Op. 16, No. 3, Pft.
By permission of The Boston Music Co.,
copyright owner.

N17

Narcissus, Op. 13, No. 4, Pft. 1st Theme
By permission of The Boston Music Co.,
copyright owner.

N18

2nd Theme

N19

A Shepherd's Tale, Op. 16, No. 1, Pft.
By permission of The Boston Music Co.,
copyright owner.

N20

NICOLAI, Otto (1810-1849)

The Merry Wives of Windsor,
Overture

Intro.

N21

1st Theme

N22

2nd Theme

N23

3rd Theme,
A

N24

3rd Theme,
B

N25

4th Theme

N26

NIN, Joaquín (1879-1949)

Vals-Serenata from Chaine de Valses, Pft.
By permission of Associated Music Publishers, Inc.

N27

Danse Ibérienne, Pft.
By permission of Associated Music Publishers, Inc.

1st Theme

N28

2nd Theme

N29

3rd Theme

N30

"1830" Variations sur un Theme Frivole
By permission of Associated Music Publishers, Inc.

N31

Suite Espagnole, Vcl. & Pft.
By permission of Associated Music Publishers, Inc.

1st Movement
Old Castile

N32

2nd Movement
1st Theme
Murciana A

N33

2nd Movement
1st Theme, B

N34

3rd Movement
Asturiana

N35

4th Movement
Andaluza

N36

NIN-KOCHANSKI

Granadina, Vn. & Pft.
By permission of Associated Music Publishers, Inc.

N37

Saeta, Vn. & Pft.
By permission of Associated Music Publishers, Inc.

N38

OFFENBACH, Jacques (1819-1880)

La Belle Hélène, Opera

Overture
1st Theme

O1

2nd Theme

O2

Act II Entr'acte

O3

Act III Entr'acte

O4

La Grande Duchesse de Gerolstein, Opera

Overture
1st Theme

O5

2nd Theme — O26

Act III Entr'acte — O27

Act IV Entr'acte
1st Theme — O28

2nd Theme — O29

Act V Entr'acte
1st Theme — O30

2nd Theme — O31

PACHELBEL, Johann (1653-1706)

Ciacona in D Minor, Organ — P1

Ciacona in F Minor, Organ — P2

Fugue in D Minor, (Dorian), Harpsi. — P3

Magnificat-Fugue, Organ & Harpsi. — P4

Toccata in C, Organ — P5

PADEREWSKI, Ignace Jan (1860-1941)

Chant Sans Paroles, Pft. — P6

Concerto in A Minor,
Op. 17, Pft. & Orch.
By permission of Associated
Music Publishers, Inc.

1st Movement
1st Theme,
A — P7

1st Movement
1st Theme,
B — P8

1st Movement
2nd Theme — P9

2nd Movement — P10

3rd Movement
1st Theme — P11

3rd Movement
2nd Theme — P12

Cracovienne Fantastique, Op. 14, No. 6, Pft.
By permission of Associated Music Publishers, Inc.

1st Theme   P13

2nd Theme   P14

Mélodie, Op. 16, No. 2, Pft.
By permission of Associated Music Publishers, Inc.

P15

Minuet, Op. 14, No. 1, Pft.
Copyright 1899 by G. Schirmer, Inc.

1st Theme, A   P16

1st Theme, B   P17

2nd Theme   P18

3rd Theme   P19

Nocturne, Op. 16, No. 4, Pft.
Copyright 1892 by G. Schirmer, Inc.

P20

PAGANINI, Niccolo (1782-1840)

Caprices, Vn.

Op. 1, No. 3   P21

Op. 1, No. 4   P22

Op. 1, No. 5   P23

Op. 1, No. 6, (Liszt)   P24

Op. 1, No. 7   P25

Op. 1, No. 8   P26

Op. 1, No. 9, "La Chasse" (Liszt)   P27

Op. 1, No. 11   P28

Op. 1, No. 13   P29

Op. 1, No. 14 "Militaire"   P30

Op. 1, No. 15   P31

Theme — P52

Le Streghe, Op. 8, Vn. & Pft.   Intro. — P53

Theme — P54

Sonata No. 11, Op. 3,
No. 5, Vn. & Guitar   1st Movement — P55

2nd Movement — P56

Sonata No. 12, Op. 3,
No. 6, Vn. & Guitar   1st Movement — P57

2nd Movement — P58

PAISIELLO, Giovanni (1740-1816)

Il Barbiere Di Siviglia,
Overture   1st Theme — P59

2nd Theme — P60

PALMGREN, Selim (1878-1951)

Finnish Romance, Op. 78, No. 5,
Vn. & Pft. — P61

May Night, Pft.
By permission of The Boston Music Co.,
copyright owner. — P61a

PARADIES, Pietro Domenico (1707-1791)

Sonata in A,
Pft. or Harpsi.   1st Movement — P62

2nd Movement
Toccata — P63

Sonata in D,
Pft. or Harpsi.   1st Movement
Napolitano — P64

2nd Movement — P65

PARADIS, Marie Therese von (1759-1824)

Sicilienne, Vn. & Pft. — P66

PASQUINI, Bernardo (1637-1710)

Aria, Harpsi. — P67

Aria, Harpsi. — P68

Aria, Harpsi. — P69

Toccata Con Lo Scherzo Del Cuccó
Harpsi. — P70

PERGOLESI, Giovanni (1710-1736)

Concertino in F Minor,
Str. Orch.   1st Movement — P71

2nd Movement — P72

3rd Movement — P73

4th Movement — P74

PESCETTI, Giovanni (1704-1766)

Sonata in C Minor,
Harpsi.   1st Movement — P75

2nd Movement — P76

3rd Movement — P77

PFITZNER, Hans Eric (1869-1949)

Palestrina, Musical Legend
Prelude to Act I   1st Theme — P78
By permission of Associated
Music Publishers, Inc.

2nd Theme — P79

3rd Theme — P80

Prelude to Act II   1st Theme — P81

2nd Theme — P82

Prelude to Act III — 1st Theme — P83

2nd Theme — P84

PHILIPS, Peter (1560-1633)

Galliardo, Harpsi. — P85

PICK-MANGIAGALLI, Riccardo (1882-1949)

Il Carillon Magico, (Ballet)
Copyright 1920 by
G. Ricordi & Co., Inc. — Intermezzo delle Rose — P86

La Danse d'Olaf,
Op. 33, No. 2
Orch. or Pft.
Copyright 1916 by
G. Ricordi & Co., Inc. — 1st Theme — P87

2nd Theme — P88

Notturno, Op. 28, No. 1,
Orch.
Copyright 1923 by
G. Ricordi & Co., Inc. — 1st Theme — P89

2nd Theme — P90

I Piccoli Soldati, Orch.
Copyright by G. Ricordi
& Co., Inc. — 1st Theme — P91

2nd Theme — P92

Rondo Fantastico, Op. 28,
No. 2, Orch.
Copyright by G. Ricordi
& Co., Inc. — 1st Theme — P93

2nd Theme — P94

3rd Theme — P95

PIERNÉ, Gabriel (1863-1937)

Cydalise et le Chèvre-pied,
Ballet Suite, Orch.
By permission of the
copyright owner,
Heugel Ltd., London. — March of the Little Fauns 1st Theme. A — P96

1st Theme. B — P97

Dance Lesson in the Hypo-Lydian Mode — P98

Finale — P99

Impressions de Music Hall, Ballet, Op. 47 — Chorus Girls 1st Theme — P100

2nd Theme — P101

L'excentrique 1st Theme — P102

2nd Theme — P103

Spanish Routine 1st Theme — P104

2nd Theme — P105

Musical Clowns (The Fratellinis) 1st Theme — P106

2nd Theme — P107

Sonata da Camera, Op. 48, Fl., Vcl. & Pft.
Permission for reprint granted by Durand & Cie, Paris.
Elkan-Vogel Co., Philadelphia, Copyright Owners, Inc.

Prelude 1st Theme — P108

2nd Theme — P109

Sarabande 1st Theme — P110

2nd Theme — P111

Finale 1st Theme — P112

2nd Theme — P113

PISTON, Walter (1894-   )

Concertino Pft. & Orch.
Copyright 1938.
by Arrow Music Press, Inc., N. Y.

1st Theme — P113a

2nd Theme — P113b

3rd Theme — P113c

The Incredible Flutist, Suite from Ballet
Copyright by Arrow Music Press, Inc., N. Y.

Intro. — P114

1st Theme — P115

2nd Theme ... P116

3rd Theme ... P117

4th Theme ... P118

5th Theme ... P119

6th Theme ... P120

7th Theme ... P121

8th Theme ... P122

9th Theme ... P123

10th Theme ... P124

Quartet No. 1, Str.
Copyright Cos Cob
Press, Inc.

1st Movement
1st Theme,
A ... P125

1st Movement
1st Theme,
B ... P126

1st Movement
2nd Theme,
A ... P127

1st Movement
2nd Theme,
B ... P128

2nd Movement
1st Theme,
A ... P129

2nd Movement
1st Theme,
B ... P130

3rd Movement
1st Theme ... P131

3rd Movement
2nd Theme ... P132

Suite for Oboe
and Pft.
Copyright 1934 by
E. C. Schirmer, Boston.

1st Movement
Prelude ... P133

2nd Movement
Sarabande ... P134

3rd Movement
Minuet ... P135

4th Movement Nocturne — P136

5th Movement Gigue — P137

PIZZETTI, Ildebrando (1880-1968)

Sonata in A, Vn. & Pft.
By permission of the copyright holders,
J. & W. Chester, Ltd., 11 Great Marlborough Street, London, W. 1.

1st Movement 1st Theme, A — P138

1st Movement 1st Theme, B — P139

1st Movement 2nd Theme — P140

2nd Movement Prayer for the Innocent — P141

3rd Movement 1st Theme — P142

3rd Movement 2nd Theme — P143

Tre Canti (Three Songs), Vn. & Pft.
Copyright 1925 by G. Ricordi & Co., Inc.

No. 1 — P144

No. 2 — P145

No. 3 — P146

PLATTI, Giovanni (1690-1762)

Sonata No. 1 in E Minor, Fl. or Vn. & Pft.

1st Movement — P147

2nd Movement — P148

3rd Movement Minuet 1st Theme — P149

3rd Movement 2nd Theme — P150

4th Movement Gigue — P151

POLDINI, Eduard (1869-1957)

Poupée Valsante (Dancing Doll), Pft.

1st Theme — P152

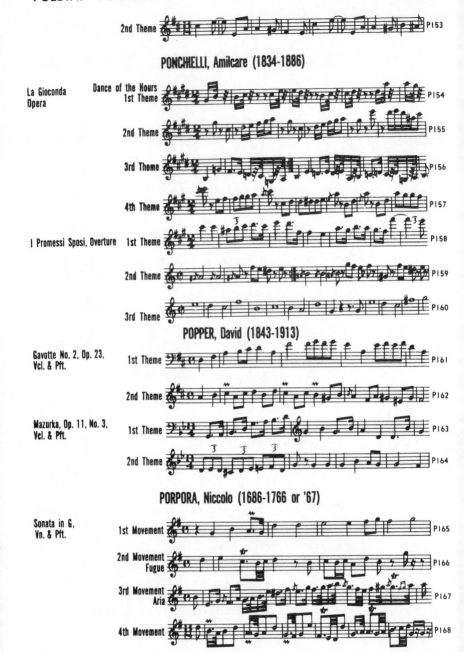

2nd Theme — P153

PONCHIELLI, Amilcare (1834-1886)

La Gioconda
Opera

Dance of the Hours
1st Theme — P154

2nd Theme — P155

3rd Theme — P156

4th Theme — P157

I Promessi Sposi, Overture   1st Theme — P158

2nd Theme — P159

3rd Theme — P160

POPPER, David (1843-1913)

Gavotte No. 2, Op. 23,
Vcl. & Pft.
1st Theme — P161

2nd Theme — P162

Mazurka, Op. 11, No. 3,
Vcl. & Pft.
1st Theme — P163

2nd Theme — P164

PORPORA, Niccolo (1686-1766 or '67)

Sonata in G,
Vn. & Pft.
1st Movement — P165

2nd Movement
Fugue — P166

3rd Movement
Aria — P167

4th Movement — P168

POULENC, Francis (1899-1963)

Mouvements Perpétuels, Pft.
By permission of the copyright holders,
J. & W. Chester, Ltd., 11 Great Marlborough Street, London, W. 1.

No. 1 — P169

No. 2 — P170

No. 3 1st Theme — P171

2nd Theme — P172

Novelette No. 1, Pft.
By permission of the copyright holders,
J. & W. Chester, Ltd., 11 Great Marlborough Street, London, W. 1.

1st Theme — P173

2nd Theme — P174

Novelette No. 2, Pft.
By permission of the copyright holders,
J. & W. Chester, Ltd., 11 Great Marlborough Street, London, W. 1.

1st Theme — P175

2nd Theme — P176

Toccata, Pft.
By permission of the copyright owner.
Heugel Ltd., London.

Intro. — P177

1st Theme — P178

PROKOFIEFF, Serge (1891-1953)

Alexander Nevsky, Cantata for Solo, Chorus and Orch., Op. 78
Copyright 1945 by Leeds Music Corp., N. Y. Reprinted here by permission of the copyright owner.

1st Movement — P179

2nd Movement 1st Theme — P180

2nd Movement 2nd Theme — P181

3rd Movement 1st Theme — P182

3rd Movement 2nd Theme — P183

4th Movement 1st Theme — P184

4th Movement 2nd Theme — P185

4th Movement 3rd Theme — P186

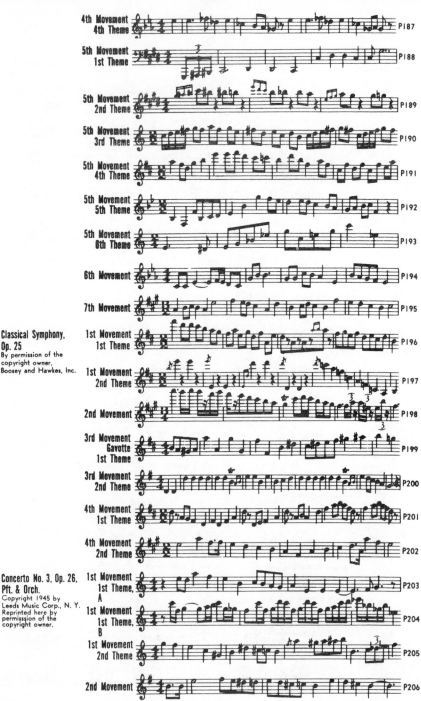

Classical Symphony,
Op. 25
By permission of the
copyright owner,
Boosey and Hawkes, Inc.

Concerto No. 3, Op. 26,
Pft. & Orch.
Copyright 1945 by
Leeds Music Corp., N. Y.
Reprinted here by
permission of the
copyright owner.

4th Movement
4th Theme   P187

5th Movement
1st Theme   P188

5th Movement
2nd Theme   P189

5th Movement
3rd Theme   P190

5th Movement
4th Theme   P191

5th Movement
5th Theme   P192

5th Movement
6th Theme   P193

6th Movement   P194

7th Movement   P195

1st Movement
1st Theme   P196

1st Movement
2nd Theme   P197

2nd Movement   P198

3rd Movement
Gavotte
1st Theme   P199

3rd Movement
2nd Theme   P200

4th Movement
1st Theme   P201

4th Movement
2nd Theme   P202

1st Movement
1st Theme,
A   P203

1st Movement
1st Theme,
B   P204

1st Movement
2nd Theme   P205

2nd Movement   P206

3rd Movement 1st Theme — P207

3rd Movement 2nd Theme — P208

Concerto No. 1, Op. 19, Vn. & Orch.
By permission of the copyright owner, Boosey and Hawkes, Inc.

1st Movement — P209

2nd Movement 1st Theme — P210

2nd Movement 2nd Theme — P211

3rd Movement 1st Theme — P212

3rd Movement 2nd Theme — P213

Concerto No. 2, Op. 63, Vn. & Orch.
By permission of International Music Co.

1st Movement 1st Theme — P214

1st Movement 2nd Theme — P215

2nd Movement 1st Theme — P216

2nd Movement 2nd Theme — P217

3rd Movement 1st Theme — P218

3rd Movement 2nd Theme — P219

3rd Movement 3rd Theme — P220

Contes de la Vieille Grand'mère, Pft.
Op. 31, No. 2
By permission of the copyright owner, Boosey and Hawkes, Inc.

Op. 31, No. 3 — P221, P222

Gavotte, Op. 12, No. 2, Pft. — P223

Gavotte, Op. 32, No. 3, Pft.
By permission of the copyright owner, Boosey and Hawkes, Inc.

Lieutenant Kije, Op. 60, Orch.
By permission of Broude Brothers

1st Movement Birth of Kije 1st Theme — P225

1st Movement 2nd Theme — P226

1st Movement
3rd Theme — P227

2nd Movement
Romance
1st Theme — P228

2nd Movement
2nd Theme — P229

2nd Movement
3rd Theme — P230

3rd Movement
Kije's Wedding
1st Theme — P231

3rd Movement
2nd Theme — P232

4th Movement
Troika — P233

Love of Three Oranges, Op. 33
Opera
By permission of the
copyright owner,
Boosey and Hawkes, Inc.

March — P234

Scherzo — P235

March, Op. 12, No. 1, Pft. — P236

Music for Children, Op. 65, Pft.
Copyright 1946 by Leeds
Music Corp., N. Y.
Reprinted here by permission
of the copyright owner.

March — P237

Waltz — P238

Overture on Hebrew Themes,
Op. 34, Cl., Pft. &
Str. Quartet
By permission of the
copyright owner,
Boosey and Hawkes, Inc.

1st Theme — P239

2nd Theme — P240

Peter and the Wolf,
Op. 67, Orch.
Copyright 1946 by
Leeds Music Corp., N. Y.
Reprinted here by
permission of the
copyright owner.

1st Theme
Peter — P241

2nd Theme
The Bird — P242

3rd Theme
The Duck — P243

4th Theme
The Cat — P244

5th Theme
The Grandfather — P245

6th Theme
The Wolf — P246

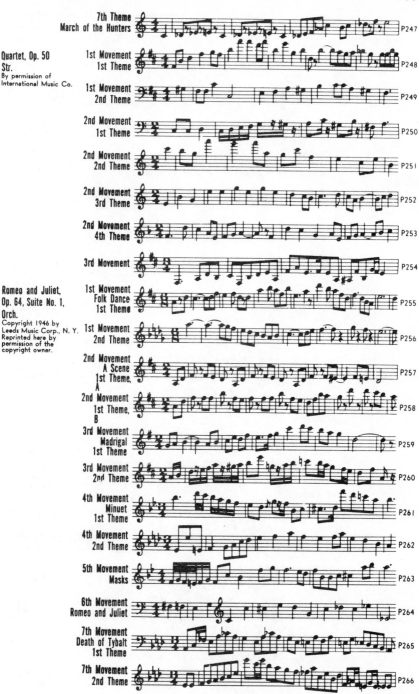

7th Theme
March of the Hunters   P247

Quartet, Op. 50
Str.
By permission of
International Music Co.

1st Movement
1st Theme   P248

1st Movement
2nd Theme   P249

2nd Movement
1st Theme   P250

2nd Movement
2nd Theme   P251

2nd Movement
3rd Theme   P252

2nd Movement
4th Theme   P253

3rd Movement   P254

Romeo and Juliet,
Op. 64, Suite No. 1,
Orch.
Copyright 1946 by
Leeds Music Corp., N. Y.
Reprinted here by
permission of the
copyright owner.

1st Movement
Folk Dance
1st Theme   P255

1st Movement
2nd Theme   P256

2nd Movement
A Scene
1st Theme,
A   P257

2nd Movement
1st Theme,
B   P258

3rd Movement
Madrigal
1st Theme   P259

3rd Movement
2nd Theme   P260

4th Movement
Minuet
1st Theme   P261

4th Movement
2nd Theme   P262

5th Movement
Masks   P263

6th Movement
Romeo and Juliet   P264

7th Movement
Death of Tybalt
1st Theme   P265

7th Movement
2nd Theme   P266

7th Movement 3rd Theme — P267

Romeo and Juliet, Op. 64, Suite No. 2, Orch.
Copyright 1946 by Leeds Music Corp., N. Y. Reprinted here by permission of the copyright owner.

1st Movement, The Montagues and the Capulets, 1st Theme — P268

1st Movement 2nd Theme — P269

1st Movement 3rd Theme — P270

2nd Movement, Juliet—The Little Girl, 1st Theme — P271

2nd Movement 2nd Theme — P272

2nd Movement 3rd Theme, A — P273

2nd Movement 3rd Theme, B — P274

3rd Movement Friar Lawrence 1st Theme — P275

3rd Movement 2nd Theme — P276

4th Movement Dance — P277

5th Movement, Romeo and Juliet Before Parting, 1st Theme — P278

5th Movement 2nd Theme — P279

5th Movement 3rd Theme — P280

6th Movement Dance of the Maids From the Antilles — P281

7th Movement Romeo at Juliet's Grave — P282

Sonata No. 6, Op. 82, Pft.
Copyright 1946 by Leeds Music Corp., N. Y. Reprinted here by permisssion of the copyright owner.

1st Movement 1st Theme — P283

1st Movement 2nd Theme — P284

2nd Movement 1st Theme — P285

2nd Movement 2nd Theme — P286

Suggestion Diabolique, Op. 4, No. 4,
Pft.

Symphony No. 5
in B Flat, Op. 100

1st Movement 1st Theme — P307
1st Movement 2nd Theme — P308
1st Movement 3rd Theme — P309
1st Movement 4th Theme — P310
2nd Movement 1st Theme — P311
2nd Movement 2nd Theme — P312
2nd Movement 3rd Theme — P313
3rd Movement 1st Theme — P314
3rd Movement 2nd Theme A — P315
3rd Movement 2nd Theme B — P316
3rd Movement — P317
4th Movement 1st Theme — P318
4th Movement 2nd Theme — P319
4th Movement 3rd Theme — P320

PUGNANI, Gaetano (1731-1798)

Sonata in E, No. 1, Vn. & Pft.

1st Movement — P321
2nd Movement — P322
3rd Movement — P323

PURCELL, Henry (c. 1659-1695)

Bonduca, or
The British Heroine
Opera

Air No. 1 — P324

Hornpipe — P325
Air No. 2 — P326

Dido and Aeneas
Opera

Overture 1st Theme — P327
2nd Theme — P328
The Triumphing Dance — P329
Sailor's Dance — P330

Fairy Queen
Opera

Hornpipe — P331
Rondeau — P332
Jig — P333
The Monkey's Dance — P334

Three-Part Fantasia, No. 3, Str. — P335
Four-Part Fantasia, No. 1, Str. — P336
Four-Part Fantasia, No. 4, Str. — P337
Four-Part Fantasia, No. 9, Str. — P338
A New Irish Tune (Lillibullero), Harpsi. — P339

Sonata No. 3, in A Minor,
2 Vns. & Harpsi.

1st Movement — P340
2nd Movement — P341
3rd Movement — P342
4th Movement — P343
5th Movement — P344

Sonata No. 6, in G Minor (also known as Chacony) 2 Vns. & Harpsi. — P345

Ground Bass — P346

Sonata No. 9, in F, "Golden Sonata", 2 Vns. & Harpsi.

1st Movement — P347

2nd Movement — P348

3rd Movement — P349

4th Movement — P350

5th Movement — P351

Suite No. 1 in G, Harpsi.

Prelude — P352

Almand — P353

Courant — P354

Minuet — P355

Suite No. 2 in G Minor, Harpsi.

Prelude — P356

Almand — P357

Courant — P358

Saraband — P359

Suite No. 7 in D Minor, Harpsi.

Almand — P360

Courant — P361

Hornpipe — P362

Suite in G Minor, Harpsi.

Overture — P363

Air — P364

Jig  P365

QUANTZ, Johann (1697-1773)

Concerto in G, Fl. & Str.

1st Movement
1st Theme,
A

1st Movement
1st Theme,
B

2nd Movement
Arioso

3rd Movement

QUILTER, Roger (1877-1953)

A Children's Overture, Orch.

1st Theme
Girls & Boys, Come Out to Play

2nd Theme
Upon Paul's Steeple Stands a Tree

3rd Theme
Dance, Get Up and Bake Your Pies

4th Theme
I Saw Three Ships Go Sailing By

5th Theme
Sing a Song of Sixpence

6th Theme
There Was a Lady Loved a Swine

7th Theme
Over the Hills and Far Away

8th Theme
The Frog and the Crow

9th Theme
A Frog He Would A-Wooing Go

10th Theme
Baa, Baa, Black Sheep

11th Theme
Here We Go Round the Mulberry Bush

12th Theme
Oranges and Lemons

RACHMANINOFF, Sergei (1873-1943)

**Concerto No. 1, in
F Sharp Minor, Op. 1,
Pft. & Orch.**
By permission of the
copyright owner,
Boosey and Hawkes, Inc.

1st Movement 1st Theme	R1
1st Movement 2nd Theme	R2
2nd Movement	R3
3rd Movement 1st Theme	R4
3rd Movement 2nd Theme	R5
3rd Movement 3rd Theme	R6

**Concerto No. 2, in
C Minor, Op. 18,
Pft. & Orch.**

1st Movement 1st Theme	R7
1st Movement 2nd Theme	R8
2nd Movement 1st Theme, A	R9
2nd Movement 1st Theme, B	R10
3rd Movement 1st Theme	R11
3rd Movement 2nd Theme	R12

**Concerto No. 3, Op. 30,
Pft. & Orch.**
By permission of the
copyright owner,
Boosey and Hawkes, Inc.

1st Movement 1st Theme	R13
1st Movement 2nd Theme	R14
2nd Movement 1st Theme	R15
2nd Movement 2nd Theme	R16
3rd Movement 1st Theme	R17
3rd Movement 2nd Theme	R18
3rd Movement 3rd Theme	R19

Elégie. Op. 3, No. 1, Pft. 1st Theme R20

2nd Theme R21

Etude Tableau, Op. 33, No. 1, Pft.
By permission of
International Music Co. R22

Etude Tableau, Op. 33, No. 2, Pft.
By permission of
International Music Co. R23

Fantasy, Suite No. 1,
Op. 5, 2 Pfts., 4 Hands
By permission of the
copyright owner,
Boosey and Hawkes, Inc. 1st Movement
Barcarolle
1st Theme R24

1st Movement
2nd Theme R25

2nd Movement
A Night for Love R26

3rd Movement
Tears R27

4th Movement
A Russian Easter
1st Theme R28

4th Movement
2nd Theme R29

The Isle of the Dead,
Op. 29, Orch.
By permission of
International Music Co. 1st Theme R30

2nd Theme R31

Mélodie, Op. 3, No. 3, Pft.
Copyright by
Charles Foley,
New York R32

Moment Musical, Op. 16, No. 2, Pft.
Copyright by
Charles Foley,
New York R33

Polichinelle, Op. 3,
No. 4, Pft.
By permission of the
copyright owner,
Boosey and Hawkes, Inc. 1st Theme R34

2nd Theme R35

Preludes, Pft.
Op. 3, No. 2,
(Famous C Sharp Minor)
Copyright renewal assigned
1925 to G. Schirmer, Inc. 1st Theme R36

2nd Theme R37

Op. 23, No. 1
Copyright renewal assigned
1925 to G. Schirmer, Inc. R38

No. 2 R39

No. 3 — R40
No. 4 — R41
No. 5 — 1st Theme — R42
2nd Theme — R43
No. 6 — R44
No. 7 — R45
No. 8 — R46
No. 9 — R47
No. 10 — R48
Op. 32, No. 5
By permission of the copyright owner, Boosey and Hawkes, Inc.
No. 10 — R49
No. 10 — R50
No. 12 — R51
Serenade, Op. 3, No. 5
Copyright by Charles Foley, New York
Sonata in G Minor, Op. 19, Vcl. & Pft.
By permission of International Music Co.
R52
1st Movement 1st Theme — R53
1st Movement 2nd Theme — R54
2nd Movement 1st Theme — R55
2nd Movement 2nd Theme — R56
2nd Movement 3rd Theme — R57
3rd Movement — R58
4th Movement 1st Theme — R59

4th Movement
2nd Theme — R60

Suite No. 2, Op. 17,
2 Pfts., 4 Hands
By permission of
International Music Co.

1st Movement
Intro. — R61

2nd Movement
Valse
1st Theme — R62

2nd Movement
2nd Theme — R63

2nd Movement
3rd Theme — R64

3rd Movement
Romance — R65

4th Movement
Tarantelle (Italian Folksong) — R66

Symphony No. 2 in
E Minor, Op. 27
By permission of the
copyright owner,
Boosey and Hawkes, Inc.

1st Movement
1st Theme — R67

1st Movement
2nd Theme — R68

2nd Movement
1st Theme — R69

2nd Movement
2nd Theme — R70

3rd Movement
Intro. — R71

3rd Movement
1st Theme — R72

3rd Movement
2nd Theme — R73

4th Movement
1st Theme — R74

4th Movement
2nd Theme — R75

Waltz, Op. 10, No. 2, Pft.
By permission of the
copyright owner,
Boosey and Hawkes, Inc. — R76

RAFF, Joseph Joachim (1822-1882)

Cavatina, Op. 85, No. 3, Vn. & Pft. — R77

La Fileuse, Op. 157, No. 2, Pft. — R78

RAMEAU, Jean Philippe (1683-1764)

Castor et Pollux, Opera	Gavotte No. 1	R79
	Gavotte No. 2	R80
	Minuet No. 1	R81
	Minuet No. 2	R82
	Passepied No. 1	R83
	Passepied No. 2	R84
Dardanus, Opera	Rigaudon No. 1	R85
	Air en Rondeau	R86
	Rigaudon No. 2	R87
Les Fêtes de Hébé Opera	Tambourin	R88
	Musette	R89
La Follette, Harpsi.		R90
Gavotte Variée, Harpsi.		R91
L'Indifferente, Harpsi.		R92
La Joyeuse, Harpsi.	1st Theme	R93
	1st Theme	R94
Minuet No. 1, Harpsi.		R95
Minuet No. 2, Harpsi.		R96
Pièces de Clavecin en Concert, No. 3, Fl., Vn. & Harpsi.	La Timide	R97

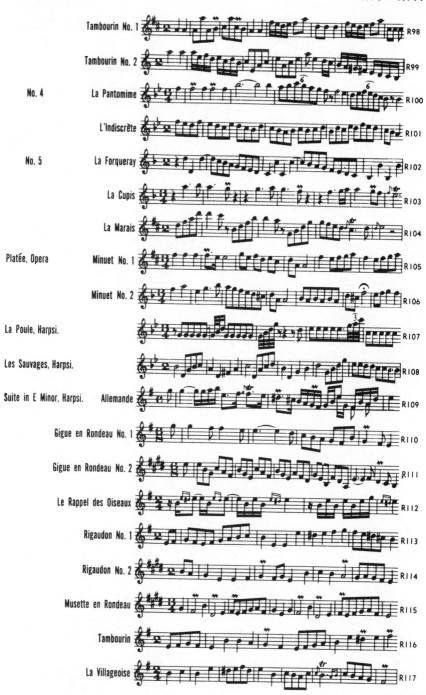

Tambourin No. 1   R98
Tambourin No. 2   R99
No. 4   La Pantomime   R100
L'Indiscrète   R101
No. 5   La Forqueray   R102
La Cupis   R103
La Marais   R104
Platée, Opera   Minuet No. 1   R105
Minuet No. 2   R106
La Poule, Harpsi.   R107
Les Sauvages, Harpsi.   R108
Suite in E Minor, Harpsi.   Allemande   R109
Gigue en Rondeau No. 1   R110
Gigue en Rondeau No. 2   R111
Le Rappel des Oiseaux   R112
Rigaudon No. 1   R113
Rigaudon No. 2   R114
Musette en Rondeau   R115
Tambourin   R116
La Villageoise   R117

Les Tendres Plaintes, Harpsi. R118

Les Tourbillons, Harpsi. R119

Les Tricotets, Harpsi. R120

Les Triolets, Harpsi. R121

La Triompante, Harpsi. R122

RAVEL, Maurice (1875-1937)

Alborada Del Graciosa (Miroirs No. 4), Pft.
By permission of Associated Music Publishers, Inc.
Theme, A R123
Theme, B R124

Bolero, Orch.
Permission for reprint granted by Durand & Cie, Paris. Elkan-Vogel Co., Inc. Philadelphia, Copyright Owners.
Theme, A R125
Theme, B R126

Concerto, Pft. & Orch.
Permission for reprint granted by Durand & Cie, Paris. Elkan-Vogel Co., Inc. Philadelphia, Copyright Owners.
1st Movement 1st Theme R127
1st Movement 2nd Theme R128
2nd Movement R129
3rd Movement 1st Theme R130
3rd Movement 2nd Theme R131

Concerto for the Left Hand, Pft. & Orch.
Permission for reprint granted by Durand & Cie, Paris. Elkan-Vogel Co., Inc. Philadelphia, Copyright Owners.
1st Theme, A R132
1st Theme, B R133
2nd Theme R134

Daphnis et Chloe, Ballet Suite No. 1, Orch.
Permission for reprint granted by Durand & Cie, Paris. Elkan-Vogel Co., Inc. Philadelphia, Copyright Owners.
1st Theme R135
2nd Theme R136

Daphnis et Chloe, Ballet Suite No. 2, Orch.
Permission for reprint granted by Durand & Cie, Paris. Elkan-Vogel Co.,Inc. Philadelphia, Copyright Owners,

Gaspard de la Nuit, Pft.
Permission for reprint granted by Durand & Cie, Paris. Elkan-Vogel Co.,Inc. Philadelphia, Copyright Owners,

Introduction and Allegro, Harp, Str. Quart., Fl. & Cl.
Permission for reprint granted by Durand & Cie, Paris. Elkan-Vogel Co., Inc., Philadelphia, Copyright Owners.

Jeux D'Eau, Pft.
Copyright 1930 by Edward B. Marks Music Co. Copyright Assigned 1932 to Edward B. Marks Music Corp. Used by Permission

Ma Mère L'Oye,
(Mother Goose Suite)
Orch.
Permission for
reprint granted
by Durand & Cie,
Paris. Elkan-Vogel Co.,
Inc., Philadelphia,
Copyright
Owners.

Pavane of the
Sleeping Beauty
(Pavane de la
Belle au Bois Dormant)

R157

Hop O' My Thumb
(Petit Poucet)

R158

Empress of the Pagodas
(Laideronnette,
Impératrice des Pagodes)

R159

Beauty and the Beast
(Les Entretiens,
de la Belle et de la Bête)

R160

The Enchanted Garden
(La Jardin Féerique)

R161

Pavane for a Dead Infanta,
Small Orch. or Pft.
By permission of Associated
Music Publishers, Inc.

R162

Quartet in F,
Str.
By permission of
International Music Co.

1st Movement
1st Theme

R163

1st Movement
2nd Theme

R164

2nd Movement
Intro.

R165

2nd Movement
1st Theme

R166

2nd Movement
2nd Theme

R167

3rd Movement
1st Theme

R168

3rd Movement
2nd Theme

R169

4th Movement

R170

Rapsodie Espagnole,
Orch.
Permission for reprint
granted by Durand &
Cie, Paris. Elkan-Vogel
Co., Inc. Philadelphia,
Copyright Owners,

1st Movement
Prélude à la Nuit

R171

2nd Movement
Malagueña
Intro.

R172

2nd Movement
1st Theme

R173

2nd Movement
2nd Theme

R174

3rd Movement
Habañera
1st Theme

R175

3rd Movement
2nd Theme

R176

3rd Movement
3rd Theme — R177

4th Movement
Feria
1st Theme — R178

4th Movement
2nd Theme,
A — R179

4th Movement
2nd Theme,
B — R180

4th Movement
3rd Theme — R181

Sonatine, Pft.
Permission for reprint
granted by Durand &
Cie, Paris. Elkan-Vogel
Co., Inc. Philadelphia,
Copyright Owners.

1st Movement
1st Theme — R182

1st Movement
2nd Theme — R183

2nd Movement — R184

3rd Movement
1st Theme — R185

3rd Movement
2nd Theme — R186

Le Tombeau de Couperin,
Pft. or Orch.
Permission for reprint
granted by Durand &
Cie, Paris. Elkan-Vogel
Co., Inc. Philadelphia,
Copyright Owners.

Prelude — R187

Fugue — R188

Forlane
1st Theme — R189

2nd Theme — R190

Rigaudon
1st Theme — R191

2nd Theme — R192

Minuet
1st Theme — R193

2nd Theme — R194

Toccata
1st Theme — R195

2nd Theme — R196

Tzigane, Vn. & Orch.
Permission for reprint granted by Durand & Cie, Paris. Elkan-Vogel Co.,Inc. Philadelphia, Copyright Owners.

Intro. Cadenza — R197
1st Theme — R198
1st Theme — R199
2nd Theme — R200
3rd Theme — R201

La Valse, Orch.
Permission for reprint granted by Durand & Cie, Paris. Elkan-Vogel Co.,Inc. Philadelphia, Copyright Owners.

1st Theme — R202
2nd Theme — R203
3rd Theme — R204
4th Theme — R205
5th Theme — R206
6th Theme — R207
7th Theme — R208
8th Theme — R209

Valses Nobles et Sentimentales Pft. or Orch.
Permission for reprint granted by Durand & Cie, Paris. Elkan-Vogel Co., Inc. Philadelphia, Copyright Owners.

No. 1 — R210
No. 2 — R211
No. 3 — R212
No. 4 — R213
No. 5 — R214
No. 6 — R215
No. 7 — R216

No. 8  R217

REBIKOFF, Vladimir (1866-1920)

The Christmas Tree, Opera — Dance of the Dolls, 1st Theme — R218

2nd Theme — R219

March of the Gnomes, 1st Theme — R220

2nd Theme — R221

Dance of the Chinese Dolls — R222

REGER, Max (1873-1916)

Balletmusik, Op. 130
By Permission of C. F. Peters,
Clayton F. Summy Co., Chicago, — Waltz — R223

Finale — R224

Gavotte, Op. 82, No 5, Pft.
By permission of Associated
Music Publishers, Inc. — R225

Konzert im Alten Stil,
Op. 123, Orch.
By permission of Associated
Music Publishers, Inc. — 1st Movement — R226

2nd Movement — R227

3rd Movement — R228

Quintet, in A,
Op. 146, Cl. & Str. Quart.
By permission of Associated
Music Publishers, Inc. — 1st Movement 1st Theme — R229

1st Movement 2nd Theme — R230

2nd Movement 1st Theme — R231

2nd Movement 2nd Theme — R232

3rd Movement — R233

4th Movement — R234

Romance, Op. 87, No. 2, Vn. & Pft. — R235

Serenade, Op. 77a, Fl., Vn. & Vla. — 1st Movement — R236

2nd Movement — R237

3rd Movement 1st Theme — R238

3rd Movement 2nd Theme — R239

Suite in A Minor, Op. 193a, Vn. & Pft. By permission of Associated Music Publishers, Inc. — 1st Movement Präludium — R240

2nd Movement Gavotte 1st Theme — R241

2nd Movement 2nd Theme — R242

3rd Movement Aria — R243

4th Movement Burleske — R244

5th Movement Minuet 1st Theme — R245

5th Movement 2nd Theme — R246

6th Movement Gigue — R247

RESPIGHI, Ottorino (1879-1936)

Adagio con Variazioni, Vcl. & Pft. — R248

Antiche Danze Ed Arie Per Liuto Copyright 1920 by G. Ricordi & Co., Inc. — 1st Movement Balletto "Il Conte Orlando" (After Simone Molinaro) — R249

Suite No 1, Orch. 2nd Movement Gagliarda (After Vincenzo Galilei) 1st Theme — R250

2nd Movement 2nd Theme — R251

3rd Movement Villanella (After Ignoto) 1st Theme — R252

3rd Movement 2nd Theme — R253

4th Movement
Passo Mezzo e Mascherada (Ignoto)
1st Theme — R254

4th Movement
2nd Theme — R255

4th Movement
3rd Theme — R256

4th Movement
4th Theme — R257

Suite No. 2, Orch.
Copyright 1924 by
G. Ricordi & Co.,
Inc.
1st Movement
Laura Soave
(After Carosio)
1st Theme — R258

1st Movement
2nd Theme — R259

1st Movement
3rd Theme — R260

2nd Movement
Danza Rustica (After Besardo) — R261

3rd Movement
1st Theme
Campanae Parisienses (Author Unknown) — R262

3rd Movement
2nd Theme
Aria (After Mersenne Marin) — R263

4th Movement
Bergamasca (After Bernardo Gianoncelli) — R264

Suite No. 3, Orch.
Copyright 1932
by G. Ricordi Italiana (After Ignoto)
& Co., Inc.
1st Movement — R265

2nd Movement
Arie di Corte (After Besardo)
1st Theme — R266

2nd Movement
2nd Theme — R267

3rd Movement
Siciliano (After Ignoto) — R268

4th Movement
Passacaglia (After Roncalli) — R269

Fountains of Rome, Orch.
Copyright 1918 by G. Ricordi & Co., Inc.
The Fountain of Valle Giulia at Dawn
1st Theme — R270

2nd Theme — R271

The Triton Fountain at Morning — R272

The Fountains of Trevi at Mid-day — R273

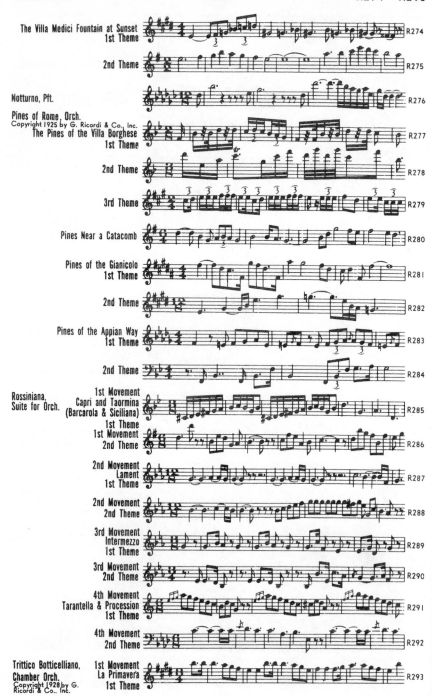

The Villa Medici Fountain at Sunset
1st Theme — R274

2nd Theme — R275

Notturno, Pft. — R276

Pines of Rome, Orch.
Copyright 1925 by G. Ricordi & Co., Inc.
The Pines of the Villa Borghese
1st Theme — R277

2nd Theme — R278

3rd Theme — R279

Pines Near a Catacomb — R280

Pines of the Gianicolo
1st Theme — R281

2nd Theme — R282

Pines of the Appian Way
1st Theme — R283

2nd Theme — R284

Rossiniana,
Suite for Orch.
1st Movement
Capri and Taormina
(Barcarola & Siciliana)
1st Theme — R285

1st Movement
2nd Theme — R286

2nd Movement
Lament
1st Theme — R287

2nd Movement
2nd Theme — R288

3rd Movement
Intermezzo
1st Theme — R289

3rd Movement
2nd Theme — R290

4th Movement
Tarantella & Procession
1st Theme — R291

4th Movement
2nd Theme — R292

Trittico Botticelliano,
Chamber Orch.
Copyright 1928 by G.
Ricordi & Co., Inc.
1st Movement
La Primavera
1st Theme — R293

1st Movement
2nd Theme   R294

2nd Movement
Adoration of the Magi
1st Theme   R295

2nd Movement
2nd Theme   R296

3rd Movement
The Birth of Venus
1st Theme   R297

3rd Movement
2nd Theme   R298

REYER, Ernest (1823-1909)

Sigurd, Overture
By permission of
the copyright owner,
Heugel & Cie, Paris.
          1st Theme   R299

          2nd Theme   R300

          3rd Theme   R301

REZNIČEK, Emil Nikolaus von (1860-1945)

Donna Diana, Overture
By permission of Associated
Music Publishers, Inc.
          1st Theme   R302

          2nd Theme   R303

RIEGGER, Wallingford (1885-1961)

New Dance, 2 Pfts.
Copyright 1940 by Arrow
Music Press, Inc., N. Y.
                                                                         R303a

Accompanying Figure
A   R303b

Accompanying Figure
B   R303c

RIMSKY-KORSAKOFF, Nicolas (1844-1908)

Antar Symphony, Op. 9
          1st Movement
          Intro.
          1st Theme   R304

          1st Movement
          Intro.
          2nd Theme   R305

          1st Movement
          1st Theme   R306

La Grande Paque Russe,
Overture, Op. 36
By permission of Associated
Music Publishers, Inc.

1st Theme   R327

2nd Theme   R328

3rd Theme   R329

4th Theme   R330

5th Theme   R331

May Night, Overture
By permission of Associated
Music Publishers, Inc.

1st Theme   R332

2nd Theme   R333

3rd Theme   R334

Mlada, Ballet
By permission of
Associated Music
Publishers, Inc.

1st Theme
Cortège des Nobles   R335

2nd Theme   R336

Scheherezade,
Op. 35, Orch.
By permission of Associated
Music Publishers, Inc.

1st Movement
The Sea & Sinbad's Ship
Intro.
A   R337

1st Movement
Intro.
B   R338

1st Movement
1st Theme   R339

1st Movement
2nd Theme   R340

1st Movement
3rd Theme   R341

2nd Movement
The Story of the Kalander Prince
1st Theme, A   R342

2nd Movement
1st Theme, B   R343

2nd Movement
2nd Theme   R344

3rd Movement
The Young Prince & the Young Princess
1st Theme   R345

3rd Movement
2nd Theme   R346

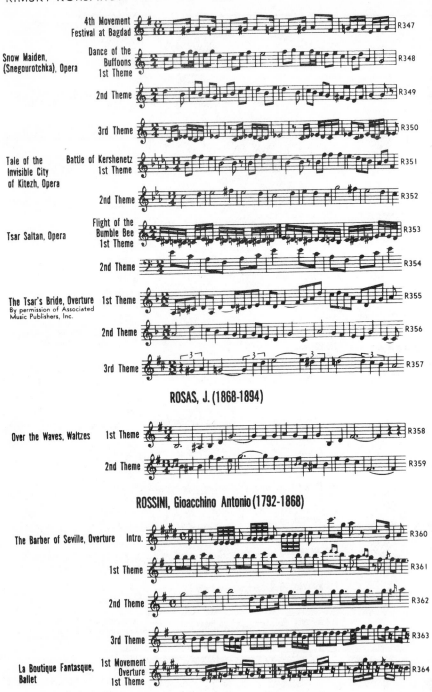

4th Movement
Festival at Bagdad   R347

Snow Maiden,   Dance of the
(Snegourotchka), Opera   Buffoons
                    1st Theme   R348

                    2nd Theme   R349

                    3rd Theme   R350

Tale of the   Battle of Kershenetz
Invisible City   1st Theme   R351
of Kitezh, Opera

                    2nd Theme   R352

Tsar Saltan, Opera Flight of the
                    Bumble Bee
                    1st Theme   R353

                    2nd Theme   R354

The Tsar's Bride, Overture   1st Theme   R355
By permission of Associated
Music Publishers, Inc.

                    2nd Theme   R356

                    3rd Theme   R357

ROSAS, J. (1868-1894)

Over the Waves, Waltzes   1st Theme   R358

                    2nd Theme   R359

ROSSINI, Gioacchino Antonio (1792-1868)

The Barber of Seville, Overture   Intro.   R360

                    1st Theme   R361

                    2nd Theme   R362

                    3rd Theme   R363

La Boutique Fantasque,   1st Movement
Ballet   Overture
                    1st Theme   R364

L'Italiana In Algeri, Overture 1st Theme — R385

2nd Theme — R386

Semiramide, Overture 1st Theme — R387

2nd Theme — R388

3rd Theme — R389

Tancredi, Overture 1st Theme — R390

2nd Theme — R391

William Tell Opera — Overture 1st Theme — R392

2nd Theme — R393

Act 3 Soldier's Ballet 1st Theme — R394

2nd Theme — R395

ROUSSEL, Albert (1869-1937)

Le Festin de L'Araignée, Ballet, Op. 17 — Prelude 1st Theme — R396

Permission for reprint granted by Durand & Cie, Paris. Elkan-Vogel Co., Inc. Philadelphia, Copyright Owners.

2nd Theme — R397

Entrée des Fourmis — R398

Danse du Papillon — R399

Danse de l'Éphémère 1st Theme — R400

2nd Theme — R401

Funerailles de l'Éphémère — R402

La Naissance de la Lyre, Op. 24, Orch. — Danse des Nymphes 1st Theme — R403

Permission for reprint granted by Durand & Cie, Paris. Elkan-Vogel Co., Inc. Philadelphia, Copyright Owners.

2nd Theme

R404

Sinfonietta, Op. 52, Str. Orch.
Permission for reprint granted by Durand & Cie, Paris. Elkan-Vogel Co., Inc. Philadelphia, Copyright Owners.

1st Movement
1st Theme

R405

1st Movement
2nd Theme

R406

2nd Movement

R407

3rd Movement
1st Theme

R408

3rd Movement
2nd Theme

R409

Symphony No. 3 in G Minor, Op. 42
Permission for reprint granted by Durand & Cie, Paris. Elkan-Vogel Co., Inc. Philadelphia, Copyright Owners.

1st Movement
1st Theme

R410

1st Movement
2nd Theme

R411

2nd Movement
1st Theme

R412

2nd Movement
2nd Theme

R413

3rd Movement
1st Theme

R414

3rd Movement
2nd Theme

R415

4th Movement
1st Theme

R416

4th Movement
2nd Theme

R417

Symphony No. 4, Op. 53
Permission for reprint granted by Durand & Cie, Paris. Elkan-Vogel Co., Inc. Philadelphia, Copyright Owners.

1st Movement
1st Theme

R418

1st Movement
2nd Theme

R419

2nd Movement

R420

3rd Movement
1st Theme

R421

3rd Movement
2nd Theme

R422

4th Movement
1st Theme

R423

RUBINSTEIN, Anton (1829-1894)

Barcarolle, Op. 30,
No. 1, Pft.
By permission of Associated
Music Publishers, Inc.

1st Theme — R424

2nd Theme — R425

Concerto No. 4 in
D Minor, Op. 70,
Pft. & Orch.
By permission of
Associated Music
Publishers, Inc.

1st Movement
1st Theme,
A — R426

1st Movement
1st Theme,
B — R427

1st Movement
2nd Theme — R428

2nd Movement — R429

3rd Movement
1st Theme — R430

3rd Movement
2nd Theme — R431

Cracovienne, Op. 5,
No. 3, Pft.

1st Theme — R432

2nd Theme — R433

Etude, Op. 23, No. 2, Pft.
"Staccato"

1st Theme — R434

2nd Theme — R435

Feramors (Lalla Rookh)
Opera
By permission of Associated
Music Publishers, Inc.

Bridal March
1st Theme — R436

2nd Theme — R437

Kamennoi-Ostrow, Op. 10,
No. 22, Pft.

1st Theme — R438

2nd Theme — R439

Melody in F, Op. 3,
No. 1, Pft.

1st Theme — R440

2nd Theme — R441

Romance, Op. 44, No. 1, Pft. 1st Theme — R442

SACCHINI, Antonio (1730-1786)

SAINT-SAËNS, Camille (1835-1921)

2nd Theme — R443

Toreador et Andalouse,
Op. 103, No. 7, from Bal
Costumé, Pft, 4 Hands
By permission of Associated
Music Publishers, Inc.

1st Theme — R444

2nd Theme — R445

Valse in F, Pft.
By permission of Associated
Music Publishers, Inc.

— R446

Valse Caprice, Pft.
By permission of Associated
Music Publishers, Inc.

1st Theme — R447

2nd Theme — R448

3rd Theme — R449

Sonata in F
Harpsi.

1st Movement — S1

2nd Movement
1st Theme — S2

2nd Movement
2nd Theme — S3

Caprice Arabe, Op. 96,
2 Pfts.
Permission for reprint granted
by Durand & Cie, Paris.
Elkan-Vogel Co., Inc.
Philadelphia, Copyright
Owners.

1st Theme — S4

2nd Theme — S5

3rd Theme — S6

Carnaval des Animaux,   Marche Royale
Orch. & 2 Pfts.   du Lion
Permission for reprint granted
by Durand & Cie, Paris.
Elkan-Vogel Co., Inc.
Philadelphia, Copyright
Owners.

— S7

Poules et Coqs — S8

Tortues (Theme from
Orpheus in Hades — Offenbach) — S9

L'Éléphant — S10

Kangorous — S11

No. 3 in B Minor,
Op. 61, Vn. & Orch.
Copyright 1905 by
Carl Fischer, Inc.,
N. Y.

Concertstück, Op. 20,
Vn. & Orch.
By permission of
J. Hamelle Music
Publishers, Paris.

Danse Macabre, Op. 40,
Orch. or 2 Pfts.
Permission for reprint granted
by Durand & Cie, Paris.
Elkan-Vogel Co., Inc.
Philadelphia, Copyright
Owners.

Elégie, Op. 143, Vn. & Pft.
Permission for reprint granted
by Durand & Cie, Paris.
Elkan-Vogel Co., Inc.
Philadelphia, Copyright
Owners.

Havanaise, Op. 83,
Vn. & Orch.
Permission for reprint granted
by Durand & Cie, Paris.
Elkan-Vogel Co., Inc.
Philadelphia, Copyright Owners.

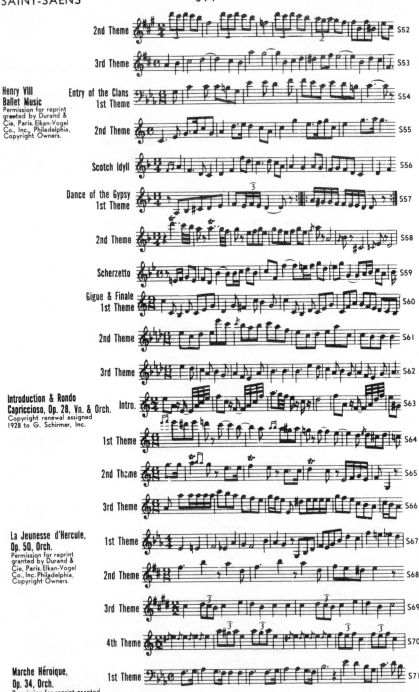

2nd Theme — S52

3rd Theme — S53

**Henry VIII
Ballet Music**
Permission for reprint
granted by Durand &
Cie, Paris. Elkan-Vogel
Co., Inc., Philadelphia,
Copyright Owners.

**Entry of the Clans
1st Theme** — S54

2nd Theme — S55

Scotch Idyll — S56

**Dance of the Gypsy
1st Theme** — S57

2nd Theme — S58

Scherzetto — S59

**Gigue & Finale
1st Theme** — S60

2nd Theme — S61

3rd Theme — S62

**Introduction & Rondo
Capriccioso, Op. 28, Vn. & Orch.**
Copyright renewal assigned
1928 to G. Schirmer, Inc.

Intro. — S63

1st Theme — S64

2nd Theme — S65

3rd Theme — S66

**La Jeunesse d'Hercule,
Op. 50, Orch.**
Permission for reprint
granted by Durand &
Cie, Paris. Elkan-Vogel
Co., Inc. Philadelphia,
Copyright Owners.

1st Theme — S67

2nd Theme — S68

3rd Theme — S69

4th Theme — S70

**Marche Héroique,
Op. 34, Orch.**
Permission for reprint granted
by Durand & Cie, Paris. Elkan-Vogel Co., Inc.
Philadelphia, Copyright Owners.

1st Theme — S71

2nd Theme — S72

3rd Theme — S73

Phaëton, Op. 39, Orch.
Permission for reprint granted
by Durand & Cie, Paris.
Elkan-Vogel Co., Inc.
Philadelphia, Copyright
Owners.

1st Theme — S74

2nd Theme — S75

3rd Theme — S76

Romance, Op. 36, Fr. Horn & Orch.
Permission for reprint granted
by Durand & Cie, Paris. Elkan-Vogel
Co., Inc. Philadelphia, Copyright
Owners.
— S77

**Le Rouet d'Omphale,
Op. 31, Orch.**
Permission for reprint granted
by Durand & Cie, Paris.
Elkan-Vogel Co., Inc.
Philadelphia, Copyright
Owners.

1st Theme — S78

2nd Thème — S79

**Samson et Dalila,
Opera, Op. 47**
Copyright 1892
by G. Schirmer, Inc.

Bacchanale
1st Theme — S80

2nd Theme,
A — S81

2nd Theme,
B — S82

3rd Theme — S83

4th Theme — S84

Scherzo, Op. 87, 2 Pfts.
By permission of
International Music Co.

Intro. — S85

1st Theme — S86

2nd Theme — S87

3rd Theme — S88

**Septet, Op. 65, Tpt.,
Str. Quin. & Pft.**
Permission for reprint
granted by Durand &
Cie, Paris. Elkan-Vogel
Co., Inc. Philadelphia,
Copyright Owners.

1st Movement
Préambule — S89

2nd Movement
Minuet
1st Theme — S90

2nd Movement
2nd Theme — S91

3rd Movement / Intermède — S92

4th Movement / Gavotte & Finale — S93

Sonatas
No. 1 in C Minor,
Op. 32, Vcl. & Pft.
Permission for reprint granted by Durand & Cie, Paris. Elkan-Vogel Co., Inc. Philadelphia, Copyright Owners.

1st Movement / Intro. — S94

1st Movement / 1st Theme — S95

1st Movement / 2nd Theme — S96

2nd Movement — S97

3rd Movement / 1st Theme — S98

3rd Movement / 2nd Theme — S99

No. 2 in F,
Op. 123, Vcl. & Pft.
Permission for reprint granted by Durand & Cie, Paris. Elkan-Vogel Co., Inc. Philadelphia, Copyright Owners.

1st Movement / Intro. — S100

1st Movement / 1st Theme — S101

1st Movement / 2nd Theme — S102

2nd Movement / Scherzo con Variazione — S103

3rd Movement / Romance — S104

4th Movement / 1st Theme — S105

4th Movement / 2nd Theme — S106

No. 1, Op. 75,
Vn. & Pft.
Permission for reprint granted by Durand & Cie, Paris. Elkan-Vogel Co., Inc. Philadelphia, Copyright Owners.

1st Movement / 1st Theme — S107

1st Movement / 2nd Theme — S108

1st Movement / 3rd Theme — S109

2nd Movement / 1st Theme — S110

2nd Movement / 2nd Theme — S111

SAINT-SAENS

3rd Movement
1st Theme — S112

3rd Movement
2nd Theme — S113

3rd Movement
3rd Theme — S114

Song Without Words, Pft. — S115

Suite Algérienne,
Op. 60, Orch.
Permission for reprint
granted by Durand &
Cie, Paris. Elkan-Vogel
Co., Inc. Philadelphia,
Copyright Owners.

1st Movement
Prélude, en Vue
d'Alger
1st Theme — S116

1st Movement
2nd Theme — S117

2nd Movement
Rapsodie Mauresque
1st Theme,
A — S118

2nd Movement
1st Theme,
B — S119

2nd Movement
2nd Theme,
A — S120

2nd Movement
2nd Theme,
B — S121

2nd Movement
3rd Theme — S122

3rd Movement
Rêverie du Soir
Intro. — S123

3rd Movement
Theme — S124

4th Movement
Marche Militaire Française
1st Theme — S125

4th Movement
2nd Theme — S126

Symphony No. 3, in
C Minor, Op. 78,
Orch., Organ & Pft.
Published and Copyrighted
(1930) by Oliver Ditson Co.

1st Movement
1st Theme — S127

1st Movement
2nd Theme — S128

1st Movement
3rd Theme — S129

1st Movement
4th Theme — S130

2nd Movement
1st Theme — S131

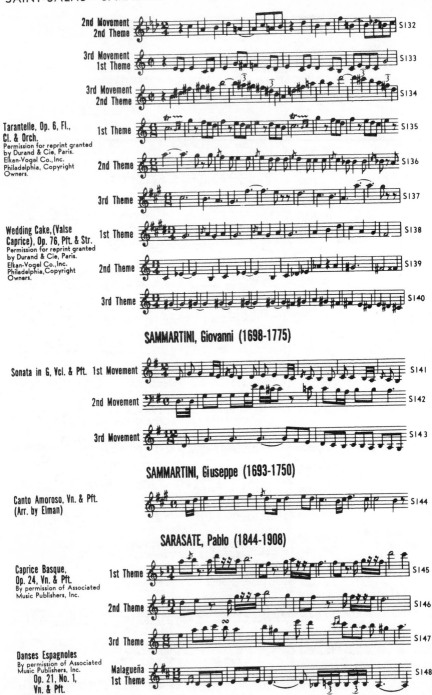

2nd Movement, 2nd Theme — S132

3rd Movement, 1st Theme — S133

3rd Movement, 2nd Theme — S134

Tarantelle, Op. 6, Fl., Cl. & Orch.
Permission for reprint granted by Durand & Cie, Paris. Elkan-Vogel Co., Inc. Philadelphia, Copyright Owners.

1st Theme — S135

2nd Theme — S136

3rd Theme — S137

Wedding Cake, (Valse Caprice), Op. 76, Pft. & Str.
Permission for reprint granted by Durand & Cie, Paris. Elkan-Vogel Co., Inc. Philadelphia, Copyright Owners.

1st Theme — S138

2nd Theme — S139

3rd Theme — S140

SAMMARTINI, Giovanni (1698-1775)

Sonata in G, Vcl. & Pft. 1st Movement — S141

2nd Movement — S142

3rd Movement — S143

SAMMARTINI, Giuseppe (1693-1750)

Canto Amoroso, Vn. & Pft. (Arr. by Elman) — S144

SARASATE, Pablo (1844-1908)

Caprice Basque, Op. 24, Vn. & Pft.
By permission of Associated Music Publishers, Inc.

1st Theme — S145

2nd Theme — S146

3rd Theme — S147

Danses Espagnoles
By permission of Associated Music Publishers, Inc.
Op. 21, No. 1, Vn. & Pft.

Malagueña 1st Theme — S148

SARASATE

2nd Theme — S149

Op. 21, No. 2 | Habañera 1st Theme — S150

2nd Theme — S151

3rd Theme — S152

Op. 22, No. 1 | Romanza Andaluza 1st Theme — S153

2nd Theme — S154

3rd Theme — S155

Op. 22, No. 2 | Jota Navarra 1st Theme — S156

2nd Theme — S157

Op. 23, No. 1 | Playera — S158

Op. 23, No. 2 | Zapateado Intro. — S159

1st Theme — S160

2nd Theme — S161

Introduction and Tarantelle, Op. 43, Vn. & Orch. or Pft. By permission of Associated Music Publishers, Inc. | Intro. — S162

Tarantelle 1st Theme — S163

2nd Theme — S164

3rd Theme — S165

Zigeunerweisen, (Gypsy Airs), Op. 20, Vn. & Pft. By permission of Associated Music Publishers, Inc. | 1st Theme — S166

2nd Theme — S167

3rd Theme — S168

4th Theme — S169

5th Theme — S170

6th Theme — S171

SATIE, Erik (1866-1925)

Gnossiennes, Pft.
No. 1 — Copyright by Editions Salabert Editions Salabert, 22 Rue Chaucat, Paris Salabert, Inc., 1 East 57 St., N. Y. — S172

No. 2 — S173

No. 3 — S174

Gymnopédies, Pft. Copyright by Editions Salabert Editions Salabert, 22 Rue Chaucat, Paris Salabert, Inc., 1 East 57 St., N. Y.
No. 1 — S175

No. 2 — S176

No. 3 — S177

Parade Ballet Copyright by Editions Salabert, 22 Rue Chaucat, Paris Salabert, Inc., 1 East 57 St., N. Y. **Rag-Time** — S178

Trois Petites Pièces Montées, (after Rabelais), Orch. De L'Enfance de Pantagruel — S179
Copyright by Editions Salabert Editions Salabert, 22 Rue Chaucat, Paris Salabert, Inc., 1 East 57 St., N. Y. **Marche de Cocagne** — S180

Jeux de Gargantua — S181

SAUVEPLANE, Henri (1892-)

Habañera, Vn. & Pft. — S182

SCARLATTI, Alessandro (1660-1725)

Fuga, Pft. — S183

SCARLATTI, Domenico (1685-1757)

Sonatas, Harpsi.
Longo 22 in E Minor — S184

Longo 23 in E   S185

Longo 33 in B Minor   S186

Longo 58 in D Minor
"Gavotte"   S187

Longo 104 in C   S188

Longo 107 in D   S189

Longo 108 in D Minor   S190

Longo 129 in G   S191

Longo 142 in E Flat   S192

Longo 152 in A   S193

Longo 205 in C   S194

Longo 208 in D   S195

Longo 232 in G   S196

Longo 239 in A Minor   S197

Longo 243 in A Minor,
"Pastorale"   S198

Longo 256 in C Sharp Minor   S199

Longo 257 in E   S200

Longo 261 in D   S201

Longo 263 in B Minor   S202

Longo 294 in F Sharp Minor,   S203

Longo 338 in G Minor
"Burlesca"   S204

Longo 345 in A   S205

Longo 352 in C Minor   S206

Longo 375 in E,   S207

Longo 382 in F Minor   S208

Longo 384 in F   S209

Longo 387 in G   S210

Longo 395 in A   S211

Longo 407 in C Minor   S212

Longo 411 in D   S213

Longo 413 in D Minor
"Pastorale"   S214

Longo 422 in D Minor
"Toccata"   S215

Longo 429 in A Minor   S216

Longo 434 in B Flat   S217

Longo 438 in F Minor   S218

Longo 449 in B Minor   S219

Longo 463 in D
"Tempo di Ballo"   S220

Longo 465 in D   S221

Longo 474 in F   S222

Longo 475 in F Minor   S223

Longo 479 in F   S224

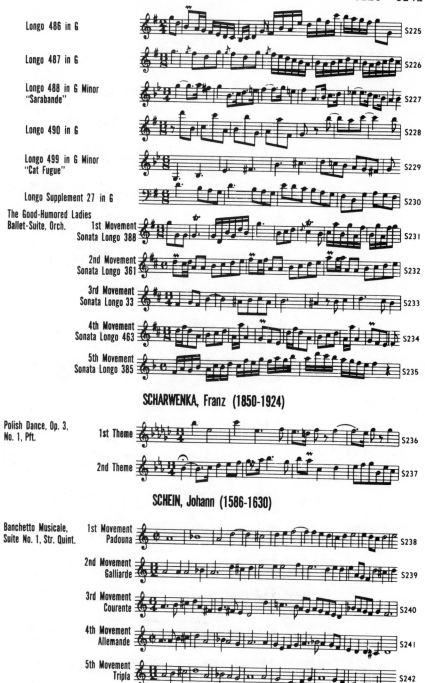

Longo 486 in G — S225

Longo 487 in G — S226

Longo 488 in G Minor "Sarabande" — S227

Longo 490 in G — S228

Longo 499 in G Minor "Cat Fugue" — S229

Longo Supplement 27 in G — S230

The Good-Humored Ladies Ballet-Suite, Orch.
1st Movement Sonata Longo 388 — S231

2nd Movement Sonata Longo 361 — S232

3rd Movement Sonata Longo 33 — S233

4th Movement Sonata Longo 463 — S234

5th Movement Sonata Longo 385 — S235

SCHARWENKA, Franz (1850-1924)

Polish Dance, Op. 3, No. 1, Pft.
1st Theme — S236

2nd Theme — S237

SCHEIN, Johann (1586-1630)

Banchetto Musicale, Suite No. 1, Str. Quint.
1st Movement Padouna — S238

2nd Movement Galliarde — S239

3rd Movement Courente — S240

4th Movement Allemande — S241

5th Movement Tripla — S242

SCHELLING, Ernest (1876-1939)

Impressions from an Artist's
Life (Variations), Orch. & Pft.
By permission of Associated
Music Publishers, Inc.

A Victory Ball, Orch.
By permission of Associated
Music Publishers, Inc.

Theme — S243

1st Theme — S244

2nd Theme — S245

3rd Theme — S246

4th Theme
A — S247

4th Theme
B — S248

4th Theme
C — S249

5th Theme — S250

6th Theme — S251

7th Theme — S252

SCHMITT, Florent (1870-1958)

Rapsodie Viennoise,
Op. 53, No. 3, Orch.
Permission for reprint granted
by Durand & Cie, Paris.
Elkan-Vogel Co., Inc.
Philadelphia, Copyright
Owners.

Reflets d'Allemagne,
Orch.

1st Theme — S253

2nd Theme — S254

3rd Theme — S255

1st Movement
Nuremberg — S256

2nd Movement
Dresden — S257

3rd Movement
Werder — S258

4th Movement
Munich
1st Theme — S259

4th Movement
2nd Theme — S260

SCHOBERT, Johann (c. 1720-1767)

Sonata in F, Op. 8, Pft.
1st Movement — S261
2nd Movement — S262
3rd Movement Polonaise — S263
4th Movement 1st Theme — S264
4th Movement 2nd Theme — S265

SCHÖNBERG, Arnold (1874-1951)

Six Little Piano Pieces, Op. 19
By permission of Associated Music Publishers, Inc.
No. 1 — S266
No. 2 — S267
No. 3 — S268
No. 4 — S269
No. 5 — S270

Verklärte Nacht, Op. 4, Str. Sextet
1st Theme — S271
2nd Theme — S272
3rd Theme — S273
4th Theme — S274
5th Theme — S275

SCHREKER, Franz (1878-1934)

Birthday of the Infanta, Orch.
By permission of Associated Music Publishers, Inc.
1st Movement "Reigen" (Rounds) 1st Theme — S276
1st Movement 2nd Theme — S277

2nd Movement Marionetten — S278

Minuet der Tanzknaben (Dancing Boys) 3rd Movement 1st Theme — S279

3rd Movement 2nd Theme — S280

4th Movement Tänze des Zwerges (Dances of the Dwarf) — S281

4th Movement 2nd Theme — S282

4th Movement 3rd Theme — S283

Kleine Suite, Chamber Orch. By permission of Associated Music Publishers, Inc.

1st Movement Präludium — S284

2nd Movement Marcia — S285

3rd Movement Canon — S286

4th Movement Fughette — S287

5th Movement Intermezzo — S288

6th Movement Capriccio — S289

SCHUBERT, Franz (1797-1828)

Allegretto in C Minor, Pft. — S290

Deutsche Tänze, Pft. Op. 33, No. 2 — S291

Op. 33, No. 6 — S292

Op. 33, No. 7 — S293

Fantaisie in C, "Wanderer" Op. 15, Pft. 1st Theme — S294

2nd Theme — S295

3rd Theme — S296

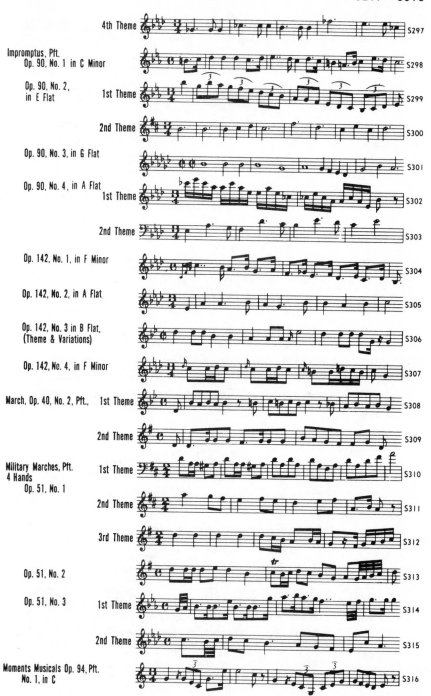

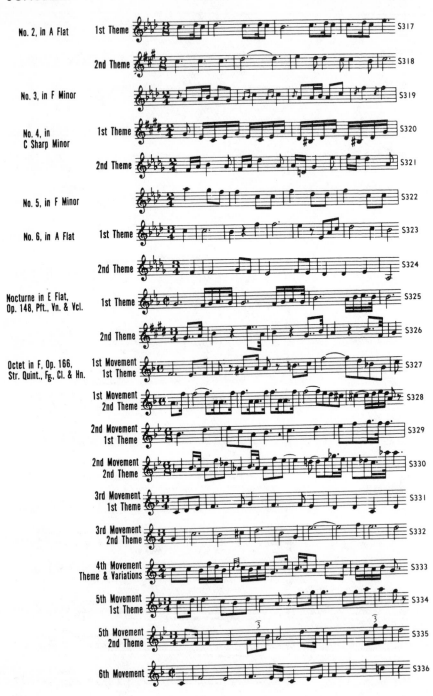

No. 2, in A Flat — 1st Theme — S317

2nd Theme — S318

No. 3, in F Minor — S319

No. 4, in C Sharp Minor — 1st Theme — S320

2nd Theme — S321

No. 5, in F Minor — S322

No. 6, in A Flat — 1st Theme — S323

2nd Theme — S324

Nocturne in E Flat, Op. 148, Pft., Vn. & Vcl. — 1st Theme — S325

2nd Theme — S326

Octet in F, Op. 166, Str. Quint., Fg., Cl. & Hn. — 1st Movement 1st Theme — S327

1st Movement 2nd Theme — S328

2nd Movement 1st Theme — S329

2nd Movement 2nd Theme — S330

3rd Movement 1st Theme — S331

3rd Movement 2nd Theme — S332

4th Movement Theme & Variations — S333

5th Movement 1st Theme — S334

5th Movement 2nd Theme — S335

6th Movement — S336

Adagio & Rondo Concertante in F, Pft. & Str. — 1st Movement — S337

2nd Movement — S338

Quartets
No. 4, in C, Str. — 1st Movement — S339

2nd Movement — S340

3rd Movement — S341

4th Movement — S342

No. 6, in D, Str. — 1st Movement — S343

2nd Movement — S344

3rd Movement — S345

4th Movement — S346

No. 8, in B Flat, Op. 168, Str. — 1st Movement — S347

2nd Movement 1st Theme — S348

2nd Movement 2nd Theme — S349

3rd Movement 1st Theme — S350

3rd Movement 2nd Theme — S351

4th Movement — S352

No. 9, in G Minor, Str. — 1st Movement — S353

2nd Movement — S354

3rd Movement — S355

4th Movement — S356

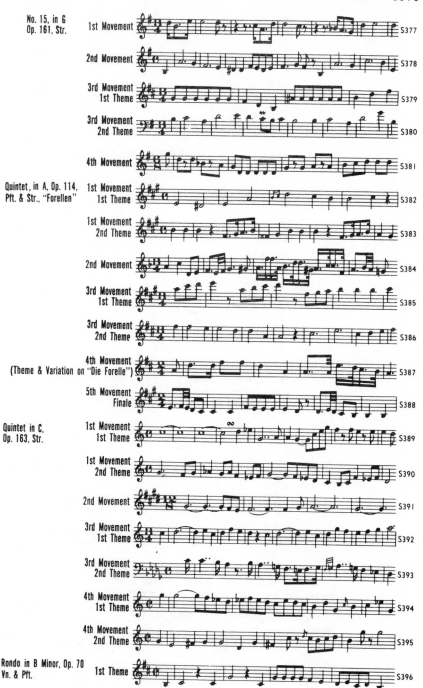

No. 15, in G
Op. 161, Str.

1st Movement — S377

2nd Movement — S378

3rd Movement
1st Theme — S379

3rd Movement
2nd Theme — S380

4th Movement — S381

Quintet, in A, Op. 114,
Pft. & Str., "Forellen"

1st Movement
1st Theme — S382

1st Movement
2nd Theme — S383

2nd Movement — S384

3rd Movement
1st Theme — S385

3rd Movement
2nd Theme — S386

4th Movement
(Theme & Variation on "Die Forelle") — S387

5th Movement
Finale — S388

Quintet in C,
Op. 163, Str.

1st Movement
1st Theme — S389

1st Movement
2nd Theme — S390

2nd Movement — S391

3rd Movement
1st Theme — S392

3rd Movement
2nd Theme — S393

4th Movement
1st Theme — S394

4th Movement
2nd Theme — S395

Rondo in B Minor, Op. 70
Vn. & Pft.

1st Theme — S396

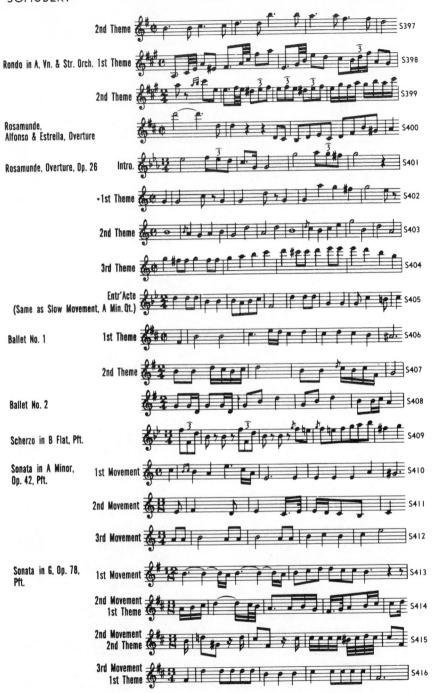

2nd Theme — S397

Rondo in A, Vn. & Str. Orch. 1st Theme — S398

2nd Theme — S399

Rosamunde, Alfonso & Estrella, Overture — S400

Rosamunde, Overture, Op. 26   Intro. — S401

•1st Theme — S402

2nd Theme — S403

3rd Theme — S404

Entr'Acte (Same as Slow Movement, A Min. Qt.) — S405

Ballet No. 1   1st Theme — S406

2nd Theme — S407

Ballet No. 2 — S408

Scherzo in B Flat, Pft. — S409

Sonata in A Minor, Op. 42, Pft.   1st Movement — S410

2nd Movement — S411

3rd Movement — S412

Sonata in G, Op. 78, Pft.   1st Movement — S413

2nd Movement 1st Theme — S414

2nd Movement 2nd Theme — S415

3rd Movement 1st Theme — S416

SCHUBERT

3rd Movement / 2nd Theme — S417

4th Movement — S418

Sonata in A, Op. 120, Pft. — 1st Movement / 1st Theme — S419

1st Movement / 2nd Theme — S420

2nd Movement — S421

3rd Movement / 1st Theme — S422

3rd Movement / 2nd Theme — S423

Sonata in A Minor, Op. 143, Pft. — 1st Movement — S424

2nd Movement — S425

3rd Movement / 1st Theme — S426

3rd Movement / 2nd Theme — S427

Sonata in B, Op. 147, Pft. — 1st Movement / 1st Theme — S428

1st Movement / 2nd Theme — S429

1st Movement / 3rd Theme — S430

2nd Movement — S431

3rd Movement — S432

4th Movement / 1st Theme — S433

4th Movement / 2nd Theme — S434

Sonata in B Flat, Pft. (Posth.) — 1st Movement / 1st Theme — S435

1st Movement / 2nd Theme — S436

2nd Movement — S437

3rd Movement — S438

4th Movement — S439

Sonata in A Minor,
Pft. & Vcl.,(Arpeggione) — 1st Movement — S440

2nd Movement — S441

3rd Movement
1st Theme — S442

3rd Movement
2nd Theme,
A — S443

3rd Movement
2nd Theme,
B — S444

Sonatina in D, Op.137,
No. 1, Vn. & Pft. — 1st Movement — S445

2nd Movement — S446

3rd Movement — S447

Sonatina in G Minor,
Op. 137, No. 3, Vn. & Pft. — 1st Movement — S448

2nd Movement — S449

3rd Movement
1st Theme — S450

3rd Movement
2nd Theme — S451

4th Movement
1st Theme — S452

4th Movement
2nd Theme — S453

Sonata in A, Op. 162,
Vn. & Pft. — 1st Movement — S454

2nd Movement — S455

3rd Movement — S456

Symphony No. 1 in D

Symphony No. 2
in B Flat

Symphony No. 3
in D

Symphony No. 4
in C Minor, "Tragic"

Symphony No. 5 in B Flat

Symphony No. 6 in C

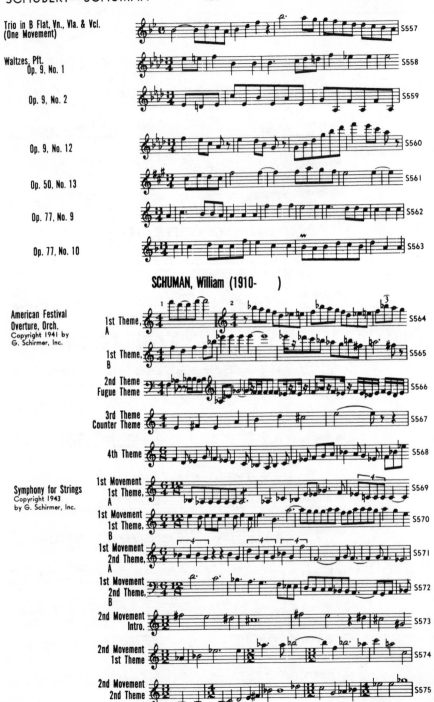

Trio in B Flat, Vn., Vla. & Vcl.
(One Movement) — S557

Waltzes, Pft.
Op. 9, No. 1 — S558

Op. 9, No. 2 — S559

Op. 9, No. 12 — S560

Op. 50, No. 13 — S561

Op. 77, No. 9 — S562

Op. 77, No. 10 — S563

SCHUMAN, William (1910-   )

American Festival
Overture, Orch.
Copyright 1941 by
G. Schirmer, Inc.

1st Theme, A — S564

1st Theme, B — S565

2nd Theme
Fugue Theme — S566

3rd Theme
Counter Theme — S567

4th Theme — S568

Symphony for Strings
Copyright 1943
by G. Schirmer, Inc.

1st Movement
1st Theme, A — S569

1st Movement
1st Theme, B — S570

1st Movement
2nd Theme, A — S571

1st Movement
2nd Theme, B — S572

2nd Movement
Intro. — S573

2nd Movement
1st Theme — S574

2nd Movement
2nd Theme — S575

3rd Movement 1st Theme — S576

3rd Movement 2nd Theme — S577

Symphony No. 3
Part I
Passacaglia & Fugue
Copyright 1942 by
G. Schirmer, Inc.

1st Theme Passacaglia — S578

2nd Theme Fugue — S579

Part II
Chorale & Toccata

1st Theme Chorale — S580

2nd Theme Toccata — S581

SCHUMANN, Robert (1810-1856)

Abegg Variations, Op. 1, Pft. — S582

Abendlied (Evening Song), Op. 85, No. 12, Pft., 4 Hands — S583

Des Abends, Op. 12, No. 1, Pft. — S584

Album for the Young, Op. 68, Pft.

Soldiers' March — S584a

The Wild Horseman — S584b

Folk Song — S584c

The Happy Farmer — S584d

Sicilienne — S584e

Little Romance — S584f

The Strange Man — S584g

Italian Sailors' Song — S584h

Arabeske, Op. 18, Pft.

1st Theme — S585

2nd Theme — S586

3rd Movement
3rd Theme S607

Concerto in A Minor,
Op. 54, Pft. & Orch.

1st Movement
1st Theme S608

1st Movement
2nd Theme,
A S609

1st Movement
2nd Theme,
B S610

1st Movement
3rd Theme S611

1st Movement
Coda S612

2nd Movement
Intermezzo
1st Theme S613

2nd Movement
2nd Theme S614

3rd Movement
1st Theme S615

3rd Movement
2nd Theme S616

3rd Movement
3rd Theme S617

Concerto in D Minor,
Vn. & Orch.

1st Movement
1st Theme S618

1st Movement
2nd Theme S619

2nd Movement S620

3rd Movement
1st Theme S621

3rd Movement
2nd Theme S622

Davidsbündler, Op. 6, Pft.

No. 1 S623

No. 2 S624

No. 5 S625

No. 9 S626

SCHUMANN

425

S647—S666

No. 4 — S647

No. 5 — S648

No. 7 — S649

No. 8 — S650

No. 10 — S651

No. 11 — S652

No. 12
Finale — S653

Phantasy in C,
Op. 17, Pft.

1st Movement
1st Theme — S654

1st Movement
2nd Theme — S655

1st Movement
3rd Theme — S656

2nd Movement
1st Theme — S657

2nd Movement
2nd Theme — S658

2nd Movement
3rd Theme — S659

3rd Movement
1st Theme — S660

3rd Movement
2nd Theme — S661

3rd Movement
3rd Theme — S662

Quartet in A Minor,
Op. 41, No. 1, Str.

1st Movement
Intro. — S663

1st Movement
1st Theme — S664

1st Movement
2nd Theme,
A — S665

1st Movement
2nd Theme,
B — S666

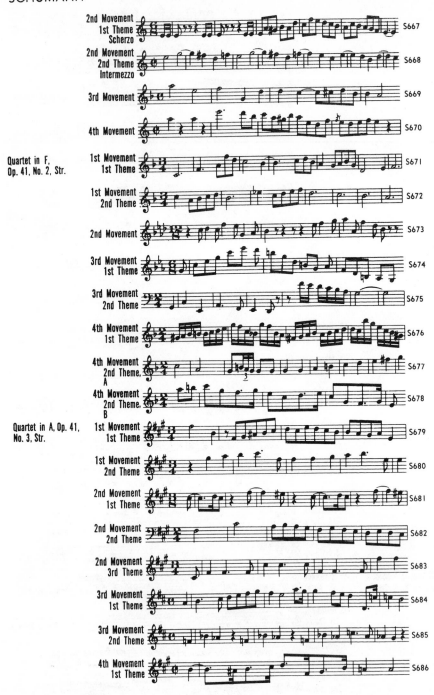

2nd Movement / 1st Theme / Scherzo — S667

2nd Movement / 2nd Theme / Intermezzo — S668

3rd Movement — S669

4th Movement — S670

Quartet in F, Op. 41, No. 2, Str.

1st Movement / 1st Theme — S671

1st Movement / 2nd Theme — S672

2nd Movement — S673

3rd Movement / 1st Theme — S674

3rd Movement / 2nd Theme — S675

4th Movement / 1st Theme — S676

4th Movement / 2nd Theme, A — S677

4th Movement / 2nd Theme, B — S678

Quartet in A, Op. 41, No. 3, Str.

1st Movement / 1st Theme — S679

1st Movement / 2nd Theme — S680

2nd Movement / 1st Theme — S681

2nd Movement / 2nd Theme — S682

2nd Movement / 3rd Theme — S683

3rd Movement / 1st Theme — S684

3rd Movement / 2nd Theme — S685

4th Movement / 1st Theme — S686

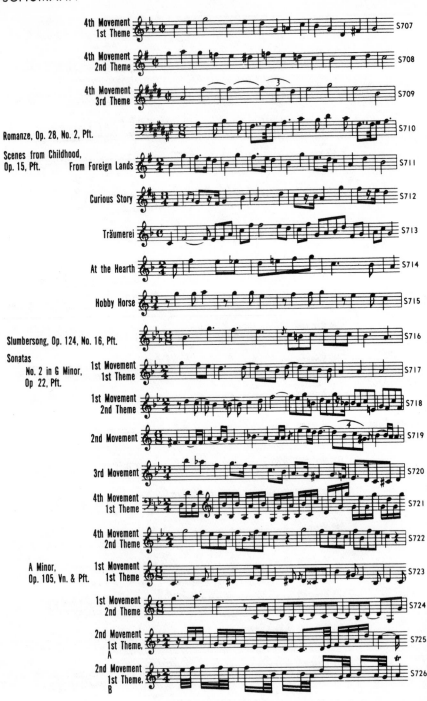

4th Movement 1st Theme — S707

4th Movement 2nd Theme — S708

4th Movement 3rd Theme — S709

Romanze, Op. 28, No. 2, Pft. — S710

Scenes from Childhood, Op. 15, Pft. From Foreign Lands — S711

Curious Story — S712

Träumerei — S713

At the Hearth — S714

Hobby Horse — S715

Slumbersong, Op. 124, No. 16, Pft. — S716

Sonatas No. 2 in G Minor, Op 22, Pft. 1st Movement 1st Theme — S717

1st Movement 2nd Theme — S718

2nd Movement — S719

3rd Movement — S720

4th Movement 1st Theme — S721

4th Movement 2nd Theme — S722

A Minor, Op. 105, Vn. & Pft. 1st Movement 1st Theme — S723

1st Movement 2nd Theme — S724

2nd Movement 1st Theme, A — S725

2nd Movement 1st Theme, B — S726

2nd Movement / 2nd Theme — S727

3rd Movement / 1st Theme — S728

3rd Movement / 2nd Theme — S729

3rd Movement / 3rd Theme — S730

D Minor, Op. 121, Vn. & Pft. — 1st Movement / Intro. — S731

1st Movement / 1st Theme — S732

1st Movement / 2nd Theme — S733

2nd Movement / 1st Theme — S734

2nd Movement / 2nd Theme — S735

2nd Movement / 3rd Theme — S736

3rd Movement / 1st Theme — S737

3rd Movement / 2nd Theme — S738

4th Movement / 1st Theme — S739

4th Movement / 2nd Theme — S740

Symphonic Etudes, in C Sharp Minor, Op. 13, Pft. — Theme — S741

Etude I — S742

Etude II — S743

Etude III — S744

Etude VI — S745

Finale / 1st Theme — S746

1st Theme — S807

2nd Theme — S808

Vogel Als Prophet,
(Bird as Prophet),
Op. 82, No. 7, Pft.

1st Theme — S809

2nd Theme — S810

Warum? (Why?), Op. 12, No. 3, Pft. — S811

SCOTT, Cyril (1879-1970)

Danse Nègre, Op. 58, No. 5, Pft.
Copyright 1911 by
Elkin & Co., Ltd.
By permission of Galaxy
Music Corporation, N. Y. — S812

Lotus Land, Op. 47,
No. 1, Pft.
Copyright 1905 by
Elkin & Co., Ltd.
By permission of Galaxy
Music Corporation, N. Y.

1st Theme — S813

2nd Theme — S814

A Song from the East,
Op. 54, No. 2, Pft.

Copyright 1907
by Elkin & Co., Ltd.
By permission of Galaxy
Music Corporation, N. Y. — S815

Etudes
By permission of The Boston Music Co.,
Op. 2, No. 1, Pft. copyright owner. — S816

Op. 8, No. 10, Pft.
By permission of Associated
Music Publishers, Inc. — S817

Op. 8, No. 12, Pft.
By permission of Associated
Music Publishers, Inc. — S818

Fantaisie, Op. 28, Pft.   1st Theme
By permission of Associated
Music Publishers, Inc. — S819

2nd Theme — S820

Mazurka, Op. 25, No. 3, Pft.
By permission of Associated
Music Publishers, Inc. — S821

Nocturne, Pft. (For Left Hand Alone)
By permission of Associated
Music Publishers, Inc. — S822

Poème, Op. 32, No. 1, Pft.
By permission of Associated
Music Publishers, Inc. — S823

Poème, Op. 32, No. 2, Pft.
By permission of Associated
Music Publishers, Inc. — S824

SCRIABIN, Alexander (1872-1915)

Poème D'Extase,
Op. 34, Orch.
By permission of Associated
Music Publishers, Inc.

1st Theme — S825

2nd Theme — S826

3rd Theme — S827

Preludes
    Op. 9, No. 1, Pft.
    (For Left Hand Alone)
    By permission of Associated
    Music Publishers, Inc.
— S828

    Op. 11, No. 2, Pft.
    By permission of Associated
    Music Publishers, Inc.
— S829

    No. 9, Pft. — S830

    No. 10, Pft. — S831

Sonata, No. 4, Op. 30,
Pft.
By permission of International
Music Co.

1st Movement — S832

2nd Movement — S833

Symphony No. 3, Op. 43
"Le Divin Poème"
By permission of
Associated Music
Publishers, Inc.

Intro. — S834

1st Movement
Luttes
1st Theme — S835

1st Movement
2nd Theme — S836

2nd Movement
Voluptés — S837

3rd Movement
Jeu Divin
1st Theme — S838

3rd Movement
2nd Theme — S839

Waltz, Op. 38, Pft.
By permission of Associated
Music Publishers, Inc.
— S840

SGAMBATI, Giovanni (1841-1914)

Serenata Napoletana, Op. 24,
No. 2, Vn. & Pft.

1st Theme,
A — S841

1st Theme,
B — S842

2nd Theme — S843

Vecchio Minuetto, Op. 18, Pft.   S844

SHOSTAKOVICH, Dmitri (1906-1975)

Concerto, Op. 35,
Pft. & Orch.
By permission of
Broude Brothers

1st Movement
1st Theme   S845

1st Movement
2nd Theme   S846

2nd Movement   S847

3rd Movement
Finale
1st Theme   S848

3rd Movement
2nd Theme   S849

3rd Movement
3rd Theme   S850

The Golden Age, Op. 22,
Ballet
Copyright 1941 by Leeds
Music Corp., N. Y.
Reprinted here by permission
of the copyright owner.

1st Theme
Polka   S851

2nd Theme   S852

3rd Theme   S853

Quartet, Op. 49, Str.
By permission of
International Music Co.

1st Movement
1st Theme   S854

1st Movement
2nd Theme   S855

2nd Movement   S856

3rd Movement
1st Theme   S857

3rd Movement
2nd Theme   S858

4th Movement
1st Theme   S859

4th Movement
2nd Theme   S860

Quintet, Op. 57,
Pft. & Str.

1st Movement
Prelude
1st Theme   S861

1st Movement
2nd Theme   S862

2nd Movement / Fugue — S863

3rd Movement / Scherzo / 1st Theme — S864

3rd Movement / 2nd Theme — S865

4th Movement / Intermezzo — S866

5th Movement / Finale / 1st Theme, A — S867

5th Movement / 1st Theme, B — S868

5th Movement / 2nd Theme — S869

5th Movement / 3rd Theme — S870

Sonata, Op. 40 / Cello & Pft.
Copyright 1947 by Leeds Music Corp., N.Y. Reprinted here by permission of the copyright owner.

1st Movement / 1st Theme — S870a

1st Movement / 2nd Theme — S870b

2nd Movement / 1st Theme — S870c

2nd Movement / 2nd Theme — S870d

3rd Movement / 1st Theme — S870e

3rd Movement / 2nd Theme — S870f

4th Movement — S870g

Symphony No. 1 in F, Op. 10
Copyright 1946 by Leeds Music Corp., N.Y. Reprinted here by permission of the copyright owner.

1st Movement / Intro. — S871

1st Movement / 1st Theme — S872

1st Movement / 2nd Theme — S873

2nd Movement / 1st Theme — S874

2nd Movement / 2nd Theme — S875

Symphony No. 5, Op. 47
Copyright 1945 by
Leeds Music Corp.,
N.Y. Reprinted here
by permission of the
copyright owner.

Symphony No. 6, Op. 53
Copyright 1946 by
Leeds Music Corp.,
N. Y. Reprinted here
by permission of the
copyright owner.

Symphony No. 7, Op. 60
Copyright 1945 by
Leeds Music Corp.,
N. Y. Reprinted here
by permission of the
copyright owner.

Symphony No. 9, Op. 70

2nd Movement / 1st Theme — S916

2nd Movement / 2nd Theme — S917

3rd Movement / 1st Theme — S918

3rd Movement / 2nd Theme — S919

4th Movement — S920

5th Movement / 1st Theme — S921

5th Movement / 2nd Theme — S922

Three Fantastic Dances, Op. 1, Pft.
Copyright 1944 and 1945 by Leeds Music Corp., N. Y. Reprinted here by permission of the copyright owner.

No. 1 — S923

No. 2 — S924

No. 3 — S925

Two Pieces for String Octet, Op. 11
Copyright 1946 by Leeds Music Corp., N. Y. Reprinted here by permission of the copyright owner.

No. 1 / Prelude / 1st Theme — S925a

2nd Theme — S925b

No. 2 / Scherzo / 1st Theme — S925c

2nd Theme — S925d

SIBELIUS, Jean (1865-1957)

The Bard, Op. 64, Orch.
By permission of Associated Music Publishers, Inc.

1st Theme — S926

2nd Theme — S927

Concerto, Op. 47, Vn. & Orch.
By permission of International Music Co.

1st Movement / 1st Theme — S928

1st Movement / 2nd Theme, A — S929

1st Movement / 2nd Theme, B — S930

2nd Movement Intro.   S931

2nd Movement   S932

3rd Movement 1st Theme   S933

3rd Movement 2nd Theme   S934

En Saga, Op. 9, Orch.
By permission of Associated Music Publishers, Inc.

1st Theme   S935

2nd Theme   S936

3rd Theme   S937

4th Theme   S938

5th Theme   S939

6th Theme   S940

Finlandia, Op. 26, No. 7, Orch.
By permission of Associated Music Publishers, Inc.

1st Theme   S941

2nd Theme   S942

3rd Theme   S943

In Memoriam, Op. 59 (Funeral March), Orch.
By permission of Associated Music Publishers, Inc.

S944

Karelia, Op. 11, Suite for Orch.
By permission of Associated Music Publishers, Inc.

1st Movement Intermezzo   S945

2nd Movement Ballade   S946

3rd Movement Alla Marcia 1st Theme   S947

3rd Movement 2nd Theme   S948

King Christian II, Op. 27, Suite for Orch,
By permission of Associated Music Publishers, Inc.

Nocturne 1st Theme   S949

2nd Theme   S950

Elégie and Musette
1st Theme
Elégie — S951

2nd Theme
Musette — S952

Serenade
1st Theme — S953

2nd Theme — S954

Ballade
1st Theme — S955

2nd Theme — S956

Lemminkäinen's Homeward
Journey, Op. 22, No. 4
Orch.
By permission of Associated
Music Publishers, Inc.
1st Theme — S957

2nd Theme — S958

3rd Theme — S959

Nightride and Sunrise,
Op. 55, Orch.
1st Theme — S960

2nd Theme — S961

3rd Theme — S962

The Oceanides,
Op. 73, Orch.
By permission of Associated
Music Publishers, Inc.
1st Theme — S963

2nd Theme — S964

Pelléas et Mélisande,
(Incidental Music)
Op. 46, Orch.
Mélisande — S965

A Spring in the Park — S966

Pastorale — S967

Entr'acte — S968

Death of Mélisande — S969

Pohjola's Daughter,
Op. 49, Orch.
Copyright by Lienau,
Licensed by SESAC, Inc., N.Y.
1st Theme
A — S970

1st Theme, B — S971

2nd Theme — S972

3rd Theme — S973

4th Theme — S974

4th Theme — S975

5th Theme — S976

Quartet, Op. 56, Str. "Voces Intimae" By permission of Associated Music Publishers, Inc.

1st Movement 1st Theme, A — S977

1st Movement 1st Theme, B — S978

1st Movement 2nd Theme — S979

2nd Movement 1st Theme — S980

2nd Movement 2nd Theme — S981

3rd Movement 1st Theme, A — S982

3rd Movement 1st Theme, B — S983

4th Movement 1st Theme — S984

4th Movement 2nd Theme — S985

4th Movement 3rd Theme — S986

5th Movement 1st Theme — S987

5th Movement 2nd Theme — S988

5th Movement 3rd Theme — S989

Rakastava, (The Lover), Op. 14, Suite for Orch. By permission of Associated Music Publishers, Inc.

1st Movement — S990

SIBELIUS

2nd Movement — S991

3rd Movement — S992

Romance, Op. 24, No. 9, Pft. 1st Theme — S993

2nd Theme — S994

The Swan of Tuonela,
(from Kalevala)
Op. 22, No. 3
Orch.
By permission of Associated
Music Publishers, Inc.

1st Theme,
A — S995

1st Theme,
B — S996

1st Theme,
C — S997

2nd Theme — S998

Symphony No. 1
in E Minor, Op. 39
By permission of Associated
Music Publishers, Inc.

1st Movement
Intro. — S999

1st Movement
1st Theme — S1000

1st Movement
2nd Theme — S1001

1st Movement
3rd Theme — S1002

2nd Movement
1st Theme,
A — S1003

2nd Movement
1st Theme,
B — S1004

2nd Movement
2nd Theme — S1005

3rd Movement
1st Theme — S1006

3rd Movement
2nd Theme — S1007

4th Movement
1st Theme — S1008

4th Movement
2nd Theme — S1009

4th Movement
3rd Theme — S1010

**Symphony No. 2
in D, Op. 43**
By permission of Associated
Music Publishers, Inc.

**Symphony No. 3
in C, Op. 52**
Copyright by Lienau,
Licensed by SESAC
Inc., N. Y.

1st Movement / 1st Theme	S1011
1st Movement / 2nd Theme	S1012
1st Movement / 3rd Theme	S1013
2nd Movement / Intro.	S1014
2nd Movement / 1st Theme	S1015
2nd Movement / 2nd Theme	S1016
3rd Movement / 1st Theme	S1017
3rd Movement / 2nd Theme	S1018
3rd Movement / 3rd Theme	S1019
4th Movement / 1st Theme	S1020
4th Movement / 2nd Theme	S1021
4th Movement / 3rd Theme	S1022
4th Movement / 4th Theme	S1023
1st Movement / 1st Theme	S1024
1st Movement / 2nd Theme	S1025
1st Movement / 3rd Theme	S1026
2nd Movement	S1027
3rd Movement / 1st Theme	S1028
3rd Movement / 2nd Theme	S1029
3rd Movement / 3rd Theme	S1030

Symphony No. 4
in A Minor, Op. 63
By permission of Associated
Music Publishers, Inc.

1st Movement 1st Theme — S1031
1st Movement 2nd Theme — S1032
1st Movement 3rd Theme — S1033
2nd Movement 1st Theme — S1034
2nd Movement 2nd Theme — S1035
2nd Movement 3rd Theme — S1036
2nd Movement 4th Theme — S1037
2nd Movement 5th Theme — S1038
3rd Movement 1st Theme — S1039
3rd Movement 2nd Theme — S1040
4th Movement 1st Theme — S1041
4th Movement 2nd Theme — S1042
4th Movement 3rd Theme — S1043
4th Movement 4th Theme — S1044
4th Movement 5th Theme — S1045

Symphony No. 5
in E Flat, Op. 82
By permission of Associated
Music Publishers, Inc.

1st Movement 1st Theme — S1046
1st Movement 2nd Theme — S1047
1st Movement 3rd Theme — S1048
1st Movement 4th Theme — S1049
1st Movement 5th Theme — S1050

SIBELIUS 446 S1051—S1070

Symphony No. 6
in D Minor, Op. 104
By permission of Associated
Music Publishers, Inc.

3rd Theme 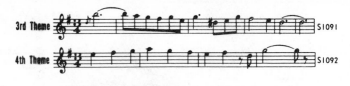 S1091

4th Theme S1092

SINDING, Christian (1856-1941)

Marche Grotesque, Op. 32, No. 1, Pft. S1093

Rustle of Spring
(Frühlingsrauschen),
Op. 32, No. 3, Pft.
Copyright renewal assigned
1931 to G. Schirmer, Inc.

1st Theme,
A
S1094

1st Theme,
B
S1095

SMETANA, Bedřich (1824-1884)

Aus Meinem Leben,
Quartet No. 1
in E Minor, Str.

1st Movement
1st Theme
S1096

1st Movement
2nd Theme
S1097

2nd Movement
1st Theme
S1098

2nd Movement
2nd Theme
S1099

3rd Movement
S1100

4th Movement
1st Theme
S1101

4th Movement
2nd Theme
S1102

The Bartered Bride,
Opera

Overture
Intro.
S1103

1st Theme
S1104

2nd Theme
S1105

Act I
Polka
1st Theme
S1106

2nd Theme,
A
S1107

2nd Theme,
B
S1108

2nd Movement 2nd Theme S1129

2nd Movement 3rd Theme S1130

3rd Movement 1st Theme S1131

3rd Movement 2nd Theme S1132

SOLER, Padre Antonio (1729-1783)

Sonatas
F, Harpsi. S1133

A Minor, Harpsi. S1134

D, Harpsi. S1135

SOUSA, John Philip (1854-1932)

El Capitan, March
© Church

1st Theme S1136

2nd Theme S1137

3rd Theme S1138

4th Theme S1139

Hail to the Spirit of Liberty, March
© Church

1st Theme S1140

2nd Theme S1141

3rd Theme S1142

The High School Cadets, March

1st Theme S1143

2nd Theme S1144

3rd Theme S1145

4th Theme S1146

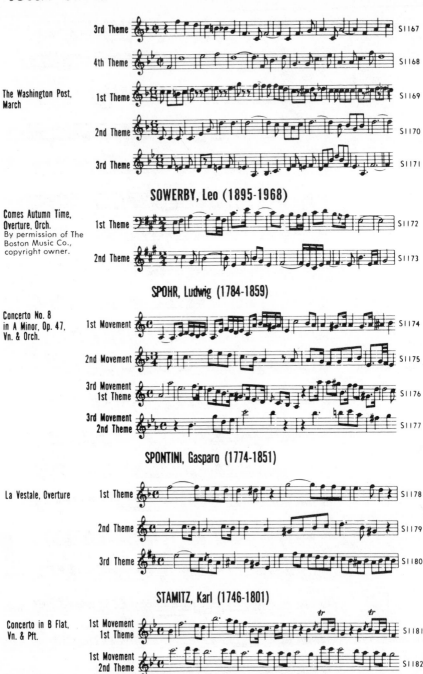

3rd Theme — S1167

4th Theme — S1168

The Washington Post, March

1st Theme — S1169

2nd Theme — S1170

3rd Theme — S1171

SOWERBY, Leo (1895-1968)

Comes Autumn Time, Overture, Orch.
By permission of The Boston Music Co., copyright owner.

1st Theme — S1172

2nd Theme — S1173

SPOHR, Ludwig (1784-1859)

Concerto No. 8 in A Minor, Op. 47, Vn. & Orch.

1st Movement — S1174

2nd Movement — S1175

3rd Movement 1st Theme — S1176

3rd Movement 2nd Theme — S1177

SPONTINI, Gasparo (1774-1851)

La Vestale, Overture

1st Theme — S1178

2nd Theme — S1179

3rd Theme — S1180

STAMITZ, Karl (1746-1801)

Concerto in B Flat, Vn. & Pft.

1st Movement 1st Theme — S1181

1st Movement 2nd Theme — S1182

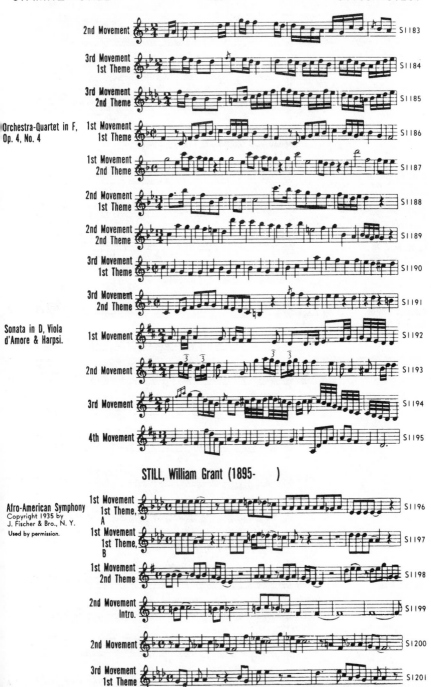

2nd Movement — S1183

3rd Movement
1st Theme — S1184

3rd Movement
2nd Theme — S1185

Orchestra-Quartet in F,
Op. 4, No. 4

1st Movement
1st Theme — S1186

1st Movement
2nd Theme — S1187

2nd Movement
1st Theme — S1188

2nd Movement
2nd Theme — S1189

3rd Movement
1st Theme — S1190

3rd Movement
2nd Theme — S1191

Sonata in D, Viola
d'Amore & Harpsi.

1st Movement — S1192

2nd Movement — S1193

3rd Movement — S1194

4th Movement — S1195

STILL, William Grant (1895-)

Afro-American Symphony
Copyright 1935 by
J. Fischer & Bro., N. Y.

Used by permission.

1st Movement
1st Theme,
A — S1196

1st Movement
1st Theme,
B — S1197

1st Movement
2nd Theme — S1198

2nd Movement
Intro. — S1199

2nd Movement — S1200

3rd Movement
1st Theme — S1201

3rd Movement
2nd Theme   S1202

4th Movement
1st Theme   S1203

4th Movement
2nd Theme   S1204

STOJOWSKI, Sigismond (1869-1946)

Chant d'Amour, Op. 26, No. 3, Pft.
Copyright renewal assigned 1939
to G. Schirmer, Inc.   S1205

Melodie, Op. 26, No. 1, Pft.
By Permission of C. F. Peters, Clayton
F. Summy Co., Chicago, Agents in the U. S.   S1206

Thème Cracovien Varié,
Op. 26, No. 4, Pft.
By Permission of C. F. Peters, Clayton
F. Summy Co., Chicago, Agents in the U. S.   S1207

STRAUSS, Eduard (1835-1916)

Doctrinen Waltzes,
Op. 79, Orch.   No. 1
                       1st Theme   S1208

                       2nd Theme   S1209

                       No. 2
                       1st Theme   S1210

                       2nd Theme   S1211

                       No. 3   S1212

                       No. 4   S1213

                       No. 5   S1214

STRAUSS, Johann, Jr. (1825-1899)

Perpetuum Mobile,
Op. 257, Orch.   Theme   S1215

                       Variation   S1216

                       Variation   S1217

Die Fledermaus, Overture   1st Theme   S1218

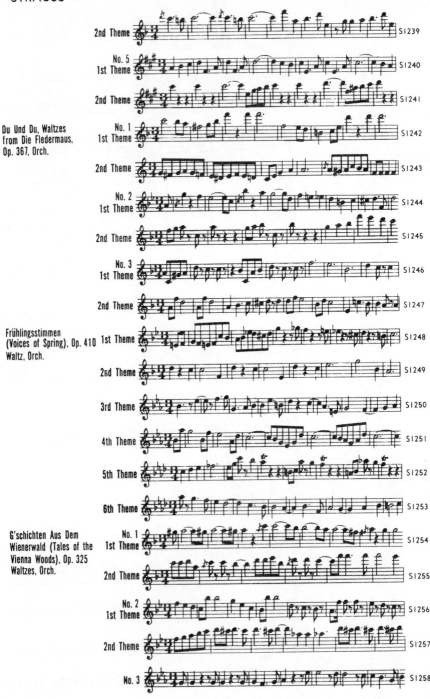

No. 4 1st Theme S1259
2nd Theme S1260
No. 5 1st Theme S1261
2nd Theme S1262

Kaiser-Waltzer (Emperor-Waltzes), Op. 437 Orch.

No. 1 1st Theme S1263
2nd Theme S1264
No. 2 S1265
No. 3 1st Theme S1266
2nd Theme S1267
No. 4 1st Theme S1268
2nd Theme S1269

Künstlerleben (Artist's Life), Op. 316 Waltzes, Orch.

No. 1 1st Theme S1270
2nd Theme S1271
No. 2 1st Theme S1272
2nd Theme S1273
No. 3 S1274
No. 4 1st Theme S1275
2nd Theme S1276
No. 5 1st Theme S1277
2nd Theme S1278

Kuss (Kiss) Waltz from Der
Lustige Krieg , Op. 400,
Orch.

1st Theme S1279

2nd Theme S1280

3rd Theme S1281

4th Theme S1282

Lagunen-Waltzes, from
Eine Nacht in Venedig
(Same as Artist's Life), Orch.

1st Theme S1283

2nd Theme S1284

3rd Theme S1285

4th Theme S1286

5th Theme S1287

Morgenblätter Waltz,
Op. 279, Orch.

1st Theme S1288

2nd Theme S1289

3rd Theme S1290

4th Theme S1291

5th Theme S1292

O Schöner Mai,
Waltzes, Op. 375, Orch.

No. 1 S1293

No. 2
1st Theme S1294

2nd Theme S1295

No. 3 S1296

Roses From the South
Waltzes, (from Queen's
Lace Handkerchief),
Op. 388, Orch.

No. 1
1st Theme S1297

2nd Theme S1298

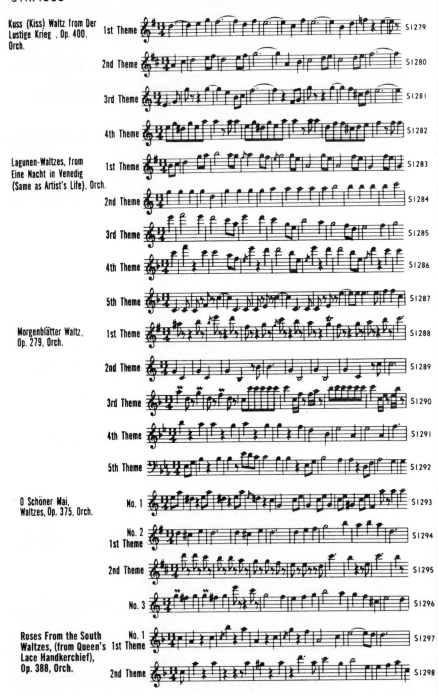

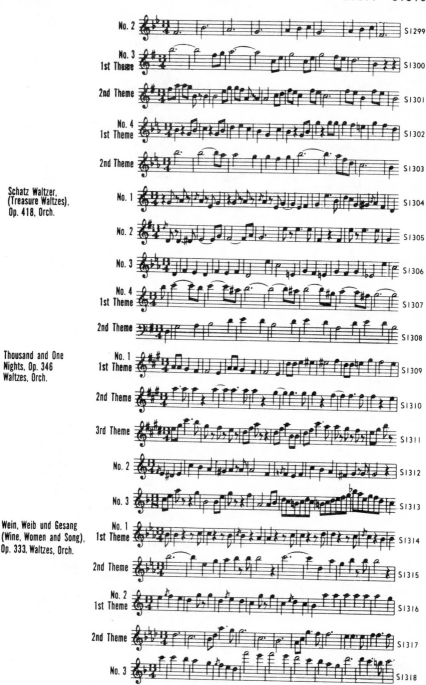

No. 4 — S1319

Wiener-Blut, Op. 354
Waltzes, Orch.

No. 1 1st Theme — S1320

2nd Theme — S1321

No. 2 — S1322

No. 3 1st Theme — S1323

2nd Theme — S1324

No. 4 — S1325

Wiener-Bonbons, Op. 307
Waltzes, Orch.

No. 1 1st Theme — S1326

2nd Theme — S1327

No. 2 — S1328

No. 3 1st Theme — S1329

2nd Theme — S1330

No. 4 — S1331

No. 5 1st Theme — S1332

2nd Theme — S1333

STRAUSS, Johann, Sr. (1804-1849)

Radetsky March, Orch.   1st Theme — S1334

2nd Theme — S1335

STRAUSS, Joseph (1827-1870)

Dorfschwalben Aus
Oesterreich (Village
Swallows of Austria),Op. 164
Waltzes, Orch.   No. 1 1st Theme — S1336

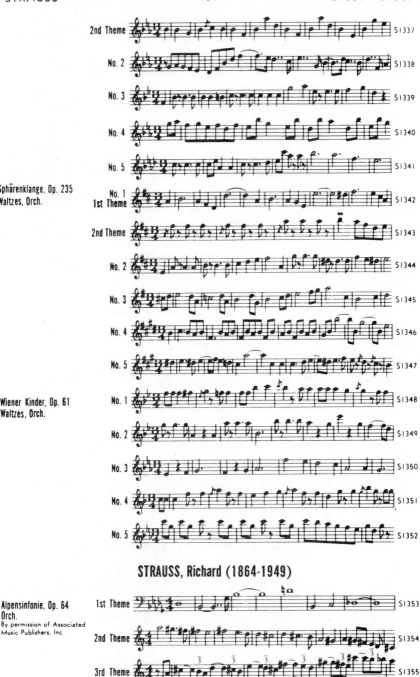

STRAUSS

Sphärenklange, Op. 235
Waltzes, Orch.

Wiener Kinder, Op. 61
Waltzes, Orch.

STRAUSS, Richard (1864-1949)

Alpensinfonie, Op. 64
Orch.
By permission of Associated
Music Publishers, Inc.

2nd Theme — S1337
No. 2 — S1338
No. 3 — S1339
No. 4 — S1340
No. 5 — S1341
No. 1 1st Theme — S1342
2nd Theme — S1343
No. 2 — S1344
No. 3 — S1345
No. 4 — S1346
No. 5 — S1347
No. 1 — S1348
No. 2 — S1349
No. 3 — S1350
No. 4 — S1351
No. 5 — S1352
1st Theme — S1353
2nd Theme — S1354
3rd Theme — S1355

4th Theme — S1356

5th Theme — S1357

6th Theme — S1358

7th Theme — S1359

8th Theme — S1360

9th Theme — S1361

10th Theme — S1362

11th Theme — S1363

12th Theme — S1364

Also Sprach Zarathustra
(Thus Spake Zarathustra),
Op. 30, Orch.

Intro. — S1365

1st Theme — S1366

2nd Theme — S1367

3rd Theme, A — S1368

3rd Theme, B — S1369

4th Theme — S1370

5th Theme, A — S1371

5th Theme, B — S1372

6th Theme — S1373

7th Theme, A — S1374

7th Theme, B — S1375

Aus Italien, Symphonic Fantasy, Op. 16

In the Campagna (Auf der Campagna)
1st Theme — S1376

2nd Theme — S1377

3rd Theme — S1378

In the Roman Ruins (In Roms Ruinen)
1st Theme — S1379

2nd Theme — S1380

3rd Theme — S1381

4th Theme — S1382

5th Theme — S1383

The Beach at Sorrento (Am Strande von Sorrent)
1st Theme — S1384

2nd Theme — S1385

3rd Theme — S1386

4th Theme — S1387

Neapolitan Folk Life (Neapolitanisches Volksleben)
1st Theme A — S1388

1st Theme B — S1389

2nd Theme — S1390

3rd Theme — S1391

4th Theme — S1392

Der Bürger Als Edelmann, Op. 60, Orch.
By permission of the copyright owner, Boosey and Hawkes, Inc.

Overture 1st Theme — S1393

2nd Theme — S1394

Minuet — S1395

4th Theme — S1436

5th Theme — S1437

6th Theme — S1438

7th Theme — S1439

8th Theme — S1440

9th Theme — S1441

Rêverie, Op. 9, No. 4,
Pft. or Pft. & Vn. — S1442

Der Rosenkavalier, Waltz Themes,
Op. 59.
By permission of the copyright
owner, Boosey and Hawkes, Inc. — S1443

S1444

S1445

S1446

S1447

Salome, Opera,
Op. 54
By permission of the
copyright owner,
Boosey and Hawkes, Inc.

Dance of the
Seven Veils
1st Theme — S1448

2nd Theme — S1449

3rd Theme — S1450

4th Theme — S1451

5th Theme — S1452

Sonata in E Flat,
Op. 18, Vn. & Pft.

1st Movement
1st Theme
A — S1453

1st Movement
1st Theme
B — S1454

1st Movement
2nd Theme — S1455

1st Movement / 3rd Theme — S1456

2nd Movement / Improvisation — S1457

3rd Movement / Finale / 1st Theme — S1458

3rd Movement / 2nd Theme — S1459

3rd Movement / 3rd Theme — S1460

Sinfonia Domestica, Op. 53
By permission of Associated Music Publishers, Inc.

1st Movement / 1st Theme, A — S1461

1st Theme, B — S1462

2nd Theme, A — S1463

2nd Theme, B — S1464

3rd Theme — S1465

4th Theme / Cradle Song — S1466

5th Theme — S1467

Till Eulenspiegels Lustige Streiche, Op. 28, Orch.

1st Theme — S1468

2nd Theme — S1469

3rd Theme (Variant of First Theme) — S1470

4th Theme — S1471

5th Theme — S1472

6th Theme — S1473

7th Theme — S1474

Tod Und Verklärung (Death and Transfiguration), Op. 24, Orch.

1st Theme — S1475

2nd Theme — S1476

3rd Theme — S1477

4th Theme — S1478

5th Theme — S1479

STRAVINSKY, Igor (1882-1971)

Apollon Musagètes, Ballet
By permission of the copyright owner, Boosey and Hawkes, Inc.

Birth of Apollo, Prologue 1st Theme, A — S1480

1st Theme, B — S1481

2nd Theme — S1482

Variation of Apollo — S1483

Pas d'Action 1st Theme — S1484

2nd Theme — S1485

Variation of Calliope — S1486

Variation of Polymnie — S1487

Variation of Terpsichore — S1488

Pas de Deux — S1489

Coda — S1490

Apotheosis — S1491

Le Baiser de la Fée, Ballet on Tschaikovsky Themes
By permission of the copyright owner, Boosey and Hawkes, Inc.

1st Movement Berceuse de la Tempête 1st Theme — S1492

1st Movement 2nd Theme — S1493

2nd Movement Fête au Village 1st Theme — S1494

2nd Movement / 2nd Theme — S1495

2nd Movement / 3rd Theme — S1496

2nd Movement / 4th Theme — S1497

2nd Movement / 5th Theme — S1498

2nd Movement / 6th Theme — S1499

3rd Movement / Au Moulin / 1st Theme — S1500

3rd Movement / 2nd Theme — S1501

3rd Movement / 3rd Theme — S1502

3rd Movement / Pas de Deux / 1st Theme — S1503

3rd Movement / 2nd Theme — S1504

3rd Movement / 3rd Theme — S1505

3rd Movement / Scène / 1st Theme — S1506

3rd Movement / 2nd Theme — S1507

Capriccio
Pft. & Orch.
By permission of the copyright owner,
Boosey and Hawkes, Inc.

1st Movement / Intro. — S1508

1st Movement / 1st Theme — S1508a

1st Movement / 2nd Theme — S1509

1st Movement / 3rd Theme — S1510

1st Movement / 4th Theme — S1511

1st Movement / 5th Theme — S1512

2nd Movement / 1st Theme. / A — S1513

2nd Movement
1st Theme,
B — S1514

2nd Movement
2nd Theme — S1515

2nd Movement
3rd Theme — S1516

3rd Movement
1st Theme — S1517

3rd Movement
2nd Theme — S1518

3rd Movement
3rd Theme,
A — S1519

3rd Movement
3rd Theme,
B — S1520

3rd Movement
Coda — S1521

Chant du Rossignol
Poème Symphonique,
Orch.
By permission of the
copyright owner,
Boosey and Hawkes, Inc.

1st Movement
1st Theme — S1521a

1st Movement
2nd Theme — S1521b

2nd Movement
Marche Chinoise
1st Theme — S1521c

2nd Movement
2nd Theme — S1521d

3rd Movement
Jeu du Rossignol Mécanique
1st Theme — S1521e

3rd Movement
2nd Theme — S1521f

Concerto,
Pft. & Orch.
By permission of the
copyright owner,
Boosey and Hawkes, Inc.

1st Movement — S1522

2nd Movement
1st Theme — S1523

2nd Movement
2nd Theme — S1524

3rd Movement
1st Theme — S1525

3rd Movement
2nd Theme — S1526

3rd Movement
3rd Theme — S1527

Concerto in D,
Vn. & Orch.
By permission of
Associated Music
Publishers, Inc.

1st Movement
1st Theme — S1528

1st Movement
2nd Theme,
A — S1529

1st Movement
2nd Theme,
B — S1530

2nd Movement
Aria,
A — S1531

3rd Movement
Aria,
B — S1532

4th Movement
Intro. — S1533

4th Movement
Theme — S1534

Dumbarton Oaks
Concerto,
Chamber Orch.
By permission of
Associated Music
Publishers, Inc.

1st Movement
1st Theme — S1534a

1st Movement
2nd Theme — S1534b

1st Movement
3rd Theme — S1534c

2nd Movement — S1534d

3rd Movement
1st Theme — S1534e

3rd Movement
1st Theme — S1534f

3rd Movement
2nd Theme — S1534g

The Fire Bird
Ballet Suite,
Orch.
By permission of
the copyright
holders, J. & W.
Chester, Ltd., 11
Great Marlborough
Street, London, W. I.

Intro. — S1535

Ronde des Princesses
1st Theme — S1536

2nd Theme — S1537

Dance of Kastchei — S1538

Berceuse — S1539

Finale — S1540

1st Movement 3rd Theme	S1601
1st Movement 4th Theme	S1602
2nd Movement 1st Theme	S1603
2nd Movement 2nd Theme	S1604
2nd Movement 3rd Theme	S1605
3rd Movement 1st Theme	S1606
3rd Movement 2nd Theme	S1607
3rd Movement 3rd Theme	S1608

SUK, Joseph (1874-1935)

Serenade, Op. 6
Str. Orch.
By permission of
Associated Music
Publishers, Inc.

1st Movement 1st Theme	S1609
1st Movement 2nd Theme	S1610
2nd Movement 1st Theme	S1611
2nd Movement 2nd Theme	S1612
3rd Movement 1st Theme	S1613
3rd Movement 2nd Theme	S1614
4th Movement	S1615

SUPPÉ, Franz von (1819-1895)

Banditenstreiche,
Overture

1st Theme	S1616
2nd Theme	S1617
3rd Theme	S1618

5th Theme — S1634

Pique Dame, Overture — 1st Theme — S1635

2nd Theme — S1636

3rd Theme — S1637

4th Theme — S1638

Poet and Peasant, Overture — Intro. — S1639

1st Theme, A — S1640

1st Theme, B — S1641

2nd Theme, A — S1642

2nd Theme, B — S1643

3rd Theme — S1644

4th Theme — S1645

Die Schöne Galathe, Overture — 1st Theme — S1646

2nd Theme — S1647

2nd Theme — S1648

3rd Theme — S1649

SVENDSEN, Johan Severin (1840-1911)

Carnival in Paris, Op. 9, Orch. — 1st Theme — S1650

2nd Theme — S1651

3rd Theme — S1652

Festival Polonaise, Op. 12, Orch.
By permission of Associated Music Publishers, Inc.
1st Theme — S1653
2nd Theme — S1654
3rd Theme — S1655

Norwegian Artists' Carnival, Op. 14, Orch.
1st Theme — S1656
2nd Theme Italian Folk Song — S1657
3rd Theme Norwegian Dance Tune — S1658

Romance, Op. 26, Vn. & Pft.
1st Theme — S1659
2nd Theme — S1660

SZYMANOWSKI, Karol (1883-1937)

The Fountain of Arethusa, Op. 30, No. 1, Vn. & Pft.
By permission of Associated Music Publishers, Inc.
1st Theme — S1661
2nd Theme — S1662

Mazurkas, Pft.
By permission of Associated Music Publishers, Inc.
Op. 50, No. 1
1st Theme — S1663
2nd Theme — S1664

Op. 50, No. 2
1st Theme — S1665
2nd Theme — S1666

Notturno, Op. 28, No. 1, Vn. & Pft.
By permission of Associated Music Publishers, Inc.
1st Theme — S1667
2nd Theme — S1668

Romance, Op. 23, Vn. & Pft.
By permission of Associated Music Publishers, Inc.
1st Theme — S1669
2nd Theme — S1670

Tarantella, Op. 28, No. 2, Vn. & Pft.
By permission of Associated Music Publishers, Inc.
1st Theme — S1671

2nd Theme — S1672

3rd Theme — S1673

TANSMAN, Alexander (1897-)

Triptyque
Str. Orch. or Str. Quartet
By permission of
Associated Music
Publishers, Inc.

1st Movement 1st Theme, A — T1

1st Movement 1st Theme, B — T2

1st Movement 2nd Theme — T3

2nd Movement — T4

3rd Movement 1st Theme — T5

3rd Movement 2nd Theme — T6

TARTINI, Giuseppe (1692-1770)

Arioso
Vn. & Pft. — T7

Concerto in D, Vcl. & Orch.
1st Movement — T8

2nd Movement — T9

3rd Movement — T10

4th Movement — T11

Concerto in D Minor, Vn. & Orch.
1st Movement — T12

2nd Movement — T13

3rd Movement — T14

Quartet in D, Str.
1st Movement — T15

2nd Movement — T16

3rd Movement — T37

4th Movement — T38

Variations on a Theme of Corelli
Vn. & Pft.
(Arr. by Kreisler)
Copyright by
Charles Foley,
New York — T39

TAYLOR, Deems (1885-1966)

Through the Looking Glass,
Op. 12
Orch.
Copyright 1923 by
J. Fischer & Bro., N. Y.
Used by permission.

1st Movement, A
Dedication — T40

1st Movement, B
The Garden of Live Flowers
1st Theme, A — T41

1st Movement, B
1st Theme,
B — T42

1st Movement, B
2nd Theme — T43

2nd Movement
Jabberwocky
1st Theme — T44

2nd Movement
2nd Theme — T45

2nd Movement
3rd Theme,
A — T46

2nd Movement
3rd Theme,
B — T47

3rd Movement
Looking-glass Insects
1st Theme — T48

3rd Movement
2nd Theme — T49

4th Movement
The White Knight
1st Theme — T50

4th Movement
2nd Theme — T51

TELEMANN, Georg Philipp (1681-1767)

Fantasias for Harpsi.

No. 1 — T52

No. 2 — T53

No. 3 — T54

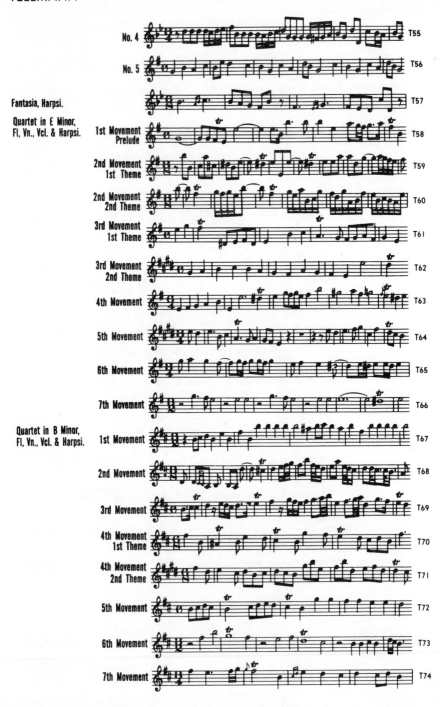

Fantasia, Harpsi.

Quartet in E Minor,
Fl, Vn., Vcl. & Harpsi.

Quartet in B Minor,
Fl, Vn., Vcl. & Harpsi.

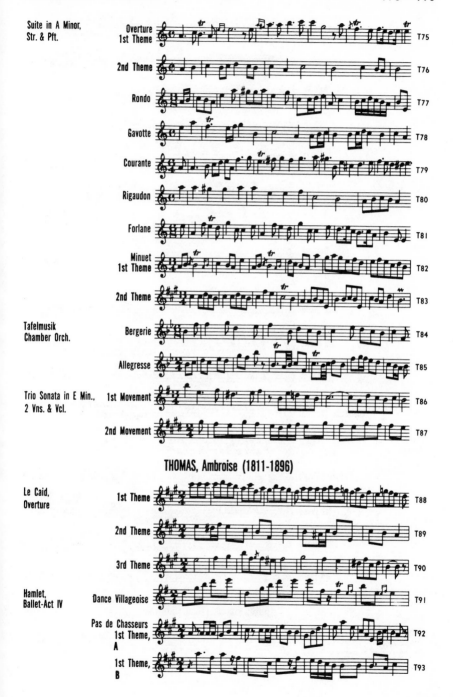

Suite in A Minor, Str. & Pft.
Overture 1st Theme — T75

2nd Theme — T76

Rondo — T77

Gavotte — T78

Courante — T79

Rigaudon — T80

Forlane — T81

Minuet 1st Theme — T82

2nd Theme — T83

Tafelmusik Chamber Orch.
Bergerie — T84

Allegresse — T85

Trio Sonata in E Min., 2 Vns. & Vcl.
1st Movement — T86

2nd Movement — T87

THOMAS, Ambroise (1811-1896)

Le Caid, Overture
1st Theme — T88

2nd Theme — T89

3rd Theme — T90

Hamlet, Ballet-Act IV
Dance Villageoise — T91

Pas de Chasseurs 1st Theme, A — T92

1st Theme, B — T93

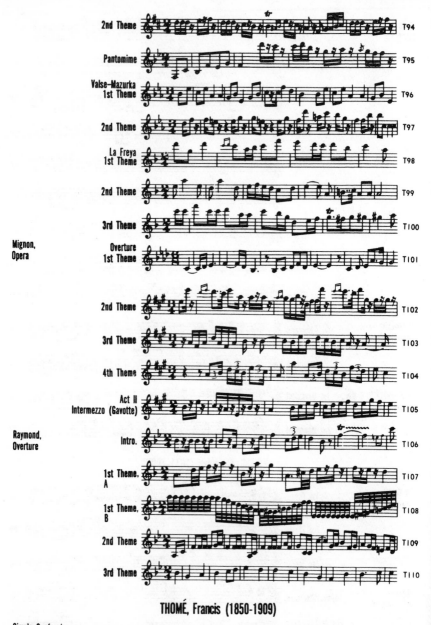

2nd Theme — T94

Pantomime — T95

Valse—Mazurka
1st Theme — T96

2nd Theme — T97

La Freya
1st Theme — T98

2nd Theme — T99

3rd Theme — T100

Mignon,
Opera

Overture
1st Theme — T101

2nd Theme — T102

3rd Theme — T103

4th Theme — T104

Act II
Intermezzo (Gavotte) — T105

Raymond,
Overture

Intro. — T106

1st Theme,
A — T107

1st Theme,
B — T108

2nd Theme — T109

3rd Theme — T110

THOMÉ, Francis (1850-1909)

Simple Confession
(Simple Aveu) — T111

THOMSON, Virgil (1896-)

Filling Station, Ballet
Copyright by Arrow Music Press, Inc., N. Y.

No. 1 Intro. 1st Theme   T111a

2nd Theme   T111b

No. 2 Mac's Dance   T111c

No. 3 Motorist and Mac   T111d

No. 4 Truck Drivers' Dance   T111e

2nd Theme   T111f

No. 7 Tango   T111g

No. 8 Waltz 1st Theme   T111h

2nd Theme   T111i

No. 9 The Big Apple   T111j

No. 11 The Chase   T111k

The Plow That Broke the Plains (Suite from film score)
Orch.
By permission of Music Press, Inc.

1st Movement Prelude 1st Theme   T112

1st Movement 2nd Theme   T113

2nd Movement Pastorale (Grass)   T114

3rd Movement Cattle   T115

4th Movement Blues (Speculation) 1st Theme   T116

4th Movement 2nd Theme   T117

5th Movement Drought (6th Movement repeats previous Themes)   T118

Quartet, No. 2 Str.
Copyright by Arrow Music Press, Inc., N. Y.

1st Movement 1st Theme   T118a

The River
Film Suite
Small Orch.
By permission of
the Composer

TOCH, Ernst (1887-1964)

The Chinese Flute,
Op. 29, Chamber Orch.
(2nd & 4th Movements
are Vocal)
By permission of Associated
Music Publishers, Inc.

3rd Movement
2nd Theme — T121

5th Movement — T122

**Pinocchio
Overture**
By permission of Associated
Music Publishers, Inc.

1st Theme — T122a

2nd Theme — T122b

3rd Theme — T122c

TSCHAIKOVSKY, Peter Ilyich (1840-1893)

Capriccio Italien, Op. 45
Orch.

1st Theme — T123

2nd Theme — T124

3rd Theme — T125

4th Theme — T126

Chanson Triste,
Op. 40, No. 2, Pft. — T127

Chant Sans Paroles
Op. 2, No. 3, Pft. — T128

Chant Sans Paroles
Op. 40, No. 6, Pft. — T129

Concerto No. 1, in B Flat
Minor, Op. 23,
Pft. & Orch.

1st Movement
1st Theme — T130

1st Movement
2nd Theme — T131

1st Movement
3rd Theme — T132

2nd Movement
1st Theme — T133

2nd Movement
2nd Theme — T134

3rd Movement
1st Theme — T135

3rd Movement
2nd Theme — T136

Marche Slave, Op. 31, Orch. — 1st Theme — T150
2nd Theme — T151
3rd Theme — T152
4th Theme — T153 *

Soldiers' March Op. 39, No 5, from Children's Album, Pft. — T154

Waltz from Eugen Onegin, 2nd Act — T155

Polonaise from Eugen Onegin, 3rd Act — T156

Hamlet, Fantasy Overture, Op. 67 — 1st Theme — T157
2nd Theme — T158
3rd Theme — T159

Romeo and Juliet, Fantasy Overture — 1st Theme — T160
2nd Theme — T161
3rd Theme — T162
4th Theme — T163

1812, Festival Overture, Op. 49 — 1st Theme — T164
2nd Theme — T165
3rd Theme — T166
4th Theme — T167

Quartet in D, Op. 11, Str. — 1st Movement — T168
2nd Movement 1st Theme — T169

*For Melodie, T153a, see page xiv.

2nd Movement 2nd Theme — T170

3rd Movement — T171

4th Movement — T172

Romance in F Min., Op. 5, Pft. 1st Theme — T173

2nd Theme — T174

The Seasons, Pft. Barcarolle (June), Op. 37, No. 6, 1st Theme — T175

2nd Theme — T176

Autumn Song (October), Op. 37, No. 10 — T177

Troika (November) Op. 37, No. 11, 1st Theme — T178

2nd Theme — T179

Serenade in C, Op. 48, Str. 1st Movement (Piece in Form of Sonatine) 1st Theme — T180

1st Movement 2nd Theme — T181

1st Movement 3rd Theme — T182

2nd Movement Waltz 1st Theme — T183

2nd Movement 2nd Theme — T184

3rd Movement Elegie 1st Theme — T185

3rd Movement 2nd Theme — T186

Finale 4th Movement (Russian Theme) 1st Theme — T187

4th Movement 2nd Theme — T188

The Nutcracker Suite, Op. 71a, Orch. Overture Miniature 1st Theme — T189

2nd Theme — T190
March 1st Theme — T191
2nd Theme — T192
Dance of the Sugar-Plum Fairy — T193
Russian Dance "Trepak" — T194
Arabian Dance — T195
Chinese Dance — T196
Dance of the Reed Flutes — T197
Waltz of the Flowers, 1st Theme — T198
2nd Theme — T199
3rd Theme — T200
4th Theme — T201
Suite No. 1, Op. 43, Orch. Marche Miniature 1st Theme — T202
2nd Theme — T203
Suite No. 3 Op. 55, Orch. 1st Movement Elegie — T204
2nd Movement Waltz — T205
4th Movement Theme & Variations — T206
The Sleeping Beauty, Suite from the Ballet, Op. 66a, Orch. 1st Movement La Fée des Lilas — T207
2nd Movement Pas d'Action — T208
4th Movement Panorama — T209

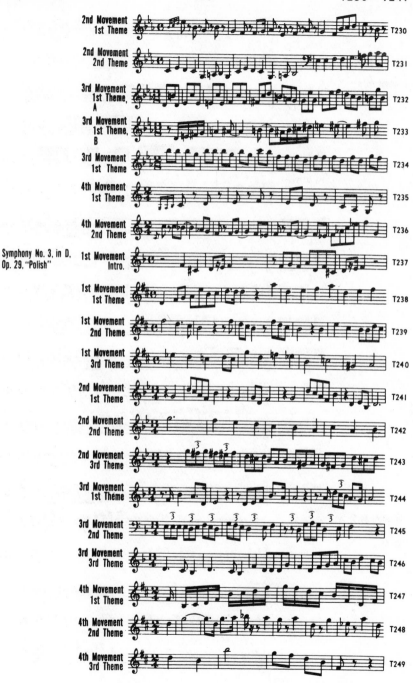

2nd Movement 1st Theme — T230
2nd Movement 2nd Theme — T231
3rd Movement 1st Theme, A — T232
3rd Movement 1st Theme, B — T233
3rd Movement 1st Theme — T234
4th Movement 1st Theme — T235
4th Movement 2nd Theme — T236

Symphony No. 3, in D, Op. 29, "Polish"

1st Movement Intro. — T237
1st Movement 1st Theme — T238
1st Movement 2nd Theme — T239
1st Movement 3rd Theme — T240
2nd Movement 1st Theme — T241
2nd Movement 2nd Theme — T242
2nd Movement 3rd Theme — T243
3rd Movement 1st Theme — T244
3rd Movement 2nd Theme — T245
3rd Movement 3rd Theme — T246
4th Movement 1st Theme — T247
4th Movement 2nd Theme — T248
4th Movement 3rd Theme — T249

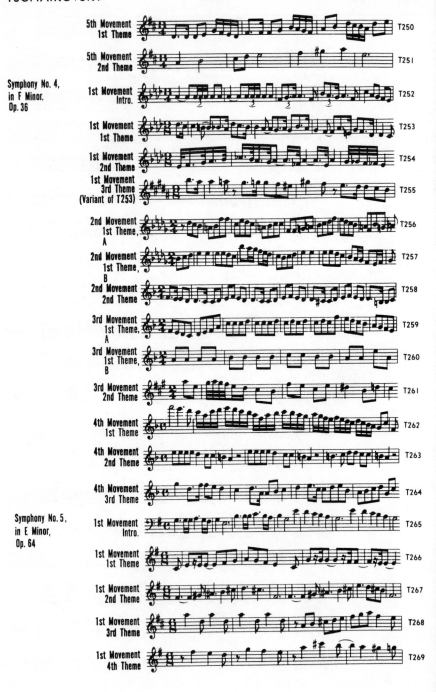

2nd Movement 1st Theme — T270
2nd Movement 2nd Theme — T271
2nd Movement 3rd Theme — T272
3rd Movement 1st Theme — T273
3rd Movement 2nd Theme — T274
4th Movement 1st Theme — T275
4th Movement 2nd Theme — T276
4th Movement 3rd Theme — T277
4th Movement 4th Theme — T278
4th Movement 5th Theme — T279

Symphony No. 6, in B Minor, Op. 74 "Pathétique"
By permission of Associated Music Publishers, Inc.

1st Movement Intro. — T280
1st Movement 1st Theme — T281
1st Movement 2nd Theme — T282
1st Movement 3rd Theme — T283
2nd Movement 1st Theme — T284
2nd Movement 2nd Theme — T285
3rd Movement 1st Theme — T286
3rd Movement 2nd Theme — T287
3rd Movement 3rd Theme — T288
4th Movement 1st Theme — T289

4th Movement, 2nd Theme — T290

Theme & Variations, Op. 19, No. 6, Pft. — T291

Trio in A Min., Op. 50, Pft., Vn. & Vcl. 1st Movement, 1st Theme — T292

1st Movement, 2nd Theme — T293

2nd Movement, Theme & Variations — T294

TURINA, Joaquín (1882-1949)

Danzas Fantásticas, Orch. or Pft. — Ensueño, 1st Theme, A — T295

1st Theme, B — T296

2nd Theme — T297

3rd Theme — T298

Orgia, 1st Theme — T299

2nd Theme — T300

Fandanguillo, Guitar
By permission of Associated Music Publishers, Inc. — 1st Theme — T301

2nd Theme — T302

Femmes d'Espagne (Mujeres Españolas)
Copyright by Editions Salabert, Editions Salabert, 22 Rue Chaucat, Paris Salabert, Inc., 1 East 57 St., N. Y. — L'Andalouse Sentimentale, 1st Theme — T303

2nd Theme — T304

3rd Theme — T305

La Oración del Torero, Quart., Str. — 1st Theme — T306

2nd Theme — T307

3rd Theme — T308

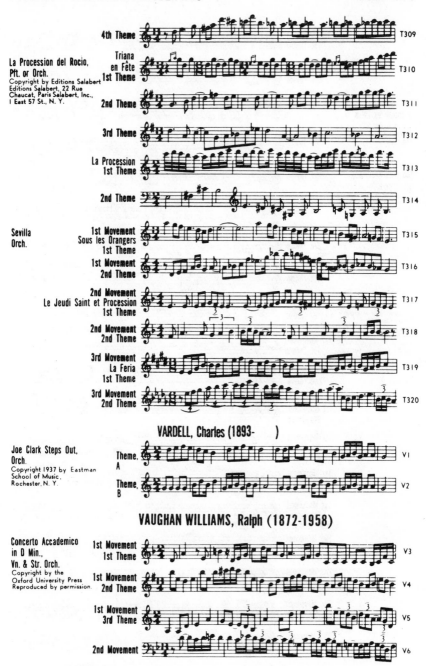

4th Theme — T309

La Procession del Rocio,
Pft. or Orch.
Copyright by Editions Salabert
Editions Salabert, 22 Rue
Chaucat, Paris Salabert, Inc.,
1 East 57 St., N. Y.

Triana
en Fête
1st Theme — T310

2nd Theme — T311

3rd Theme — T312

La Procession
1st Theme — T313

2nd Theme — T314

Sevilla
Orch.

**1st Movement
Sous les Orangers
1st Theme** — T315

**1st Movement
2nd Theme** — T316

**2nd Movement
Le Jeudi Saint et Procession
1st Theme** — T317

**2nd Movement
2nd Theme** — T318

**3rd Movement
La Feria
1st Theme** — T319

**3rd Movement
2nd Theme** — T320

VARDELL, Charles (1893-   )

Joe Clark Steps Out,
Orch.
Copyright 1937 by Eastman
School of Music,
Rochester, N. Y.

**Theme,
A** — V1

**Theme,
B** — V2

VAUGHAN WILLIAMS, Ralph (1872-1958)

Concerto Accademico
in D Min.,
Vn. & Str. Orch.
Copyright by the
Oxford University Press
Reproduced by permission.

**1st Movement
1st Theme** — V3

**1st Movement
2nd Theme** — V4

**1st Movement
3rd Theme** — V5

2nd Movement — V6

Symphony No. 4,
in F Minor
Copyright by the
Oxford University Press.
Reproduced by permission.

The Wasps
(Aristophanes)
Orch.

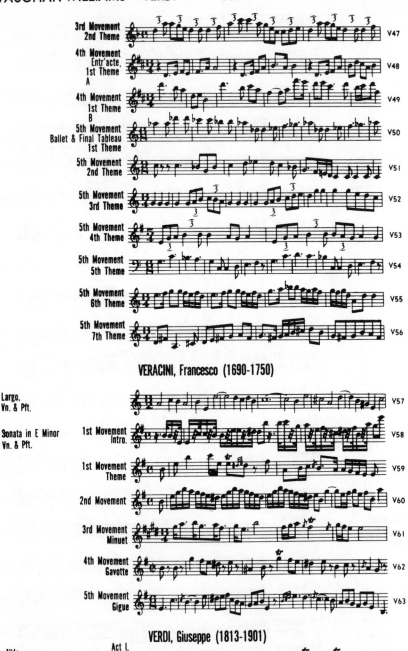

3rd Movement
2nd Theme — V47

4th Movement
Entr'acte,
1st Theme
A — V48

4th Movement
1st Theme
B — V49

5th Movement
Ballet & Final Tableau
1st Theme — V50

5th Movement
2nd Theme — V51

5th Movement
3rd Theme — V52

5th Movement
4th Theme — V53

5th Movement
5th Theme — V54

5th Movement
6th Theme — V55

5th Movement
7th Theme — V56

VERACINI, Francesco (1690-1750)

Largo,
Vn. & Pft. — V57

Sonata in E Minor
Vn. & Pft. — 1st Movement Intro. — V58

1st Movement
Theme — V59

2nd Movement — V60

3rd Movement
Minuet — V61

4th Movement
Gavotte — V62

5th Movement
Gigue — V63

VERDI, Giuseppe (1813-1901)

Aïda,
Opera — Act I,
Dance of the Priestesses
1st Theme — V64

2nd Movement — V85

3rd Movement
1st Theme — V86

3rd Movement
2nd Theme — V87

4th Movement — V88

La Traviata, Opera

Act I,
Prelude
1st Theme — V89

2nd Theme — V90

I Vespri Siciliani,
Overture

1st Theme — V91

2nd Theme — V92

VIEUXTEMPS, Henri (1820-1881)

Ballade et Polonaise
Op. 38
Vn. & Pft.

1st Theme — V93

2nd Theme — V94

3rd Theme — V95

4th Theme — V96

5th Theme — V97

Concerto No. 4
in D Minor,
Vn. & Orch.

1st Movement
1st Theme, A — V98

1st Movement
1st Theme, B — V99

1st Movement
2nd Theme — V100

2nd Movement
1st Theme — V101

2nd Movement
2nd Theme — V102

3rd Movement
1st Theme — V103

VILLA-LOBOS, Heitor (1887-1959)

VINCI, Leonardo (1690-1730)

VIOTTI, Giovanni (1753-1824)

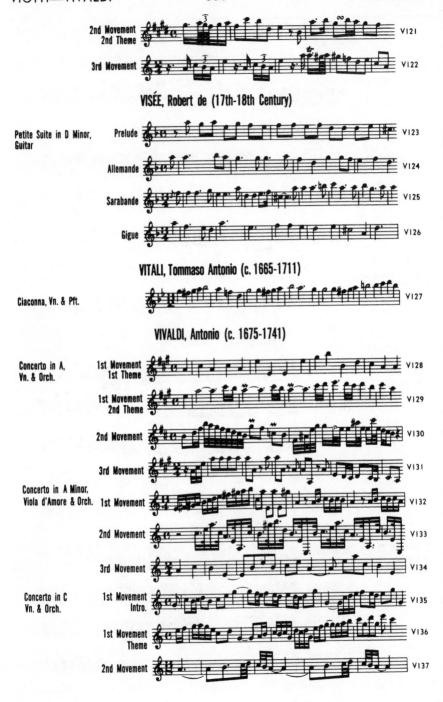

2nd Movement 2nd Theme — V121

3rd Movement — V122

VISÉE, Robert de (17th-18th Century)

Petite Suite in D Minor, Guitar — Prelude — V123

Allemande — V124

Sarabande — V125

Gigue — V126

VITALI, Tommaso Antonio (c. 1665-1711)

Ciaconna, Vn. & Pft. — V127

VIVALDI, Antonio (c. 1675-1741)

Concerto in A, Vn. & Orch. — 1st Movement 1st Theme — V128

1st Movement 2nd Theme — V129

2nd Movement — V130

3rd Movement — V131

Concerto in A Minor, Viola d'Amore & Orch. — 1st Movement — V132

2nd Movement — V133

3rd Movement — V134

Concerto in C Vn. & Orch. — 1st Movement Intro. — V135

1st Movement Theme — V136

2nd Movement — V137

3rd Movement — V138

Concerto in C Minor,
Vn. & Orch.
1st Movement — V139

2nd Movement — V140

3rd Movement — V141

Concerto in G Minor,
Op. 6, No. 1,
Vn. & Orch.
1st Movement — V142

2nd Movement — V143

3rd Movement — V144

Concerto in G Minor,
Vn. & Str. Orch.
1st Movement — V145

2nd Movement — V146

3rd Movement — V147

Concerto Grosso
in G Minor,
Op. 3, No. 2
(L'Estro Armonico)
Orch.
1st Movement — V148

2nd Movement — V149

3rd Movement — V150

Concerto Grosso in A Minor,
Op. 3, No. 6
(L'Estro Armonico)
1st Movement — V151

2nd Movement — V152

3rd Movement — V153

Concerto Grosso
in A Minor,
Op. 3, No. 8
2 Vns. & Orch.
1st Movement — V154

2nd Movement — V155

3rd Movement — V156

Concerto Grosso in D,
Op. 3, No. 9
Orch.
1st Movement — V157

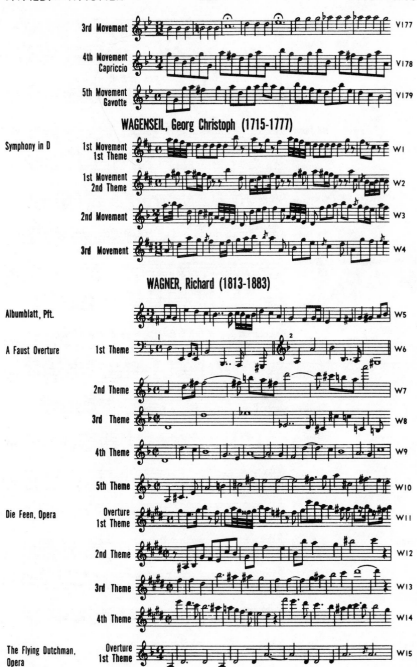

3rd Movement — V177

4th Movement
Capriccio — V178

5th Movement
Gavotte — V179

WAGENSEIL, Georg Christoph (1715-1777)

Symphony in D

1st Movement
1st Theme — W1

1st Movement
2nd Theme — W2

2nd Movement — W3

3rd Movement — W4

WAGNER, Richard (1813-1883)

Albumblatt, Pft. — W5

A Faust Overture — 1st Theme — W6

2nd Theme — W7

3rd Theme — W8

4th Theme — W9

5th Theme — W10

Die Feen, Opera — Overture 1st Theme — W11

2nd Theme — W12

3rd Theme — W13

4th Theme — W14

The Flying Dutchman, Opera — Overture 1st Theme — W15

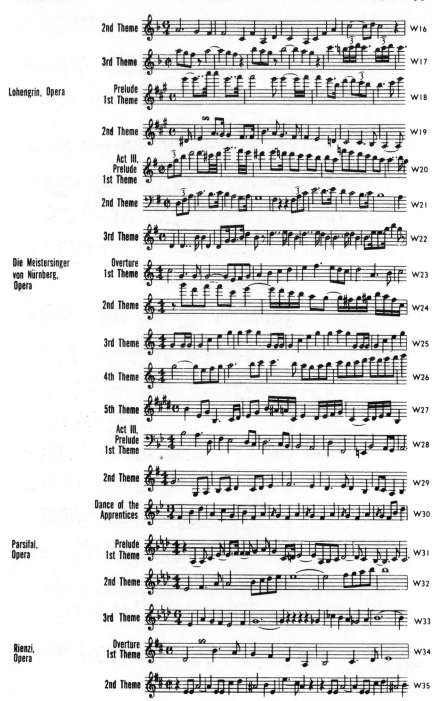

Lohengrin, Opera

Die Meistersinger
von Nürnberg,
Oper

Parsifal,
Opera

Rienzi,
Opera

2nd Theme — W16
3rd Theme — W17
Prelude 1st Theme — W18
2nd Theme — W19
Act III, Prelude 1st Theme — W20
2nd Theme — W21
3rd Theme — W22
Overture 1st Theme — W23
2nd Theme — W24
3rd Theme — W25
4th Theme — W26
5th Theme — W27
Act III, Prelude 1st Theme — W28
2nd Theme — W29
Dance of the Apprentices — W30
Prelude 1st Theme — W31
2nd Theme — W32
3rd Theme — W33
Overture 1st Theme — W34
2nd Theme — W35

Der Ring Der Nibelungen
(The Ring of the Nibelungs)
Das Rheingold,
Opera — Prelude — W36

Entrance of the
Gods Into Valhalla
1st Theme — W37

2nd Theme — W38

Die Walküre,
Opera — Ride of the Valkyries
1st Theme — W39

2nd Theme — W40

Magic Fire Music
1st Theme — W41

2nd Theme — W42

Waldweben
Siegfried, Opera (Forest Murmurs)
1st Theme — W43

2nd Theme — W44

3rd Theme — W45

4th Theme — W46

5th Theme — W47

6th Theme — W48

Götterdämmerung
Opera — Siegfried's
Rhine Journey
1st Theme — W49

2nd Theme — W50

3rd Theme — W51

4th Theme — W52

5th Theme — W53

6th Theme — W54

Siegfried's
Funeral Music
1st Theme — W55

2nd Theme — W56

3rd Theme — W57

4th Theme — W58

5th Theme — W59

6th Theme — W60

7th Theme — W61

Siegfried-Idyll
Orch.

1st Theme, A — W62

1st Theme, B — W63

2nd Theme — W64

3rd Theme — W65

4th Theme — W66

5th Theme Bird Calls — W67

Tannhaüser, Opera

Overture 1st Theme, A — W68

1st Theme, B — W69

2nd Theme (Also in Bacchanale) — W70

3rd Theme (Also in Bacchanale) — W71

4th Theme — W72

5th Theme — W73

6th Theme — W74

7th Theme — W75

8th Theme — W76

Act II, March Intro. — W77

1st Theme — W78

2nd Theme — W79

3rd Theme — W80

Bacchanale (Venusberg Music) 1st Theme — W81

2nd Theme — W82

3rd Theme — W83

4th Theme — W84

Tristan und Isolde, Opera — Prelude 1st Theme — W85

2nd Theme Act III — W86

Act III Prelude 1st Theme — W87

2nd Theme — W88

3rd Theme — W89

Love Death 1st Theme — W90

2nd Theme — W91

WALDTEUFEL, Emil (1837-1915)

Dolores Waltzes Op. 170, Orch.
Courtesy Carl Fischer, Inc., N.Y.

No. 1 1st Theme — W92

2nd Theme — W93

España, Waltzes
Op. 286, Orch.
Courtesy Carl Fischer,
Inc., N. Y.

Estudiantina, Waltzes
Op. 191, Orch.
Courtesy Carl Fischer,
Inc., N. Y.

1. Same as C71.   2. Same as C72.   3. Same as C75.

Frühlingskinder Waltz (Violettes), Op. 148 Orch.

1st Theme — W114
2nd Theme — W115
3rd Theme — W116
4th Theme — W117

Ganz Allerliebst (Très Jolie), Waltz Op. 159, Orch.

1st Theme — W118
2nd Theme — W119
3rd Theme — W120
4th Theme — W121

Immer Oder Nimmer (Toujours ou Jamais), Waltzes Op. 156, Orch.

No. 1 — W122
No. 2 1st Theme — W123
2nd Theme — W124
No. 3 1st Theme — W125
2nd Theme — W126
No. 4 — W127

Mein Traum, Waltzes, Op. 151, Orch.

No. 1 — W128
No. 2 1st Theme — W129
2nd Theme — W130
No. 3 1st Theme — W131
2nd Theme — W132
No. 4 — W133

Sirenenzauber (Sirens)
Waltzes, Op. 154
Orch.

No. 1
1st Theme — W134

2nd Theme — W135

No. 2
1st Theme — W136

2nd Theme — W137

No. 3
1st Theme — W138

2nd Theme — W139

No. 4 — W140

The Skaters, Waltzes
Op. 183, Orch.
Courtesy Carl Fischer,
Inc., N. Y.

No. 1
1st Theme — W141

2nd Theme — W142

No. 2
1st Theme — W143

2nd Theme — W144

No. 3
1st Theme — W145

2nd Theme — W146

No. 4 — W147

WALLACE, William Vincent (1812-1865)

Maritana,
Overture

1st Theme — W148

2nd Theme — W149

3rd Theme — W150

4th Theme — W151

5th Theme — W152

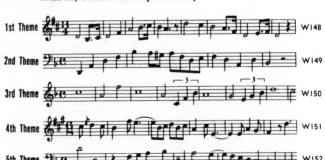

WALTON, William Turner (1902-   )

Concerto Viola & Orch. Copyright by the Oxford University Press. Reproduced by permission.

1st Movement 1st Theme — W153
1st Movement 2nd Theme — W154
2nd Movement 1st Theme — W155
2nd Movement 2nd Theme — W156
2nd Movement 3rd Theme — W157
3rd Movement 1st Theme — W158
3rd Movement 2nd Theme — W159

Concerto Vn. & Orch. Copyright by the Oxford University Press. Reproduced by permission.

1st Movement 1st Theme — W160
1st Movement 2nd Theme — W161
2nd Movement 1st Theme, A — W162
2nd Movement 1st Theme, B — W163
2nd Movement 2nd Theme — W164
2nd Movement 3rd Theme — W165
3rd Movement 1st Theme — W166
3rd Movement 2nd Theme — W167

Crown Imperial, Coronation March, Orch. Copyright by the Oxford University Press. Reproduced by permission.

1st Theme — W168
2nd Theme — W169
3rd Theme — W170
4th Theme — W171

Façade, Suite No. 1, Orch.
Copyright by the Oxford University Press.
Reproduced by permission.

Polka 1st Theme — W172

2nd Theme — W173

3rd Theme — W174

Valse 1st Theme — W175

2nd Theme — W176

A Swiss Yodeling Song 1st Theme — W177

2nd Theme (Parody on William Tell) — W178

3rd Theme — W179

Tango-Pasodoble 1st Theme — W180

2nd Theme — W181

Tarantella-Sevillana 1st Theme — W182

2nd Theme — W183

Façade, Suite No. 2, Orch.
Copyright by the Oxford University Press.
Reproduced by permission.

Fanfare — W184

Scotch Rhapsody 1st Theme — W185

2nd Theme — W186

Country Dance — W187

Noche Española 1st Theme — W188

2nd Theme — W189

Popular Song — W190

Old Sir Faulk W191

Portsmouth Point,
Overture
Copyright by the Oxford
University Press.
Reproduced by permission.

1st Theme,
A W192

1st Theme,
B W193

2nd Theme W194

WARLOCK, Peter (1894-1930)

Capriol, Suite for Orch.

1st Movement
Basse Dance W195

2nd Movement
Pavane W196

3rd Movement
Tordion W197

4th Movement
Bransles W198

5th Movement
Pieds-en-l'air W199

6th Movement
Mattachins W200

Serenade for Str. Orch.
Copyright by the Oxford
University Press.
Reproduced by permission.

1st Theme W201

2nd Theme W202

WEBER, Carl Maria Von (1786-1826)

Abu Hassan,
Overture

1st Theme W203

2nd Theme W204

Concertstück,
Op. 79, Pft. & Orch.

1st Theme W205

2nd Theme W206

3rd Theme W207

4th Theme W208

3rd Theme — W229

4th Theme — W230

5th Theme — W231

Jubel-Ouvertüre

Intro. 1st Theme — W232

2nd Theme — W233

1st Theme — W234

2nd Theme — W235

3rd Theme — W236

4th Theme God Save the King — W237

Oberon, Overture

Intro. — W238

1st Theme — W239

2nd Theme — W240

3rd Theme — W241

Peter Schmoll und Seine Nachbarn, Overture

Intro. — W242

1st Theme — W243

2nd Theme — W244

Polacca Brillante, Op. 72, Pft.

1st Theme — W245

2nd Theme — W246

Preciosa, Overture

1st Theme — W247

2nd Theme — W248

Rondo Brillant
"La Gaîté"
Op. 62, Pft.

Sonata No. 1 in C,
Op. 24, Pft.

Sonata No. 2 in A Flat
Op. 39, Pft.

Trio in G Minor,
Op. 63,
Vn., Vcl. & Pft.

3rd Theme — W249
1st Theme — W250
2nd Theme — W251
1st Movement — W252
2nd Movement — W253
3rd Movement — W254
3rd Movement 2nd Theme — W255
4th Movement (Perpetual Motion) — W256
1st Movement — W257
2nd Movement — W258
3rd Movement 1st Theme — W259
3rd Movement 2nd Theme — W260
4th Movement — W261
1st Movement 1st Theme — W262
1st Movement 2nd Theme — W263
2nd Movement Intro. — W264
2nd Movement Theme — W265
3rd Movement — W266
4th Movement 1st Theme — W267
4th Movement 2nd Theme — W268

4th Movement 3rd Theme — W269

WEINBERGER, Jaromir (1896-1967)

Schwanda, Opera
By permission of Associated
Music Publishers, Inc.

Polka — W270

Fugue — W271

Under the Spreading
Chestnut Tree,
(Variations and
Fugue on an
old English tune),
Orch.
By permission of Associated
Music Publishers, Inc.

1st Theme
Theme for Variations — W272

2nd Theme
Theme for Fugue — W273

WIENIAWSKI, Henri (1835-1880)

Concerto No. 2
in D Minor, Op. 22,
Vn. & Orch.

1st Movement
1st Theme — W274

1st Movement
2nd Theme — W275

2nd Movement
Romance — W276

3rd Movement
1st Theme — W277

3rd Movement
2nd Theme — W278

Dudziarz (Mazurka),
Op. 19, No. 2
Vn. & Pft.

1st Theme — W279

2nd Theme — W280

Kuiawiak, Op. 3,
Vn. & Pft.

Intro. — W281

1st Theme — W282

2nd Theme — W283

3rd Theme — W284

Legende, Op. 17
Vn. & Pft.

1st Theme — W285

2nd Theme — W286

Obertass
(Mazurka)
Op.19, No. 1,
Vn. & Pft.

1st Theme   W287

2nd Theme   W288

Polonaise Brillante,
Op. 4,
Vn. & Pft.

1st Theme   W289

2nd Theme   W290

3rd Theme   W291

Polonaise Brillante,
No. 2, Op. 21,
Vn. & Pft.

1st Theme   W292

2nd Theme   W293

3rd Theme   W294

Souvenir de Moscou,
Airs Russes, Op. 6
Vn. & Pft.

1st Theme   W295

2nd Theme,
A   W296

2nd Theme,
B   W297

WOLF, Hugo (1860-1903)

Italian Serenade,
Str. Quart. or Str. Orch.
By permission of Associated
Music Publishers, Inc.

1st Theme   W298

2nd Theme,
A   W299

2nd Theme,
B   W300

WOLF-FERRARI, Ermanno (1876-1948)

The Jewels of the Madonna,
Copyright renewal assigned
1939 to G. Schirmer, Inc.

Act II
Intermezzo   W301

Act III
Intermezzo,
1st Theme   W302

2nd Theme   W303

Apache Dance
1st Theme   W304

2nd Theme — W305

The Secret of Suzanne,
Overture
Copyright 1910 by
Josef Weinberger, Leipzig.

1st Theme — W306

2nd Theme — W307

3rd Theme — W308

YSAŸE, Théo (1865-1918)

Variations, Op. 10,
2 Pfts.
By permission of Associated
Music Publishers, Inc.

Theme — Y1

ZANDONAI, Riccardo (1883-1944)

Giulietta E Romeo
Symphonic Episode, Orch.
Copyright 1928
by G. Ricordi & Co., Inc.

1st Theme — Z1

2nd Theme — Z2

3rd Theme — Z3

ZARZYCKI, Alexander (1834-1895)

Mazurka, Op. 26,
Vn. & Pft.
Copyright 1899
by Carl Fischer, Inc., N. Y.

1st Theme — Z4

2nd Theme — Z5

3rd Theme — Z6

ZIMBALIST, Efrem (1889-   )

Quartet in E Minor,
Str.
Copyright 1938
by G. Schirmer, Inc.

1st Movement — Z7

2nd Movement
1st Theme — Z8

2nd Movement
2nd Theme — Z9

3rd Movement
1st Theme — Z10

3rd Movement
2nd Theme — Z11

4th Theme — Z12

TRANSPOSITION KEY

C	D	E	F	G	A	B	C	
C#	D#	E#	F#	G#	A#	B#	C#	} enharmonic[x]
Db	Eb	F	Gb	Ab	Bb	C	Db	}
D	E	F#	G	A	B	C#	D	
Eb	F	G	Ab	Bb	C	D	Eb	
E	F#	G#	A	B	C#	D#	E	
F	G	A	Bb	C	D	E	F	
F#	G#	A#	B	C#	D#	E#	F#	} enharmonic[x]
Gb	Ab	Bb	Cb	Db	Eb	F	Gb	}
G	A	B	C	D	E	F#	G	
Ab	Bb	C	Db	Eb	F	G	Ab	
A	B	C#	D	E	F#	G#	A	
Bb	C	D	Eb	F	G	A	Bb	
B	C#	D#	E	F#	G#	A#	B	} enharmonic[x]
Cb	Db	Eb	Fb	Gb	Ab	Bb	Cb	}

x Sounding the same but written differently.

This chart, though not necessary to the use of the notation key, should be helpful to the reader in explaining key relationships. For example, the fifth note in the key of C is G, its equivalent in the key of A is E.

HOW TO USE
THE NOTATION INDEX*

To identify a given theme, play it in the key of C† and look it up under its note sequence using the following alphabet as a guide:

A Ab A♯ **B** Bb B♯ **C** Cb C♯ **D** Db D♯
E Eb E♯ **F** Fb F♯ **G** Gb G♯

Double flats follow flats; double sharps follow sharps.

The letter and number to the right of the definition indicate the place in the alphabetic section of the book where the theme may be found in its original key with the name of the composition and the composer.

Trills, turns, grace notes, and other embellishments are not taken into consideration here. However, it must be remembered that the appoggiatura is a regular note. In rare cases the grace note may be of such nature as to give the aural impression of being a regular note, in which case it is included in this section.

Keys are, in the main, determined by the harmonic structure of the opening bars, not by the cadence. The phrase that begins in C and goes to G is considered to be in C. Themes that may be analyzed in two keys are listed under both keys. There are themes that defy key definition. However, if the melodic line carries a key implication of its own, if only for the first few notes, that key is used. If the theme carries no such implication, then, for the sake of convenience, the first note is assumed to be C and the rest transposed accordingly.

Memory plays strange tricks and it is possible that the desired theme may be remembered inaccurately. We have occasionally listed a theme incorrectly as well as correctly if there is a popular misconception about it.

Each definition has been carried to six places except in the case of duplication. Duplicates are continued to a point of difference, but in no case to more than eleven places. When a note is repeated many times, for space conservation an exponent is used, *i.e.* $G G G G G G = G^6$.

H. B.

* Publisher's note: The Notation Index was conceived by Harold Barlow.
† C Major for major themes, C Minor for minor themes.

NOTATION INDEX

A C E F G A	E53
A C F A C D	D15
A C F D# G# E	P212
A C G A C G	D242
A C G C F A	H817
A C G E G F	S1110
A D A B C# D	S679
A D A D A D#	R207
A D A D B E	B1294
A D A D G C	S1276
A D A G E F	T98
A D A G F E	D356
A D B G C A	B635
A D C D C B	B1291
A D C D E D	L247
A D D A D D	B786
A D D C# D E	W278
A D D E A G	G200
A D E C# D A	T41
A D E E D A	H808
A D E F D G	L153
A D E F E F	S18
A D E F G G#	S700
A D E G A E	D34
A D F# C D D#	S924
A D G F E D	H742
A D G F# F# E	C469
A D# E G A A#	D206
A E A E E E	E41
A E A G C D	S1094
A E C D C D	S1491
A E D B G C	T241
A E D E C A	M125
A E D G A E	R140
A E F Bb A E	D66
A E G C A D	S1527
A E G C D G	S1173
A E G D F C	W66
A E G D F E	N16
A E G F C F	W89
A F A B A G	C352
A F A F A F	T3
A F C D E A	S833
A F C# D E F	S1496
A F E D D C	M274
A F E D E F	B599
A G A A C A	B1711L
A G A B C C	B613

A G A B C D	C360
A G A C A G	C415
A G A C D C	G365
A G A G A G C	S789
A G A G A G E	C342
A G A G C D	S995
A G A G C F	S1005
A G A G E A	R191
A G A G F E C#	R124
A G A G F E D	C105
A G A G F E F	S1581
A G A G G F	P213
A G B A D G	C290
A G B C B A	B1597
A G B D F F	S1322
A G B G B A	M128
A G B G C G	F147
A G C B E Bb	F153
A G C D E D	H821
A G C D G E	M1025
A G C E D A	L86
A G C E F# A	R160
A G C E G A	T178
A G C G A G	H285
A G C G E A	S260
A G D B G F	D445
A G D C G G	C418
A G D# E G B	I38
A G E A G D	R379
A G E A G E	I37
A G E C A G	S614
A G E C G A	S470
A G E C G B	B1771
A G E C G F	S560
A G E D C A C	W48
A G E D C A G	K116
A G E D C B	D362
A G E D E G	D71
A G E E A G	K58
A G E E F D	H573
A G E F E E	C358
A G E F E F	B1462
A G F A G F	I33
A G F D C D	W282
A G F D E F	D210
A G F E A A	M142
A G F E D C B A	B1071
A G F E D C B C	H451

INDEX OF TITLES

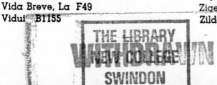